Oc

To my dear Sister Sandy,

I love you and I pray that the Lord will use you powerfully as an agent of healing and reconciliation.

Blessings,

Wendy Habicht

HEALING WOUNDED
RECONCILING PEOPLES & RESTORING PLACES
HISTORY

RUSS PARKER

THE
PILGRIM
PRESS
Cleveland

Published in the USA, Canada and the Philippine Republic by
The Pilgrim Press
700 Prospect Avenue East
Cleveland, Ohio 44115-1100
pilgrimpress.com

Originally published in 2001 by
Darton, Longman and Todd Ltd
1 Spencer Court
140-142 Wandsworth High Street
London SW18 4JJ

06 05 04 03 02 5 4 3 2 1

A catalogue record for this book is available from the Library of Congress

Parker, Russ.
Healing wounded history: reconciling peoples and healing places / Russ Parker.
p. cm.
ISBN 0-8298-1502-3 (alk. paper)
1. Spiritual healing. 2. Healing—Religious aspects—Christianity I. Title.

BT732.5 .P368 2002
253—dc21

2002034589

For Sylvia and Wally

Thanks for a lifetime of friendship

CONTENTS

ACKNOWLEDGEMENTS

First and foremost I would like to thank Michael Mitton without whom this book could not possibly have been written. He has accompanied me for some years now upon a journey of discovery while we explored together our interest in healing wounded history, which led to our jointly writing the workbook that accompanies this one. He is the best friend I have ever had and his support and loving shoves to get me writing have really been appreciated. Along the way I have met a host of people who are too many to name, but who have been pioneers and explorers in the whole field of reconciliation and whose passion for healing group relationships has been an inspiration to me. In particular, I would like to thank John and Yvonne Presdee for their friendship; their Reconciliation Prayer Walks have been of enormous insight to me. I have benefited greatly from my times with Brian Mills, Peter Hocken and Roger Mitchell of the English Reconciliation Coalition, who have been putting into practice for years the issues and causes within this book. I would particularly like to thank John Dawson, the Director of the International Reconciliation Coalition, for a most enjoyable conversation in the back of a bus as we were driven to a service of repentance and apology in Turkey. His vision and warmth are some of the riches I still carry. I would like to thank Jeannette Sagar for supplying me with innumerable articles and publications on this subject, and for her sparkly heart. My thanks also to Trevor Sullivan and his wife Doris who have given me so much welcome into their home in Ireland. In many ways my journey into this subject began with a 'chance' meeting with Trevor on a hillside near Keswick, England in 1966. I would like to thank Charles Longbottom, both in his capacity as Chairperson of the Acorn Christian Foundation Trustees and as my good friend, for supporting me as I tried to balance my duties as his Director with getting this book finished. I am indebted to friends like Jacquie and John Peat of the Redhill Christian Centre, Ray Simpson, Guardian of the Community of Aidan and Hilda, John Marsh, Archdeacon of Blackburn, Stephen Baker and Dr Ken McAll of Family Tree Ministries, Francis and Judith MacNutt of Christian Healing Ministries and Don Brewin of SOMA, UK, who have all been there to talk, discuss and dig deeper into this subject with me. I would like to thank Gerald Hughes who has been my soul friend on this long journey – he perhaps more than most knows what it has cost me. Finally, I would like to record my appreciation and gratitude to Brendan Walsh, my editor, and his staff at Darton, Longman and Todd, who have had to wait until I recovered from a (literal) flood followed by surgery before I could, at last, complete this book.

Epiphany 2001

FOREWORD

I thank God for this book. The revolutionary concepts here taught have only recently been restored to the church and, as pioneering practitioners like Russ Parker deliver their treasures to paper, we are released from the uncertainty that hinders bold united action. Have you heard? Something wonderful is happening. The church of Jesus, divided for so long, is beginning to function again as an agent of healing, not just for individuals and families but also for institutions, nations, communities and cultures struggling with the memory of wounded history. In today's prayer networks and missionary movements, small bands of forerunners have taken up the cross, willingly applying it to their lives, not only through such disciplines as fasting but also applying the cross to the pride of personal and corporate identity such as ethnicity, nationality and gender. Intercessors are beginning to address the root issues of group history. In an attempt to cleanse and heal the foundations of everything from the nation state to the dynastic family, all kinds of events have been organised, books have been written, documentary films have been produced, in fact, a whole new vocabulary has entered the conversation of the international church.

Who can help us to understand what Jesus is doing in our day? I believe that Russ Parker has given us the most comprehensive biblical survey on the subject to date. *Healing Wounded History* is a true gift to pastors, prayer leaders and Bible teachers, indeed anybody seeking to serve the purposes of God in this generation. However, this book is more than a thoroughly researched Bible study, it is a practical guide to action, worth reading for the closing chapters alone which deal with the processes involved in healing the wounded memory of families, churches and cities.

The author is a respected and trusted leader in the international reconciliation movement. Seasoned by many years of experience, Russ has personally implemented the teachings found in this text. For this reason, we should respect and ponder the ideas he has gathered and then implement them. This is not a 'me too' book that simply parrots a popular theme; this is a careful analysis of the best contemporary teachings matched with the treasures of church history and flavoured with original insights presented in a readable way, touching the emotions as well as the mind. In other words, a book infused with the wisdom that only comes from the Spirit of God.

John Dawson, Founder, International Reconciliation Coalition
Los Angeles
May 2001

INTRODUCTION

> We have to learn how to heal our history. Not forget it, but heal it in full knowledge and acceptance of what has gone before. We have to learn how to accept responsibility, without admitting personal guilt, for what our ancestors have done to others.
>
> (John Lucal, 'The Berlin Wall, 1992 and beyond', *The Way* 31/1 (January 1991), p. 56)

It has often been said that healing is not an event, but a journey. This is because, essentially, Christian healing is not just the wonder of physical or mental recovery, however startling the occasion; it is ultimately the repairing and developing of relationships with God, with others, with ourselves and with the world and society in which we live. This is the journey of a lifetime and it will involve mystery and mess, failure and growth, but our final destination is to look God in the face for the brilliance of an eternity. Healing is the ongoing resource which will enable us to walk this path where we will grow into wholeness, into God's likeness. Consequently, each experience of healing is not a terminus where we can stop and believe that we have arrived at the end of our journey but a stepping stone on the way to becoming complete in Christ. We also quickly discover that we are not alone in this quest, it is a journey in the company of others.

In more than twenty-five years of praying with people and seeking help for myself it soon became apparent that the profile of healing was more complex than I had first thought. It has become increasingly important to approach people not just as individuals but as *individuals in community*. In other words, we must take into account the past and present world of shaping circumstances that people bring within them when they come to the place of prayer. For example, when I was a pastor of a church in an urban priority area on Merseyside, I was approached by a member of the church who was suffering from depression. She asked for healing but it was inappropriate simply to pray for healing of her mental trauma without paying respect to the fact that she had long been unemployed, lived in a run-down part of the town where she was constantly harassed by vandalism, and was subjected to bouts of violent and physical abuse by a partner who struggled with cycles of drunkenness. I found myself involved in helping them to find work, in combating the indifference of over-harassed councillors who had given up on trying to improve the local living conditions, and in arranging counselling sessions for the couple to try and understand the nature and effects of the drink problem they both suffered from. It would have been cheap simply to pray with the laying on of hands and then send the woman back to the environment that constantly threatened to reabuse her. This experience brought home to me that healing is essentially not just an individual enterprise of care but a team effort.

There is a parallel discipline going on within the counselling world where one of the emerging issues is that of *psychosystemics*. This refers to the shaping factors of environment, employment, family history and culture. Larry Kent Graham describes this process as a reciprocal interplay between the psyche of individuals and the social, cultural and natural orders. He says that the interplay is not neutral or static: it is value laden and teeming with possibilities. Consequently, the classic pastoral care tasks of healing, sustaining, guiding and reconciling are to be expanded to include prophetic efforts towards emancipatory liberation, justice-seeking, public advocacy and ecological partnership.[1] In other words, the recovery of sight to the blind must never be separated from releasing the captives or binding up the broken hearted (Isaiah 61:1). Very often these conditions are linked and combined in the same person.

It was from beginnings like these that I began to realise that the agenda for Christian healing involved much more than I had bargained for. We may well begin with the individual request for prayer, but we are soon required to comprehend and engage with the network of issues that form the pattern which shapes each life. This network or context in which we each live our life takes the form of a story or, to be more precise, a collection of group stories with all their memories and emotions. Like all important stories they are a mixture of blessings and wounds and from time to time events remind us of these stories and we tell them once again. For example, within months of taking office the Labour Prime Minister, Tony Blair, issued an apology on behalf of the British for their contribution to the infamous Irish potato famine. His declaration was met with almost universal approval from Irish political leaders in both the Republic and Northern Ireland. There was no surprise registered regarding the raising of this issue; in fact it was felt that the apology was long overdue, and many believed that it was a stepping stone along the road of dialogue and healing within the troubled negotiations for an honourable peace settlement for the North. There was a real sense in which the wound of the famine which lay just beneath the surface of the Irish Republican memory and story was being recognised, located and its healing worked at. Apology offers a climate for dialogue, the beginning of all healings. Confession at a group level suggests that it is possible to work towards healing wounded-group stories and to change the destructive and often repeated cycle such stories generate, which still entangle tribes and communities.

I am quite convinced that the predominantly emerging theme in the work of care both on a political and spiritual scale is going to be the relationship between reconciliation and the healing of relationships at a group and institutional level. Therefore, *Healing Wounded History* attempts to offer a theological and practical examination of reconciliation, the healing of group stories and their relationship to and effect upon the land or place where these stories are located. We shall also observe how unhealed history repeats itself, recognise recurring patterns of dysfunction, and offer some appropriate healing routines and liturgies.

> It's all about belonging.
> The wish of the Unionists to belong to the UK.
> The wish of the Nationalists to belong to Ireland.
> Both traditions are reasonable.
> There are no absolutes.
> The beginning of understanding is to realise that.
>
> (Tony Blair)
> (First speech given by a British Prime Minister to the Oireachtas, Dublin, Thursday 26 November 1998)

1 HEALING THE LAND: AN OVERVIEW

> If my people, who are called by my name, will humble themselves and pray and seek my face and turn from their wicked ways, then will I hear from heaven and will forgive their sins and will heal their land. Now my eyes will be open and my ears attentive to the prayers offered in this place. I have chosen and consecrated this temple so that my Name may be there. My eyes and my heart will always be there.
>
> (2 Chronicles 7:14–16)

The expression 'heal the land' occurs only here in the whole of scripture and yet it contains principles of engagement between God, community and land which are threaded throughout the Old and New Testaments. The background to this disclosure of intimacy and exhortation is the completion of the first temple in Israel. Before this time all sacrifices and prayers were confined largely to the portable tabernacle and the temporary shrine of Shiloh. The completion of the temple underlined the fact that they were no longer a wandering collection of tribal families but a nation in the making who were settled upon their own land. As part of the consecration ceremony, Solomon had prayed that the coming of the Ark of God to its proper resting place would usher in an unprecedented time of blessing and power, because now the presence of God was at the heart of community and worship (2 Chron. 6:14–41). Then we are told that the glory of the Lord came down like fire from heaven and filled the temple (2 Chron. 7:1–3). The whole focus for the dedicating of the temple is this, that God was among his people as a living presence. Worship was the route to intimacy and wholeness.

All this is the backcloth to the challenge to both king and people to keep their covenant with God so as to prosper in the land. Failure to meet the challenge meant expulsion from the land and the disintegration of community as they went into exile – exile which is constantly regarded in the Old Testament as a return to captivity in Egypt. Consequently, healing the land raises a number of interconnected issues:

- the effectiveness of the place of ministry for the healing of community;
- the importance of land, the place of affected human actions;
- the power of wounded stories;
- the witness of confession.

Before continuing, we do need to establish an exegetical issue: is this an exclusive transaction between God, the virgin Jewish nation and the first temple in Jerusalem? Can it be applied beyond its cradle within Israelite society to the Christian community? Without implying that the Christian community is to be considered or treated as the replacement nation of God's people, Israel, this is a serious question, because it underlines the way we use the Old Testament as a resource for our understanding of the New Testament and the way we practise our Christian faith. Are we, for example, still bound by the Jewish dietary laws or the rites of passage into the worshipping community such as circumcision? Most Christian thinkers think not: we live our lives by the model and example of Jesus Christ and the principles he outlined in his teachings. Yet the Old Testament does contain principles for life such as the commandments, which Christians still believe and even write on the walls of their churches.

Therefore, in order to understand what a text of scripture may mean, we ask two questions of it. What did it mean to the people to whom it was first given and does this offer us any insights as to what it can mean to us today? For example, when Isaiah the prophet said to King Ahaz that a young woman would bear a son called Immanuel (Isa. 7:14), what did it mean at the time it was said? The king was afraid for the future of his rule because of the hostile alliances between surrounding kingdoms, and he was not sure what to do. He vacillated between making political alliances or trusting in Yahweh. The prophet challenged him to ask God for a sign, but the king could not bring himself to do even this. So the prophet said that before the child with the significant name 'God is with us' reached maturity, the threat would have disappeared from sight. Christians, however, see this prophecy as applying most fully and profoundly to the coming of Jesus, who most truly embodied the meaning of 'God is with us'. The text had an initial special application but by principle had a further application. So too, this passage from Chronicles has an initial application to the Jewish nation and the first temple. But a further and later application is to all those who consider themselves to be the people of God and who serve him in their place of ministry for the good and health of their community.

The effectiveness of the place of ministry for the healing of community

Over and over again in this passage we are given wonderful insights into the attentiveness and care of God for the place in which his ministry is conducted. We are told that the temple is a chosen place (2 Chron. 7:12). Whatever skills and craftsmanship have gone into the designing and the making of the place, at its heart it is only viable because God has chosen it for himself as the place where he wants to be intimately present with the gathered community. In the strongest anthropological language imaginable, God reveals himself almost as a lover, intent on missing nothing that takes place between himself and those seeking him out. It is not only that his eyes, ears and heart are attentive to the prayers offered: the language used conveys the fact that God's presence is connected with and in the place of ministry. We must not lose sight of this prime objective in the Old Testament ceremonies with their detailed instructions of the sacrificial rites and routines of ministry. God wants above all to connect, to be present and intimate with his people, however complicated the road to this encounter is. However, we are not perfect and we often rebel or drift away from God and become entangled in our sins. The awful fact is that the breakdown of the worshipping community also affects the location and the people whom they are to serve. This is why God promises that when the people of God bring their collective breakdown to God in confession and acts of repentance, not only will there be forgiveness for the community of faith but also healing for the land. As we shall see, land does not only mean geographical location in the Bible but also the community connected with that location.

As we apply this insight to the Christian places of ministry, the church, we are challenged to reconsider our calling to be a resource for the healing and wholeness of our society. It is here that the challenge begins, because we so often discover that the church itself is wounded and in need of healing. Yet how seldom do we bring our church story before God for healing and renewal. Part of what is involved in the healing of the land is the healing of the Christian place of ministry so that it can be the place of ministry for the healing of its community. Surely Jesus was meaning this for the temple and if so for us also, when he said that his house was to be a house of prayer for the healing of the nations (Mark 11:17; Isa. 56:7). 'Healing the land' therefore involves learning our church's story and where necessary asking for forgiveness for all of it in order for the church to be healed and released to be a healing community.

The importance of land, the place of affected human actions

Throughout scripture we are taught that there is a direct connection between human story and the land or ground on which this story occurs. In challenging the people of God to seek forgiveness and healing for their shared sins, God promises to forgive those sins and much more, to heal their land. One of the recurring threads in the prayers of consecration for this first temple is the connection between forgiveness of the sins of the nation and a restored connection with the land. For example, defeat in war at the hands of an enemy (2 Chron. 6:24–5) is thought to be the result of national sin, and returning to the land is a consequence of confession and repentance. When the nation is not living the community lifestyle which reflects God's principles the land suffers with drought, but forgiveness brings rain and a restored community life (2 Chron. 6:26–7). There are over 2,500 references to land in the Old Testament and over 250 in the New. The themes which emerge from these texts are judgement, redemption and healing. Perhaps the first reference of significance for us is that in Genesis 3 which outlines in story form the breakdown of cohesion between humanity and land. Before the act of rebellion we are given the picture of Adam as the shepherd and master of his world: he names the animals and walks in the garden with the blessings of God.

However, when he and Eve rebel against the injunction of God they are expelled from the land of favour and the very ground now becomes hard to till because of the curse which comes upon it from the act of rebellion. I want to shout out and say that it is not fair that the land itself should suffer for our actions. However, what we are to take from this passage is that there is an intimacy between people and the very soil from which they have come. The earth responds to us as much as it responds to God. This is not to credit the earth with a Gaia or goddess status, but to recognise that the earth itself is living and able to respond to the human story as well as declare the glory of the Lord (Ps. 19:1–4; 98:7–9). Perhaps an even more powerful text to consider is that in Genesis 4 where Cain kills his brother Abel. The murderer is confronted by the God who notes the very place where the sinful deed was done: '"Your brother's blood cries out to me from the ground. Now you are under a curse and driven from the ground, which opened its mouth to receive your brother's blood from your hands"' (Gen. 4:10–11). Here is the listening God who knows the stories attached to places and challenges the living to take note of them also. Ever since this moment God's agenda has included healing the land and the wounded stories associated with such places.

Incidentally, it is interesting to contrast this story with the words in Hebrews 12:24 which say that the blood of Jesus speaks better things than the blood of Abel. The spilling of the blood of the righteous Abel meant that Cain could not dwell in or engage with the land; he was put out because his relationship to the place was dysfunctional. Jesus died on a site believed to be on the slopes of the valley of Hinnom, a rubbish dump outside the city walls of Jerusalem, a place which had a bad memory of child sacrifices. Yet what does the spilling of the blood of Jesus mean? It tells us that by that supreme act of redemptive sacrifice we who believe in Jesus can come in, we can return to the forgiveness and love of God. In fact, the passage in Hebrews is all about coming closer in to God, to the communion of 'just men made perfect', to the cradling arms of Christ and the angels in joyful assembly (Heb. 12:22–3). Perhaps one of the strongest and most basic needs of the whole human race is to belong and to belong in the place or on the land where we can connect, be rooted and grow. We should not be surprised then to see that the consummation of the purposes of God is described in terms of land and community. In the penultimate chapter of the book of Revelation, almost the final vision given to John is that of the new creation: 'Then I saw a new heaven and a new earth . . . I saw the Holy City, the new Jerusalem, coming down out of heaven from God' (Rev. 21:1–2). The disruption between community and land, described in the stories of Genesis, is finally to be redeemed in almost the last healing recorded in scripture. The new heaven and earth provide the context for the new community. Therefore we must explore and understand the significance of land and its connections with the human story, and learn routines of healing which we can bring to painful places which still cry out their story for those who have an ear to hear.

The power of wounded stories

At the heart of this great exhortation from God is the need to heal the blighted story of the people of God. The core of such healing is the recognition that the actions of one affect the well-being of the many. The particular one outlined here is the challenge to the king to make sure that he does not worship a foreign god, one alien to the land given to the people of the covenant with Yahweh. If the king becomes an idolater the people will pay the price by being removed from the land and sent into exile. The idea of corporate personality was developed by H. Wheeler Robinson when he sought a rationale for the biblical stories where the innocent were punished for the wickedness of the sinful individual, as in the case of Aachan in Joshua 7, where his entire family and his cattle were destroyed along with him for the crime of stealing what God had devoted to destruction. Robinson wrote:

> The larger or smaller group was accepted without question as a unity; legal prescription was replaced by the fact or fiction of the blood-tie, usually traced back to a common ancestor. The whole group, including its past, present and future members, might function as a single individual through any one of those members conceived as representative of it.[1]

However, Robinson's carte-blanche use of this term as an explanation for such stories was heavily criticised for adopting a corporate understanding of humanity at the expense of individuality, and his ideas gradually went out of fashion among scholars. Today there has been a revival of interest in the subject of corporate or group identity with particular emphasis on understanding principles for the development and healing of community.

E. A. Martens traces the focus on groups throughout the Old Testament. He rightly points out that when God made promises to Abraham, Isaac and Jacob that they would inherit land, he always included their descendants (Gen. 12:7; 13:14ff; 15:7; 17:18ff). He explains this by saying that the group is the important focus for God, and the keyword to describe this in Hebrew thought is *solidarity*. He says that the unity of the group reached back in time to include the ancestors. In burial, for example, the dead were spoken of as being gathered to their fathers. The borderline between individual and group was fluid.[2] The same belief is behind the lists of genealogies which not only appear throughout the Old Testament, but serve as a key foundation for understanding the good news according to Matthew and Luke. They emphasise the importance of belonging beyond our individuality to the group that in various ways gave birth to us.

Joel Kaminsky strongly challenges the earlier assumption that corporate personality reflects the more primitive material in the Hebrew Bible and that individuality is a mark of the evolution of theological thought. He writes:

> Ancient Israel considered it quite normal for divine and sometimes even human punishment to be corporate in nature. Corporate ideas of retribution are not confined to a few unusual cases; rather, a corporate understanding of punishment pervades the major theological systems found in the Hebrew Bible.[3]

Kaminsky then proceeds to examine accounts throughout the Old Testament where this theme of the one being representative of the many occurs. He begins with the story of King Manasseh and the horrific consequences to the nation for his outrageous desecration of the temple of God (2 Kings 21:1–18; 23:26–7; 23:36—24:6). He points out that the nation of Israel was exiled for the sins of the dead king even though it subsequently had the services of the righteous King Josiah. Kaminsky describes this as the phenomenon in which sin spreads vertically across numerous generations as trans- or intergenerational retribution.[4] At the heart of this idea of corporate personality or identity stands the covenant which God makes with his chosen people. At their core, covenants are made with groups and not individuals. J. D. L. Levenson identifies two basic covenants in the Old Testament, one made with Israel as God's special people (Josh. 24), and which he calls the Sinaitic, and one made with David and his progeny (2 Sam. 7; 2 Chron. 6 and 7), called the Davidic.[5] In both covenants there are exhortations to faithfulness to that covenant coupled with warnings of the consequences which will harm the nation if those covenants are broken by the individuals who represent them.

The Sinaitic covenant specifically stated that exile would be the punishment of those who were disobedient to God's laws. Consider for example, 'I will scatter you among the nations and I will unsheathe the sword against you. Your land will be a desolation and your cities a ruin' (Lev. 26:33; cf. Deut. 4:27; 28:64). It seems that the royal covenant of David is one where the ability of the nation to overcome its enemies and dwell in safety in their land depends upon the faithfulness of the monarch (2 Chron. 7:19–20). Kaminsky believes that this royal convenant underlines how the one can represent the many when that one is the special person of the king. He describes the king as God's vicar upon earth, the single most important mediator between the people and their God.[6] If the king sinned he endangered the welfare of the nation, not only because he was his nation's representative but because, as monarch, his example would invariably be followed by the people. However, we must put alongside the example of the king's capacity to represent and affect his nation that of the Sinaitic covenant which heavily underlined the fact that any one person could affect the well-being of the many. Deuteronomy 29 sets out the terms of this covenant and indicates that the covenant applies horizontally to everyone in this present generation (29:10–11) and also vertically to those who are not yet born and thus not actually present when the covenant was made (29:14–15):

> All of you are standing today in the presence of the Lord your God – your leaders and chief men, your elders and officials, and all the other men of Israel, together with your children and your wives and the aliens living in your camps . . . You are standing here in order to enter into a covenant with the Lord your God . . . to confirm you this day as his people, that he may be your God as he promised you and as he swore to your fathers, Abraham, Isaac and Jacob. I am making this covenant, with its

> oath, not only with you who are standing here with us today in the presence of the Lord our God but also with those are not here today.

What these two covenants underline for us is that as individuals we can affect and are affected by the group of which we are a part. In the case of these two covenants and what we have examined so far in the Bible, the groups in question are those of tribe and family. I would like to suggest, however, that there are a number of group stories with which we interact. The book of Revelation builds its prophecies around a number of references to the particular group stories that feature in the purposes of God from the beginning until the climax of the ages. The four in particular are *nation, tribe, people* and *language*.[7] There are five truths which reflect the interaction between God and these group stories:

- The blood of Jesus has been shed to redeem those from every tribe and language and people and nation (Rev. 5:9).
- The worshippers around the throne in heaven represent every nation, tribe, people and language (Rev. 7:9).
- John is encouraged to give his prophecy about many peoples, nations, languages and kings (Rev. 10:11).
- Spiritual warfare is directed against every tribe, people, language and nation (Rev. 13:7).
- Moral and spiritual decay is focused upon peoples, multitudes, nations and languages (Rev. 17:15).

So it is apparent that in some way we are caught up in the group stories which we carry within us and of which we are a part; and it is clear that these are in fact wounded-group stories. This book will concentrate on four major group stories which contribute to the shaping of us and they are family, church, community, and tribe or nation. No doubt there are other important group stories to examine such as gender, race, the companies we work for and their corporate philosophies and practices, and the colleges and schools which trained us. However, I have chosen to focus on just four, as those that have a more general impact on the shaping of Christians and their outlook on society. If it is true that we are to some degree a product of a number of group stories and that we carry them within us, then it is also true that we can and do have a role of witness, reconciliation and healing to these groups.

The witness of confession

The core of Solomon's night-time encounter with God after the consecration of the temple and its ministry, is that when the need is there, confession is the key to healing the community's sin and pain. In this dream interview, God introduces a future scenario when the nation will have forsaken God and gone its own way and the land is suffering the consequences. The key to redemption is for the people of God to confess their own sins first, in response to which God will favour them with forgiveness and move beyond their need to bring healing to the land, the wider community and its geographical location. The passage focuses upon the confession of the worshipping community and also the monarch. Both have a role of representing their community. As we shall see in more detail later, confession involves an identification and ownership of the group story in question in order for there to be healing and restoration for that group. We must not think that this idea of the one representing the many is confined to the Old Testament. Notice how Paul, in his letter to the Roman church, contrasts the effects of death upon society through the sin of Adam with the overflowing of life through Jesus Christ:

> For if the many died by the trespass of the one man, how much more did God's grace and the gift that came by the grace of the one man, Jesus Christ, overflow to the many! (Romans 5:15)

Paul uses this theme, of contrasting the consequences of the choices of Adam and Jesus for the many, as his major building block for the doctrines of salvation and justification (cf. Rom. 5:17–21). Consequently, we need to model our work of healing on this example of Jesus who confessed and took upon himself the group story of mankind in general. One present-day example of this is that of John and Yvonne Presdee who are cofounders of the Reconciliation Prayer Walks. On the nine hundredth anniversary of the First Crusade they had the conviction that they should walk the original Crusader route and visit as many mosques, synagogues and Orthodox churches as possible, these being the principal targets of destruction and slaughter by the Crusaders. They felt that they had a calling to represent the western Christian church of which they are members and therefore representatives. Gripped by their belief in the power of confession they met with leaders, Muslim, Jewish and Orthodox Christian, and read out an apology for the actions of the Christian Crusaders; they were not in any way apologising for Christ or their faith, only the deeds committed by fellow Christians. Everywhere they did this they were met with a mixture of disbelief and warm acceptance of their confession. One rabbi of a synagogue in Bosnia surprised them. John had forgotten to bring his written apology and asked if the rabbi could wait ten minutes while he returned to his hotel to fetch his apology. The rabbi replied by saying, 'We have waited nine hundred years for this – ten more minutes won't make much more difference!' It demonstrated how long unhealed stories can linger in people's hearts and memories. For reconciliation between peoples or groups even to begin to happen, there does need to be a process of recognition and confession of what that wounded-group story is. This does not solve all the problems, but it does furnish us with a climate for ongoing dialogue and healing of relationships.

Healing the land, therefore, brings together the strands of unhealed history and the locations where such stories continue to exert a shaping of the peoples living there. It needs a recognition of the repeated patterns of such woundedness, which are the windows through which we can see and feel something of the unhealed story of a particular group. It means we must listen to unhealed history and, if appropriate, own it as ours and go on the journey of reconciliation and healing. This is the agenda we will explore throughout the rest of this book, and we will begin by looking at the significance and importance of land in human experience.

2 LAND AS GIFT AND SACRAMENT

We are guests in this world. (Columbanus)

One of the important phenomena to emerge from both the prayer and healing movements of our day is that of 'prayer-walking' on sites where unhealed or unacknowledged wounded stories are located. This is done in the belief that such wounds still speak out their pain today and affect those living on those sites. It is in this connection that Jeanie Wyle-Kellerman notes: 'Seemingly in response to cries from the earth itself, hundreds of people are gathering to pray in places where blood has been shed.'[1] She goes on to see a connection between the unacknowledged pain and blood in the soil in North America with that nation's tendency to transience and alienation from a sense of the sacred in land and place. These prayer locations, widely scattered in time and space, include the fields of Culloden near Inverness where Scottish hopes of independence were crushed by the ascendant English, the gas chambers of Auschwitz in Poland, the battle site of the Somme, the massacre site of Wounded Knee, and the sacred Hawai'ian island of Kaho'alawe which the US navy had used for bombing practice. These are only a small sample of sites that have been visited and this work is being more and more encouraged and co-ordinated by the International Reconciliation Coalition.[2] What fuels this ministry is the belief that human story affects the location it happens in and that this serves as a window of opportunity to locate and understand unhealed history. This then allows the possibility of bringing reconciliation between the living representatives of the story in question, who to some degree relive or repeat the damaging script of the past event. An example of this is the annual service of reconciliation which is held at the site of the battle of the Boyne, near Slane Bridge, which is close to Drogheda in the Republic of Ireland. For the last ten years or more, representatives of Christian churches from the Republic, Northern

Ireland and Great Britain have gathered to learn the lesson of history and engage in apology and reconciliation between the peoples of these three countries. Irish representatives spoke of how this battle has been used to rally nationalist sympathies to acts of violence against the English and the loyalist community in Northern Ireland. They asked forgiveness from God and those whom they had harmed. Representatives of the English victors at that battle asked for forgiveness for presuming to invade Ireland, a country to which they had no right whatsoever. In July 2000 I gave the main address at this service and also preached in three local Roman Catholic churches in Drogheda. As I prepared my talks, I felt guided to include an apology for what the English under Cromwell did in destroying their town. Each time this was greeted with a spontaneous and enthusiastic applause, which apparently had never happened in these churches before. It served to remind us all that unhealed history is still a live issue in both the locality and the community and will go on influencing and shaping us until we find appropriate healing routines to release us from its hold.

Wyle-Kellerman goes further by saying that the healing process also affects the dead who were the original victims or perpetrators of the story in question. She picks up the theme of the God who listens to and locates the scream of the spilled blood of Abel and so focuses our attention on attending to the wounds of the dead as well as the living. She writes that 'people who have head the cries of the dead say they feel the quieting of the land after prayers are offered. They say they feel a peace and a deep connection to the earth afterwards.'[3]

What emerges from these examples is the importance of land and its capacity to hold, reflect and repeat the human story sown into its soil. In order to understand the significance of land and its role in the healing and reconciliation of wounded history, we need to examine a number of themes:

- the biblical view of land as gift and place of belonging;
- Jubilee and Sabbath: reconciling, renewing and resting the lands;
- environmentalism and the reverencing of the earth;
- the power of holy places and the pain of hurting places.

The biblical view of land as gift and place of belonging

At the core of human experience there seem to be three great needs, *to belong, to be secure and to be powerful*. They have all been embraced to some degree by the pursuit and possession of land. These themes are indeed basic to the Old Testament, which focuses upon a displaced people whose founding patriarchs were energised by the repeated promise that they would dwell in a land of richness and security and that God will cohabit the land with them. We need to recognise that land in the Bible must be understand as both geographical location – the place that gives the security of being one's own land, and as a symbol to represent the wholeness of joy and well-being that is illustrated by social cohesion and personal comfort. Walter Brueggemann in his book, *The Land,* unpacks the word 'place' and describes it as

> space which has historical meanings, where some things have happened which are now remembered and which provide continuity and identity across generations . . . where important words have been spoken which have established identity, defined vocation and envisioned destiny . . . where vows have been exchanged and promises have been made.[4]

As we shall see, all these are the ingredients which form a group story in its locality.

However, the Israelites did not come by this land through their own powers, it was through promise. Consequently the Bible demonstrates that the core quest of humanity is to belong, to find roots rather than just the meaning of life. Remarkably enough, the lessons of history for the Old Testament faithful came more from the times of being landless. They were to understand the purposes of God at work in their captivity, wilderness wandering and exile in order, when the time came, to dwell securely in their own promised land. The times of being wanderers, those on the journey to nowhere in particular, and sojourners, those who temporarily dwell in land not their own, were designed to teach principles of living once the promised land became the homeland.

The first principle is that the presence of God makes land a blessing. This is starkly revealed when in the wilderness the wandering tribes are sustained with the provision of manna. The writer of

Exodus points out that as far as Yahweh is concerned, the miracle is performed not just to feed the hungry but so that they will know that it is the Lord who has brought them out of Egypt (Exod. 16:6–7). The point is that even in the wilderness God is present. He does not live just among the powerful, nor does he wait for their arrival in the land of promise, but he shares the wilderness journey. It is here that God's presence is revealed by the column of fire and the pillar of cloud (Num. 14:14). The same effect is produced when the landless captives in Egypt or Babylon witness the miraculous presence of God, whether through acts of powerful judgement upon the oppressors in Egypt, or through Yahweh's ability to touch the heart of a despot (Cyrus), and use him to set God's people free to return to their homeland. All these encounters with Yahweh, in land not their own, are to convey that land is made the place of provision and blessing through the presence of the Lord with his people and not through any quality of the land in itself. The Psalmist captured this simple but profound truth when he wrote 'Yahweh is my Shepherd, I shall not be in want' (Ps. 23:1). Two other truths emerge from this experience: Yahweh is not confined to the soil of Israel, and ownership or possession of land does not belong to Israel but to God, because 'the earth is the Lord's and everything in it, the world, and all who live in it' (Ps. 24:1).

The second principle, therefore, is that land is gift. Israel had land because God kept his promise to the nation. They are reminded of this constantly throughout the formative period when they had entered the promised land and were beginning to build community in the land God had given them:

> Not one of all the Lord's good promises to the house of Israel failed; every one was fulfilled. (Joshua 21:45)

> When the Lord your God brings you into the land he swore to your fathers, to Abraham, Isaac and Jacob, to give you – a land with large, flourishing cities you did not build, houses filled with all kinds of good things you did not provide, wells you did not dig, and vineyards and olive groves you did not plant – then when you eat and are satisfied, *be careful that you do not forget the Lord* who brought you out of Egypt, out of the land of slavery. (Deuteronomy 6:10–12, italics mine)

Here the anticipation of living in the homeland and enjoying its fruits is coupled with living in the intimacy of a relationship with Yahweh. Indeed, it may be said that the fruitfulness of the land is a consequence of living in harmony with Yahweh and his laws. As Brueggemann reminds us, gifted land is also covenanted land.[5] The promised land is the place to celebrate this relationship and all the festivals such as Passover, Firstfruits, the Feasts of Weeks and of Trumpets and of Tabernacles (Lev. 23:4–44) are designed to celebrate this connection between the land yielding its harvest of provision and the saving relationship between Yahweh and his people. To forget God was to risk harming the land and facing the possibility of eviction (Deut. 6:15, 20–5). This is starkly set out in the chapter of blessings and curses in Deuteronomy 28, for both blessing and curse touches both the land and the community that lives upon it:

> You will be blessed in the city and blessed in the country.
>
> The Lord will grant you abundant prosperity – in the fruit of your womb, the young of your livestock and the crops of your ground – in the land he swore to your forefathers to give you.
>
> (Deuteronomy 28:3, 11)

> You will be cursed in the city and cursed in the country.
>
> The fruit of your womb will be cursed, and the crops of your land. (Deuteronomy 28:16, 18)

The land was not a passive bystander to the affairs of human society but a player in the game. At the heart of this link is Yahweh who challenges us all to live according to his principles on the land which is his gift to us. It is not just simply that what we do on the land affects that land for good or ill; it is how we relate to the presence of God which affects the land, because the land is a living link with the presence of God. This interconnectedness of human story in relationship with God and land runs like a thread throughout scripture, perhaps never more graphically than in the time of the judges. The whole book revolves around the recurring scenario of the loss of land through the rebellion of the people against the rule and governance of Yahweh. They are brought into a time of oppression within their land by an alien tribe; then the people call on Yahweh in repentance and in response a deliverer or judge is raised up by the gifting of the Spirit, the enemy is routed and the cycle ends with the 'land having peace' for a certain number of years, usually coinciding with the length of rule of the judge.[6] After the judge's death, the cycle is repeated. This continues more or less until the period of the monarchy, when the oppressing despot is invariably the king himself. From the time of Solomon and the rest of his long dynasty, with the notable exceptions of Hezekiah and Josiah, the history of the monarchy is all about getting land, keeping it and defending it against all comers, and losing it finally to an alien despot. Coupled with this was the obsessional belief that no matter what the lifestyle or beliefs of the kings, Yahweh would always defend Jerusalem against all its enemies. In fact, this obsession served to shield the rulers from the challenges of living according to the rule of God's holy presence among his people. Prophet after prophet warned the kings of the dire consequences of their oppressive acts and the hoarding of land but they were invariably rejected. Jeremiah speaks perhaps more than any other prophet about the subject of land, its dependence upon the good gift of God and how easily it could be lost through idolatry and pride.[7]

Finally, land must be managed by the principles of justice and care. One of the constant themes presented to the Israelites once they entered their homeland was to remember their time of dispossession in Egypt when they were slaves. This acts as a recurring motif for the establishing of principles for managing the land and caring for the community on it. 'Remember' is in fact the key word in the book of Deuteronomy and it serves as a challenge not to lose touch with the reality of Yahweh's delivering presence, and as a call to live a life where freedom and honouring and not bondage and slavery are the guiding passions (Deut. 8:2–20). Land came also to signify belonging and identity both for the tribal group as a whole and for each person in particular. To forget this abiding provision of Yahweh was to run the danger of slipping into the illusion that land and society is something we possess or own. This is the beginning of the downward path on which the strong begin dispossessing the weak.

A classic example of this is the killing of Naboth by King Ahab so the king could take possession of Naboth's vineyard which he coveted (1 Kings 21). Naboth refused to sell, saying that such an act would dishonour the memory of his ancestors whose names lived on through his occupation of the inherited land. For the crime of stealing land and destroying the identity of the one who lived there, the prophet proclaims to Ahab that the memory of his own clan name will be extinguished. There is an embedded loathing of acquiring land for personal power and possession in the Old Testament and this is reflected in the lament of the prophet Isaiah: 'Woe to you who add house to house and join field to field till no space is left and you live alone in the land' (Isa. 5:8). This remark is undoubtedly aimed at the monarchy who alone would have had the muscle and the motivation to acquire land just for the purposes of power and personal prestige. When Ezekiel was in exile, waiting for the return to his homeland which had been destroyed as a consequence of a disastrous monarchy, he looked for a time of better equality in caring for people's right to live on their own land, their gift from God. He wrote, 'The Prince must not take any of the inheritance of the people, driving them off their property. He is to give his sons their inheritance out of his own property, so that none of my people will be separated from his property (*or land*)' (Ezek. 46:18; words in brackets are mine).

In the New Testament, to a large degree, the focus of land is replaced by the kingdom of God, which is not tied down to earthly cities and places but which offers as its ultimate prize the citizenship of heaven. W. D. Davies thinks that the history of Christianity has been to spiritualise the issue of land and replace its importance with the person of Jesus himself.[8] This is perhaps a narrow view of the gospel presentation because, although Jesus may not say a great deal about land, he certainly picks up the land lifestyle which Yahweh encouraged his people to adopt. Jesus taught about the kingdom of God, which was about the quality of life we should embrace whether we have land to live upon or not; this is precisely the lesson of Israel in captivity, wilderness and exile. When his disciples asked him questions about when God would overthrow the Romans so that they could have their land back, he refused to talk politics but encouraged them to be open to the Holy Spirit so that they could live a life of godly witness to their scattered and dispossessed communities (Acts 1:6–8). Jesus' whole teaching was a challenge for people to return to the concept of land as gift; it is the meek who will inherit (not conquer) the earth. Therefore his healings, his acts of forgiveness, his saving touch and transformation of lives, and his death and resurrection, are all invitations to live within the kingdom of God. And this kingdom is to come upon earth, not in terms of possession of territory but in the living of godly community which is to bless the soil upon which it is lived. A further illustration of community and land is illustrated by Jesus's interaction with the story of Jerusalem with which he seemed to be well aquainted (Matt. 23:37–9). Yet there are hints about the significance of land in the repeated references to Abraham as a model of faith, and his stories cannot be separated from his tenacious belief in the promise of a homeland (Gal. 3:6–9; 4:21–6; Rom. 4). However, the subject of land comes once more into view with the climax of the ages when a holy community will finally be established on the soil of a new earth (Rev. 21:1–2). Moltmann points out that because humanity plays the key role in the ordering of God's world, human reconciliation and healing will lead ultimately to the restoration of creation, just as human sin led to creation's fall. He goes on to say, 'At present the world as a whole remains unaware of the reconciliation achieved on the cross, of the fact that God will eventually remake the world and its power structures so that they reflect his glory instead of human arrogance.'[9]

In conclusion therefore, we see that land has come to represent a woven cord of the three themes of God's grace-giving presence making land fruitful, living in the spirit of giftedness and not possessiveness, and building holy society. We must read the laws and regulations for community and temple ministry as being the vehicle to remind us of and renew this vision of living in holiness and harmony with the land. There are in fact two particular healing liturgies for land which will help us to understand something of why land can hold, either for blessing or curse, the story of the people who lived upon it. I am referring to Jubilee and Sabbath.

Jubilee and Sabbath: reconciling, renewing and resting the land

Both Jubilee and Sabbath are presented as an intertwined package in the Law Codes of Moses (Lev. 25). Both alike are focused on the pastoral care of land and community. The year of Jubilee is introduced as the year following seven Sabbath years (a Sabbath year was held every seventh year) which meant that it was to be observed every fiftieth year. It was to be announced on the Day of Atonement and so immediately it is part of God's redemptive action for his people and is an opportunity for forgiveness and reconciliation between families and peoples (Lev. 25:9). Like all the Sabbath years before it, Jubilee was an opportunity to give the land a time of rest from its labours, and so the land was to lie fallow and no sowing or planting was to take place. In other words, this was a challenge to trust in the God who gifted them in slavery, wilderness and exile, to provide for them in the land of promise. It was a twofold response of faith: faith in God, the carer and provider for community, and faith for a time to bless and respect the land which had given them home and sustenance. Because it was a celebration of God's liberation of the Israelites from captivity, the nation was to extend this selfsame liberty to all their countrymen in the land. This included the returning of land to the true owners who may have sold its lease either to repay debts or because they were too impoverished to work the land. As such, this legislation presented the most radical programme for continuous social reform to be found in the Old Testament. Peter Ackroyd saw it as no less than an opportunity to heal and restore true community to the land, a time of new covenant when not only people but the earth itself may be renewed through resting.[10] Jubilee was an extraordinary generosity, where the consequences of debts were cancelled, and as such it prefigures the very gift of Jesus upon the cross whereby he cancelled our debt of sins and made new life and community possible (cf. Col. 2:14; Eph. 2:19–20).

The impact of Jubilee, the year of release, was in fact far-reaching in its scope. It was at the very least a stern rebuke to the whole system of large-scale collectivisim or nationalisation of land. It was also a major resource for the healing and renewal of community and the very land itself. Jeffrey Fagar fleshes out the contents of this renewal as four essential elements:[11]

- to prevent the accumulation of land by the rich at the expense of the poor;
- to reattach people to the land as an act of belonging;
- to make the family group economically viable again;
- to renew family solidarity.

Jesus seems to sum up the spirit of Jubilee when he describes the content of his mission in the language of Isaiah 61 as the freeing of captives and the oppressed, and transfers the focus on land to that of the kingdom of God (Luke 4:16ff). It doesn't take much imagination to see in Jesus' use of the words from Isaiah 61, 'the year of the Lord's favour', an echo of the Jubilee promise. John Yoder picks out threads of Jubilee criteria in the prayer which Jesus taught us, which understands God's kingdom as the establishment of justice and right relations on the earth – which is nothing else but God's will being done on earth. He says that the hope for earthly renewal is spelled out in three terse statements: Give us this day our daily bread, forgive us our debts as we forgive our debtors, do not bring us to the time of trial. The reference to debts here he sees as being the Jubilee tradition of liquidation of debts, and not simply debts spiritualised as 'sins'.[12] The early church certainly took on something of the Jubilee manifesto when it sought to live in community where the day-to-day needs of the members were met (Acts 4:32–5). Although there is no actual account of the year of Jubilee being implemented within the nation of Israel, it is nonetheless a vital aspect of the biblical vision for bringing healing to the land and its tenant community under the Lordship of God.

Dr J. H. Wright challenges us with a wonderful vision of the implications of Jubilee in our lives today even though he makes no reference to our God-given mandate to care for the earth:

> To apply the jubilee model, then, requires that people face the sovereignty of God, trust his providence, know his redemptive action, and hope in his promise. The wholeness of the model embraces the church's evangelistic mission, its personal and social ethics and its future hope.[13]

Whereas the word for Jubilee (*yobel*) means 'release', the word 'Sabbath' can mean either 'to cease' or 'to rest'. Although there is no clear rule of Sabbath observance put upon the church, the church simply took the Jewish Sabbath and transferred its core principles to the first day of the week to coincide with a statement of faith on the resurrection of Christ from the dead. This has by and large been universal in the church's practice but could only be enjoyed by everyone from the time of the fourth century when the Emperor Constantine made Christianity the official state religion. There seem to be two basic reasons for the introduction of Sabbath as a regular rhythm of the community of God's people: as a reminder of the nation's redemption from slavery in Egypt, and to celebrate the role of God in creation.

Although the Sabbath was a cessation of work on the seventh day, it was not to be an inactive or deadly dull day. It was to be an occasion to celebrate salvation from slavery and a sign of the everlasting covenant which God had made with the nation (Lev. 23:3; Isa.

58:13; Exod. 31:12–17; Deut. 5:12ff). Sacrifices could be offered and praises given (Lev. 24:5–8; Num. 28:9–10). Sabbath was also for the unemployed, children and the retired and so the emphasis is not totally upon giving up industry for a day, but giving time to recognise and give thanks for healing and salvation. The second reason for the Sabbath is that we are called to work and rest after the example of the Almighty himself. We are told that with each strand of his creation, God pronounced it 'good' (*tovah*). He affirmed it, honoured it and nourished it even in its making. There is that truly astonishing statement in Exodus 31:17 referring to God resting from his labours on the seventh day, where we are told that the Lord paused to 'get his breath back' (Heb. *wayyinaphash*).[14]

When we come to the New Testament there is a radical freedom in Jesus to engage in Sabbath rest. In the middle of an onslaught of healing requests, he suddenly withdraws to the quiet places to rest and connect with God. The continuous references to him being alone or in lonely places serve to underline the importance of what we have been saying about meeting God through the wonder of his creation (Mark 1:32–3, 35–6; Luke 5:15–16). The other side to Jesus' attitude towards the Sabbath is his sharp rebuke of the Pharisees who seem to have emptied the Sabbath of its humanitarian character and imprisoned it in minutiae of rules and regulations. You can feel the rush of his anger when he turns upon his critics in the synagogue who condemned him for healing someone on the Sabbath (Matt. 12:9–14). Jesus overturned their approach to Sabbath by saying that it was made for people and not people for it (Mark 2:27). A final and developing thought regarding Sabbath in the New Testament is from the pen of the writer to the Hebrews, who uses the Sabbath rest as a way of describing the Christian life as one which is dependent upon the Lord who provides, and not just on our own abilities to provide for ourselves.

The Sabbath is an occasion to recreate through honouring God for his creative gifts to us, the chief one being land – without it there is no community. It is also an opportunity to honour and celebrate land itself, to change the dynamic of relationship from one of work on the land to one of wonder at the land. This theme is taken up well by Michael Mayne in his book *This Sunrise of Wonder*, which is an invitation to take the Sabbath rhythm to heart in a contemplative way and let God nourish us through the wonders of his creation.[15] He sees

Sabbath as a calling to slow the pace of industry within our souls and, through listening and contemplation of creation, to reconnect with land and God in a new and vital way. We would see the extraordinary in the ordinary if only we would stop beside the Creator and look and listen. As the poet Gerard Manley Hopkins wrote,

> The world charged with the grandeur of God,
> It will flame out like shining from shook foil.[16]

It is in this sense that God makes the land a sacrament of his grace to us. Within it he has woven the presence of his Spirit in every leaf of every tree, and to behold it we must engage in Sabbath rest and celebrate the presence of God in and through his creation. This is what lies at the heart of pilgrimage and it connects us to God through places made holy by his touch.

Both Jubilee and Sabbath invite us to celebrate and honour both the land and the God who gives it. More than this, it is a call to live wholesomely upon the land and to respect its intimate connection with our human story. If we live within God's principles we are told that the land will prosper and be a blessing to us; if we neglect God's ways it is tantamount to neglecting the earth and results in an inevitable destruction of the land and, thereby, ourselves. We have the capacity to wound our earth or enrich it. We now live in an age where the survival of the planet is a serious issue and inevitably the Christian church is accused of being one of the chief culprits. In the light of what we have discovered about land and its carrying of our human story, we must now give some thought to the issue of the environment and the need to reverence the earth as God's gift.

Environmentalism and reverencing the earth

We now live in an age when care and survival of the planet is a mainstream subject and no longer a fringe topic for so-called New Agers. The threat of global warming resulting from the discharge of toxic gases into the atmosphere has galvanised a range of disciplines to consider the issues and effects of a declining earth. Michael Northcott said that the environmental disaster we all now face is the biggest single cause of the movement of peoples across the globe.[17] We are barraged on our televisions with unforgettable scenes –

of flooding in numerous countries in which thousands have lost their lives, of the many homeless who wander like dazed zombies through the rubble of what was once their homeland, now ravaged by war and famine. The levels of starvation in Ethiopia which attracted the generosity of millions for the dying is now threatening to become the norm in the majority of Third World nations. There have been two world summits on the environment, in Brazil and Japan, but there does not seem to be any constructive solution to the problems threatening to collapse the planet's ecosystems. It is an obvious thing to say, but without the planet we have no healing for ourselves.

> The well-being of the ecosystem of the planet is a prior condition for the well-being of humans. We cannot have well-being on a sick planet, not even with our medical sciences. So long as we continue to generate more toxins than the planet can absorb and transform, the members of the earth community will become ill. Human health is derivative. Planetary health is primary.[18]

My main purpose in this section is not to give an exhaustive treatment of environmentalism, its causes and solutions – others have done that more eloquently. I want to focus upon the postmodern reawakening to the reverence of the earth and how our Christian faith helps us to make a healing contribution to the land. However, before we can do this we must face up to the charge that it is western Christianity which set the trend of plundering the earth. This accusation was first levelled in 1967 by the historian Professor Lynn White. Coming from a Christian family himself, he argued that the ecological problem began with the marriage of science and technology which gave birth to power machinery and labour-saving devices. However, what lay behind of this marriage was the Christian view of humankind and nature that arose in the Middle Ages. What he describes here is nothing short of a quantum shift in thinking and consequent actions. It was during this time that people began to see themselves no longer as a part of nature but as having dominion over nature. According to White, this ruthless attitude toward nature later joined forces with a new technology to wreak environmental havoc. The villain of this lethal scenario is the church, which had earlier displaced animism (in which every tree, spring and stream had its own guardian spirit), and allowed the domination of nature for the sole benefit of human beings to whom the creation had been made subordinate by God. White wrote that Christianity had now made it possible to exploit nature in a mood of indifference because it had opted for a militant anthropocentric faith where nature's sole *raison d'être* was to serve humanity.[19] To be fair to White, he does mention the example of St Francis and his reverence for nature, but Francis is more the exception than the rule. It became fashionable to blame organised religion in general and Christianity in particular for the destruction of the planet. In his books *Creation Spirituality* and *The Coming of the Cosmic Christ* Matthew Fox argued that because the dominant branch in western Christendom has been the evangelicals who begin with the fall of humankind and the cursing of the earth, Christianity has failed to get back to its beginning, which is God's divine act of creation. Consequently, with its focus on fall and redemption, it has channelled all its energies into saving mankind at the expense of caring for the earth which has a role to play in the making whole of all humanity.[20] But is this true? I think that Christian theology has largely neglected the importance of creation, and has not tried to provide a process of incorporating creation into its activities of mission and evangelism.

However, there have been notable exceptions which have served to recall the church to a much more inclusive style of living and witnessing. Among examples would be John Calvin, who in his teaching on stewardship of creation wrote the following injunction:

> Let him who possesses a field, so partake of its yearly fruits, that he may not suffer the ground to be injured by his negligence; but let him endeavour to hand it down to posterity as he received it . . . Let everyone regard himself as the steward of God in all things which he possesses.[21]

In the village of Selborne in Hampshire, the Revd Gilbert White wrote his observations of local wildlife in his famous book *The Natural History of Selborne* (1789); writing about the humble earthworm and its indispensable activity in reinvigorating soil, he described such as the wisdom of God in creation. A more recent exponent of creation-affirming teaching would be that of Francis Schaeffer who rejected on the one hand the inadequacy of pantheism, and a world-rejecting Christianity on the other. He set out some of his ideas in his book

Pollution and the Death of Man (1970). He recognised our shared creatureliness with the earth and called on churches to become 'pilot plants' demonstrating the possibility of a substantial healing of the damage brought about by human greed.

Let us then explore some of the biblical themes which describe the relationship between creation and human story.

Creation and humanity share an intimacy and interconnectedness with God

> God saw all that he had made, and it was very good.
>
> (Genesis 1:31)

> The Lord God formed the man from the dust of the ground.
>
> (Genesis 2:7)

We need to recognise that humanity was made with the same lovingkindness as the earth with all its teeming variety of life, and that we should remember that God has pronounced us both 'good'. In this sense, we share a solidarity with the soil from which we came and to which we shall return. These opening passages from Genesis teach us some important truths about our links with the land. Ron Elsdon points out that they set humanity's life in terms of two relationships, with the Creator and with creation, and they must never be pulled apart.[22] And like humanity, creation can and does respond to the majesty and love of Almighty God. We read of the earth singing to the Lord (Ps. 96:1, 11); of the heavens declaring God's glory (Ps. 19:1; 89:5); of the calves leaping with joy on being let out of their stalls (Mal. 4:2); and, in the final day, of the lamb and the wolf feeding together in redeemed harmony (Isa. 11:6; 65:25). Professor Ian Bradley, an enthusiastic commentator on Celtic Christianity, says that perhaps one of the most fruitful and suggestive images we can use to picture the dynamic and reciprocal relationship between God and nature is that of the dance of creation.[23] He picks up this theme of creation's song and focuses upon the mountains and trees taking on animal characteristics and moving around in a mixture of joy and trembling in the presence of the Lord; the mountains skip like rams, and the hills like lambs (Ps. 114:4; cf. Isa. 55:12).

Creation and humanity share a common fallenness and need of redemption

> The whole creation is eagerly waiting for God to reveal his sons . . . [it] still retains the hope of being freed, like us, from its slavery to decadence, to enjoy the same freedom and glory as the children of God. From the beginning till now the entire creation, as we know, has been groaning in one great act of giving birth. (Romans 8:19–22 JB)

This scripture paints a graphic picture of a creation anxious to see humankind redeemed and renewed in the image of God because it signals that its own re-creation is at hand. This is not to subscribe to the Gaia hypothesis of Sir James Lovelock, a member of the Royal Society, who suggests that the earth is a living self with a mind and a will of its own.[24] Together with Lynn Margulis, a microbiologist, his teachings have formed a central corpus for the wide variety of green and 'Gaia' movements that are now popular ecofriendly concerns around the world. What scripture teaches us is that there is such a close connectedness between humanity and land that the creation is drastically impacted and shocked by the fall of humankind. We read that the land is cursed and that the Edenic partnership, 'this affectionate relationship'[25] has been disrupted so that the working of the land is now a struggle. However, we need to remember that even though God may well have cursed the ground, this does not mean that creation has been condemned or written off. For us to understand the full vista of God's plan of redemption we need to take on board an ecospirituality as well as a human spirituality. Ecospirituality recognises the universe as an indispensable partner on the journey towards our healing; the earth's story is the literal ground of there being any human story at all.[26] We need to open our eyes to the full impact of Christ's incarnation, death and resurrection upon the welfare of society as well as the land. A New Testament illustration of this is the great hymn in praise of Jesus in Colossians 1:15–20, where he is sung as the image of the invisible God and the firstborn of all creation. Most commentators believe this to have been a Christian adaptation of an earlier hymn to the cosmological Logos or divine Word. If so, then Paul has adapted it to emphasise that Jesus is Lord of both salvation and creation.

One of the early modern exponents of this truth was Archbishop William Temple. He wrote that Christianity was the most materialistic of all great faiths. Because Christianity is based on the belief that Jesus Christ is God incarnate in the flesh, all matter can become the instrument of God's Spirit.[27] In other words, creation is a vehicle of God's presence, and so the death and resurrection of Christ was for the whole of God's creation, not just for humanity. Northcott wrote that in the saving purposes of God, Christ, through his incarnation, has become part of the created order and in his sacrifice upon the cross he has lifted up the creation to God.[28] If this is so, then we have a special vocation as Christ's servants to go and do likewise – and be a channel of healing and salvation for creation itself. This is perhaps one of the reasons for the revival of interest in Celtic Christianity and Celtic spirituality. They are regarded as being more creation-affirming than their Roman counterparts. They certainly paid more attention to the presence of God outside the walls of the church and its regulations and saw the presence of God written loud and large in his creation. This is evidenced by the range of prayers threaded through their writings, perhaps the most well known being the poem attributed to Patrick:

> I arise today
> Through the strength of Heaven:
> Light of the sun,
> Radiance of moon,
> Splendour of fire,
> Speed of lightning,
> Swiftness of wind,
> Depth of sea,
> Stability of earth,
> Firmness of rock.[29]

We can learn from our Celtic forebears who saw in the resurrection of Christ that the destiny of the whole world was made manifest. 'All the world rose with him, for the essence of all the elements dwelt in the body in which Christ arose.'[30] This is not a fanciful idea, because it should challenge us to think of ways in which we can bring Christian principles to our industrial and agricultural policies. This truth is in fact written into the celebrations of the church. One such example is the Communion service. In it we handle bread and wine, the things of the earth, and they become a sacrament for the presence of God to touch and bless us as we take these things into our hearts in the name and life of Jesus our saviour.

> Every Sunday Eucharist is a powerful ecological parable of the capacity of matter itself to be redolent of the redemptive purposes of God for the creation and to mediate God's grace to the Eucharistic participants. The transformation of bread and wine into elements which mediate the presence of Christ is a reiteration of the potential of all material existence to reveal God's grace.[31]

I think this is true, and we must not separate ourselves from creation when we think of our call to be witnesses to God's love. There may well be wounded places upon the earth that need to hear the words of repentance of those who have damaged the ground with their unhealed story. It may just be that, as this piece of earth stands on tip-toe waiting to see its own redemption come, we can signal the coming of that healing by holding a Communion service in such places and celebrating the death and resurrection of Jesus, the healer of us all. This would at least give us the energy and the faith to go further and tackle the unhealed stories that went into the place and caused it to be wounded.

Creation and humanity share a partnership of stewardship

> God blessed them and said to them, 'Be fruitful and increase in number; fill the earth and subdue it. Rule over the fish of the sea and the birds of the air and over every living creature that moves on the ground.' (Genesis 1:28)

The key words in this passage are *rule* and *subdue*. The two Hebrew words from which they are derived are respectively *radah* and *kabash*. The first literally means to crumble off or scrape out; the word for 'subdue' is more aggressive and means to tread down or bring into subjection. We can understand from these words how it might so easily be conceived that God was giving us carte blanche to do with the earth as we see fit; our survival, regardless of the cost to creation, is all that matters. The western church does not have a very good track record in this department, particularly as it came to possess more and more land as it grew in power in society. We have much to repent of, both before the peoples we dispossessed, and before the land itself. I think the day has come when we must begin to show a new approach to land: we must find new models of stewardship of the earth where well-being of the community, not profit, is the prime motive. Be that as it may, we must read this particular passage in the context of the land being a gift from God. We must not confuse dominion or rule with domination or rape of the earth. We have already seen that the giving of Jubilee was a God-given mandate to prevent the accumulation of land for purely selfish reasons; it was a means to maintain identity and community on the land. Winkey Pratney is very helpful here when he interprets the use of these words in terms of maintaining a garden. 'Subduing' becomes the necessary discipline to convert the jungle overgrowth into manageable garden. The call to rule is that vigorous thinning out of what is overgrown, and transplanting of the surplus elsewhere.[32] However, to rule and subdue in this ecological sense means that we must recover a spirituality that is true to scripture and that reflects the caring heart of God who pronounces all of his creation 'good'.

Chris Park does in fact suggest eight principles of stewardship of the earth which he lays down as a challenge to the church:

1. God retains ownership of the earth; we are only stewards or tenants.
2. Stewardship is a gift of God and not an achievement of man.
3. Stewardship is a gift to man collectively. Attempts to monopolise land as private gain is a violation of this underlying rule.
4. Man, unlike God, does not create from nothing.
5. Man must honour the integrity of pre-existing material.
6. Man is always answerable to God for his use of the land.
7. Man must exercise authority over the rest of creation on behalf of God and with responsibility.
8. Our stewardship of nature should reflect the good shepherd.[33]

We can conclude from these themes that there is an intimacy of interaction between the human story and the welfare of creation; creation often acts like a mirror image of the spirituality of its community. It is for this reason that we can either bless or pollute the land according to whether we live in harmony with God or not. Embedded within the Mosaic laws of Leviticus (which are all designed for people living on the land) there is the stark fact that the land does respond to how it is treated: by our arrogance we can make it uninhabitable for us. 'If you defile the land, it will vomit you out as it vomited out the nations that were before you' (Lev. 18:28). At the heart of our intimacy with creation is learning to discover the holy places within it and cultivating the presence of God there, and learning where the land weeps, understanding why, and so finding ways to bring release and healing there.

The power of holy places and the pain of hurting places

One of the growth ministries within the church in the last fifteen years has been the desire for pilgrimage. More and more people are looking for escape from the busyness of their routines and go on a quest for inner silence and spaciousness. This is not new, of course, for people have been going on retreat or hermitage since the time of the Desert Fathers in the second century. What is different is that the growth is within the Evangelical wing of the church. This reflects perhaps a growing maturity and catholicity of spirituality which is prepared to look outside and beyond its own certainties to discover riches not yet found. Many take on spiritual directors or soul friends whose function is to walk alongside them as they go on their journey of growth and discovery. For many, it includes retreat to a quiet monastic community for a time. Hundreds flock to the islands of Iona and Lindisfarne and for a day explore at the fringe or more substantially what it is to be closer to God. Many are taking up personal growth courses such as the Myers Briggs Personality Type Indicator, while others make a retreat in the Ignatian tradition which has been seeing something of a revival not least among Protestants, many for the first time. At the heart of all this variety of pursuits is a deep desire to connect with the holy.

Pilgrimage is all about connecting with God at the holy place. Again, this is true for Catholics and Evangelicals alike. Whether we go to Lourdes in search of the God who heals or to the former Vineyard church in Toronto to find the God who cherishes us with a passion, we are all looking for holy places. There are a number of common elements about holy places. They are places where God has touched the earth, either through a saint or in some dynamic vision. They are places where the immanent presence of God still remains like an imprint upon the land and he is there to touch us and change us. They are places where God has focused on some aspect of his truth and the place still proclaims this message, whether it be healing, or repentance and confession as in the case of the church in Pensacola, Florida where there has been a remarkable flood of conversions. The power of holy places is that they reconnect us with the God who is here, alive and active within and through his creation. They are often places where we feel empowered and renewed to serve God in a new and living way. Holy places are often the places where we see afresh the wonder of God's creation, and it comes alive again for us. In 1995 I had a month's sabbatical exploring the Celtic holy places in the islands and highlands of Western Scotland. It was a wonderful time of being still and letting creation point the path back to God for me. I especially appreciated being in Ninian's cave on the Galloway coast which had been prayed in since the fifth century; I felt that I had walked into a cloud of God's presence and was silenced with adoration for a very long time. Sitting just inside the cave mouth and gazing out at the sea, I felt the rolling-in rhythm of God's love, coming in on the waters for me in all seasons of my life – when I am enthusiastic for God and when I am too lazy to seek him. I hardly said a word all the time I was there and yet I was in conversation all the time. Part of the human quest is the inbuilt desire to connect with the holy, and God has set in the earth places where his presence remains.

However, there are also places where the land is hurting and this is invariably because of the effect of our wounded stories being sown into the ground and into the community that goes on living there. Often these stories are very old but their potency to affect the living is remarkable. Some years ago I was given a guided tour around the walls of Derry in Northern Ireland. I came to a certain place where I could look down and across the steep valley to the largely Catholic Bogside estates. As I did so I suddenly felt I could hear the sounds of angry screaming. When I mentioned this to my guide, who was a Presbyterian minister, he said that I was not the first to comment on this. He said it was as if the anger of the Catholic population was crying out in protest over years of oppression, crowded and badly built housing and high unemployment. The walls had come to represent English and Protestant military might and, as such, had become the target of so much hate.

I well remember being approached by a number of people who lived in the Walton area of Liverpool when I visited the site where the body of the young boy Jamie Bulger was found brutally murdered. They said that they felt guilty by association because the crime had happened in their own community. There was a sense that they did not know how to deal with the shame that they carried. As a result that violent death still spread a poisonous influence into that community. This is true for all sites of violent death and atrocities. It is for this reason that there has been a growth of healing prayers on the sites of historical wounding around the world. Healing services in the form of Communion services, silent vigils and public confessions have been held in a variety of locations around the world: at Warren Point and numerous other places in Northern Ireland where soldiers and civilians have been killed by terrorist bombs; in North America at sites such as Wounded Knee where indigenous peoples have been massacred; in Rwanda, Sudan and Bosnia Hercegovina (to name only a few), where ethnic cleansing has been carried out by one dominant group over another. The English Reconciliation Coalition has led healing initiatives on a number of issues affecting the nation and its relationship with other people-groups, ranging from the slave trade, the attempts to destroy the Welsh language, the enforced Scottish clearances, and the deporting of prisoners to Australia. It is apparent that these wounded stories still exert an influence not only between people-groups but also on the place in which the original damage was done.

Drawing from all our discussions about the land, it becomes quite clear that one of our commissions from God is to bring healing to wounded places and attend to the unhealed human story located there. We can see that God's plan of redemption and healing is one indivisible action focused on both humanity and the rest of creation. This is one reason why much of today's prayer and healing initiatives are taking seriously the need to engage in reconciliation between peoples in the localities where the hurts and wrongdoings were initially inflicted. It is important to do this, to know where the equivalent of the blood of Abel cries out from the ground for recognition and healing. Yet this is only one aspect of the reconciliation and healing that is needed. Not only must we deal with the sins of our forebears and their consequences upon others and ourselves –

we must find ways to reconnect with the land for our own identity and growth. Peter Berg calls this *bioregionalism,* by which he means that each earth region has its own unique, interdependent regional culture and identity and that we must learn to become native to our own place and be aware of the ecological relationships which operate within it.[34] I would go further than this and say that one of the ways we find healing for ourselves is to know something of the story of the land which gave us nurture and something of the people of whom we are a part. In order to do this we must learn something about memories and how they shape individuals, people-groups and their localities.

3 THE IMPORTANCE AND POWER OF MEMORIES

I remember, therefore I am.

The first step in liquidating a people is to erase its memory.

(Milan Kundera[1])

On Father's Day in 1997 I was seated in a side ward at Clatterbridge Hospital in Birkenhead. I had come with my brothers and sisters to visit our father who was dying. He was finding it difficult to speak and we in our turn were struggling to say anything meaningful during what was to be our last meeting with him before he died. As he fidgeted in his bed the covers fell back to reveal his bare legs. I found myself staring at them and was struck by the fact that they looked beautiful; there was no discolouring, no varicose veins or any unsightly scars. They looked like the legs of a man in his prime. However, I also became aware of the fact that although his legs were beautiful, it brought up inside of me feelings of great pain and discomfort. The vision and the feelings have stayed with me ever since. As I later reflected on the experience it became more apparent why I felt such anxieties – it was the simple but stunning fact that I had never seen his legs before. Then from out of my unconscious there tumbled a collection of memories from my childhood and they were all to do with negatives. I had never seen my father's legs before because we had never gone to the swimming baths together, never sat on a beach and played together, never played football in the park or cuddled up in bed together. I was surprised at the strength of the feelings after all these years, but the experience did help to illuminate some insights into my own personality and behaviour and I understood myself a little better than before. I also realised that I was responsible for my responses and choices in life on these occasions. Finally, the engagement with these memories helped me to see, at a level I had not allowed myself for some time, that I loved my father and missed him very much.

We all have memories and they hold the map of our hearts and from time to time, in order to know who we are and how we perceive ourselves in relationship to others, we need to explore the inner terrain of our lives. Of course there are many times when we are plunged into this journey almost against our will when we are 'hooked' by some event which takes us by surprise whether it be through smell, touch, something we see or some particular words we hear which had impact upon us once. Whether we have been 'triggered' into remembering or whether it is by deliberate choice, it is useful to understand memory as 'that mental process or faculty of representing in consciousness an act, experience, or impression, with recognition that it belongs to time past'.[2] By properly exploring these memories we can gain some insight and explanation about how we conduct our lives and why we respond to people and circumstances as we do. Such illumination offers us the chance, not to change the past, but to change the way we respond to the past. This is in fact the dynamic behind the work of inner healing or healing the memories. It is the core material upon which most counselling and therapy is focused. However, there are some who feel that such memory work may not be much more than introspective idling and that it is rather over self-indulgent. There is no doubt that memories can be selective in content and become distorted through time and prejudice. Consequently there has been much research on the value of personal narratives and the need to provide appropriate means for testing their accuracy and relevance. There is also the need to recognise that our memories are not just our own individual enterprise, but are often shaped by the communities of which we are a part. One of the pioneers in this research, Maurice Halbwachs, said that individual and social memory are umbilically linked in the sense that we can have very few memories that do not depend in some way upon our membership of a group of some sort.[3] A simple illustration of this fact was brought home to me when I addressed a conference entitled 'Healing the Land' in Newport, South Wales, some years ago. On the whole the day had gone very well, and there was much warmth and enthusiasm from everyone for the teaching they were receiving. At one stage I then introduced a story to see what their immediate responses to it would be. I asked them to imagine that the whistle had just been blown for the ending of a rugby match at the old Cardiff Arms Park between England and Wales and that the final score was England 33, Wales 15. When I asked them how they felt about that, I received a mixture of fairly hostile emotions. At the core of these feelings were statements such as 'You English are not welcome in our land', and 'It may be just a game to you, but it's war for us'. Just beneath the surface lay a whole subtext of their nation's story as it related to the invading English who had robbed them of land and language. They were not joking with me: they were very serious, and I respected that seriousness.

It seems that memories, and wounded memories in particular, have a shaping influence not just on the individual but on communities, places, peoples and tribes as well. It is the purpose of this chapter to look at the functioning of memories and see their relevance for bringing reconciliation and healing to people-groups and their places. In order to do this we shall explore the following themes:

- the Bible and memory;
- memory and identity;
- memory and group stories.

The Bible and memory

There are over 250 references to memory and remembering in scripture. 'Scripture writers keep going back to five memories as the core of their faith history; Abraham's calling, slavery in Egypt, wandering in the desert, the giving of the Law at Mount Sinai and the gift of promised land.'[4] All these memories are taken up from time to time and used as an authoritative reference to encourage, exhort or challenge the nation and its leaders to keep true to Yahweh and to honour his covenant. Nehemiah, fired up with a passion to rebuild the broken city of Jerusalem, encouraged the frightened population to stand and fight against those who would stop them restoring the city (Neh. 4:14ff). Prophets like Isaiah and Micah challenged the affluent and backsliding leaders of the nation to remember how God had delivered them from their enemies and given them the Law of Moses so that they could follow it and dwell secure in the land (Isa. 17:10; 46:9; Mic. 6:5). The renewal of the nation's spiritual and social life was to be resourced by a combination of festivals and memorials which would be a re-enacting and a re-presenting of the communal story of their deliverance, the wilderness wanderings, the conquest and settlement of the land, and the giving of a covenant to live by. To forget where they had come from and by whose hand was tantamount to risking the destruction of the nation. Consequently the Passover and Feast of Tabernacles, to name but two, were to be the vehicles by which to bind the people together in solidarity of worship and service to God (cf. Exod. 23:14–17; Lev. 23:4–44). It is fascinating to witness the revival of these two festivals in particular among Evangelical and charismatic Christians, who feel the need for a greater degree of identity and belonging, and find it more within the story of the Hebrew nation than the story of their Christian denomination. Another resource for remembering was the setting up of memorial stones as a testimony and a reminder of God's deliverances of his people – for example those set up by Joshua when he led the tribes over the Jordan and into battle at Jericho (Josh. 4:7).

'Remember' is the key word in the book of Deuteronomy: the purpose of the book is to look back at the shared story of the birth of the nation, not as a boring repetition of the facts, but this time to see it from God's perspective and remember to learn the right lessons from it. The people are to remember the covenant and not to lose sight of the fact that the nation's story is incomplete without God (Deut. 4:10–14). They are to remember their freeing from slavery in Egypt, and to keep their commitment to the Sabbath rest, which is an image of the spiritual rest of their liberation (Deut. 5:15). They are to remember that it was God who brought them into the land of promise, and so they must keep God at the centre of the community's growth and expansion (Deut. 7:17–24; 8:2–9). Consequently, to remember is to identify with a shared story and to understand how the present life is, or is to be, still shaped by it. As far as the Old Testament is concerned, the focus of memory is upon God and the ways and purposes in which he acts for our benefit. To fail to remember means abandoning the Lord and losing the point and the power of the story that was meant to give us life and a future.

This theme of the purpose of memory is continued in the New Testament and is uniquely present in the passion of Jesus and his death on the cross. At the heart of the Last Supper, indeed, at the moment that was to become the focus and turning point of the whole meal, Jesus took the bread, blessed it and broke it and gave it to his disciples. As he did so he said, 'This is my body given for you; do this in remembrance of me' (Luke 22:19; cf. 1 Cor. 11:23–6). In his *Theological Dictionary of the New Testament* Gerhard Kittel said that the act of remembering here is not the mere calling to mind or recollection of a past event or person, but takes the form of active representation as the action of Jesus is repeated.[5] At one level therefore, the Holy Communion is a memorial feast inviting us to identify ourselves with Jesus' death and crucifixion for our forgiveness. At another level it is an opportunity to connect with the person of Jesus, who, from a human perspective, asks that we do this. As such it reflects his need to belong also, to be a member of his gathered people. Yet in his desire to belong with us, connecting with us through faith and sacrament as in the Holy Communion, Jesus brings his healing into our hurt memories as a powerful resource to change and deliver us from the destructive grip of the pattern of old stories. This is what lies behind the invitation of Jesus to 'learn of him' (Matt. 11:29). The Holy Spirit enables us to understand lessons from Jesus' story which we then apply to our own story in our quest to be transformed and made whole. We can learn, for example, from the death of Jesus that he was abused physically and tormented by cruel words and abandoned like many of us but that this was not the end of the story. In response to abuse he offered forgiveness and his resurrection declared that God would free him from the effects of his sufferings on the cross. No matter what horrors he suffered from others, God would redeem the pain in newness of life. So we, often tortured by what others have done to us, can change our response by trusting God to give us the power to go free from such bondage and to walk in newness of life. This is the central thesis to Charles Elliott's book *Memory and Salvation*, where he says that 'in this sense the memories of Jesus bring the past into contact with the future'.[6] Such healed memories therefore help to create a less destructive world for ourselves and, as we shall see later, for the groups which we represent, carrying them within us, such as our families, churches or even nations.

It can be said therefore that memory is an act of re-membering, of ownership and belonging and of learning again the story of which we are a part and with which we need to identify in order to understand who we are. Such understanding brings the possibility of healing and wholeness.

Memory and identity

On the basis of what we have discussed so far it seems apparent that all memories consist of three major elements, *story, conclusion and consequence*. For as long as we have been able to communicate, we have done so largely through the sharing of personal stories whose narrative and feelings give some description of what is important to us. Anton Boisen, writing in the nineteenth century, conceived the notion of a person as being a 'living human document'.[7] By this he meant that we are all shaped by distinctive stories and the meanings we have derived from them. Stories are important to us because they are ours, no matter how much we may distort, re-edit or repeat them. They perform a number of critical functions in terms of making sense of experience, constructing individual and group identity, providing a map of our 'reality', giving a guide and impetus to moral action and maintaining social relationships.[8] The telling of stories is how we wish to be known and how we believe we know ourselves.

From our stories we draw conclusions about ourselves. These become the windows through which we look upon the world around us. If, in the past, I was constantly told that I was a failure or could do better, and I believe this, then, no matter how much I may achieve, there will be a part of me that will never be pleased with myself. I will be tempted constantly to push myself harder in order to attain that elusive feeling of being OK. If, however, my family story contains times of being affirmed and supported for who I am rather than for what I do, then I am more likely to take risks of exploration in life or feel more assured and confident about myself. A story like this will stand me in good stead when the times of testing come. Such conclusions have as their consequence a lifestyle that will shape my present and future and, because of this, I recycle this story and invest it with whatever important feelings and perceptions I choose. Elliott speaks about winners' and losers' memory and the different consequences this will have upon the carrier.[9] It is a fact of life that we can have two quite different accounts of the same event depending upon whether we were losers or winners. We are told that history has been written by the winners and this is certainly true from my experience. When working in Ireland I had to learn to shut up and do a lot more listening and relearn history in all its complex levels. In my school history lessons I was never introduced to Irish literature and culture, only English victories in that country. History may be written by the winners but the so-called losers carry their own version of the same story and it colours their outlook on life in general and relationships with the winners (in their story) in particular. I well remember being deeply moved when I listened to a Welsh clergyman praying for the healing of his nation with great passion: 'Lord, forgive our people for not being willing to receive the Gospel from English people because they stole our language and robbed us of our land.' When I wanted to include this story in another book my editor wanted me to change the words to 'suppressed our language'. My response was to challenge him to ask a Welshman whether he felt robbed or suppressed!

Of course, the loser's is the oldest memory as it seems that we are more prepared to remember what we have lost than what we have gained. One example of this is the story of the Celtic races: theirs is a common story of being pushed ever westwards across the globe in a continuous story of losing land to one conquering army after another. In a conference I led in the Republic of Ireland, I asked the group attending what was their greatest fear if they suddenly were made redundant and could not pay their mortgage. Almost unanimously they replied 'death and starvation and loss of land'. The spectre of the infamous famine of the 1840s was just beneath the surface along with the fear that their land would once again be taken from them. Seven hundred years of English domination cannot easily be extinguished from the Irish story. This was brought home to me some years ago when, in a conversation with the then President of the Republic of Ireland, Mrs Mary Robinson, she told me that one of the reasons for the troubles in Ireland is that they were still fighting the battles of the dead and the sooner they were healed of it the better.

Memory and group stories

> History, despite its wrenching pain,
> Cannot be unlived, but if faced
> With courage, need not be lived again.
>
> (Maya Angelou[10])

So far in this chapter we have been looking at personal memories and how they affect us, but now we are discovering that we also carry and are shaped, though not determined, by group stories. This reflects the fact that from the very beginning God has created us for community. This in turn is a reflection of the Godhead which is a triune community of Father, Son and Holy Spirit. Jesus often referred to this divine community and its collegiality by saying that he only did what he observed his Father doing in the first place (John 5:19); that to love him or really look at him was to love and see the Father (John 14:21, 9); that to receive Jesus was also to receive the Holy Spirit (John 15:26). In fact, the nature and character of the Trinity is a prophetic challenge and contrast to the autocratic rule of individuals and to those groups who would seek to dominate another. 'The Trinity corresponds to a community in which people are defined in their relationship with one another and in their significance for one another.'[11] As the people of God, we are to reflect the community of the Trinity and be a people known for our love rather than as a community shaped by the will to dominate. It is necessary therefore that we too discover something of the group stories which we carry and have some insight into how they shape our lives from time to time. Writers have identified a number of corporate stories that we carry; for the purposes of this book we will be exploring family, church, community and tribal or national group stories in particular. This is because I believe that it is in these areas that the focus of reconciliation work is largely, though not exclusively, needed.

There has been ongoing research into the group stories of larger multinational companies and political parties. In his book *Naming the Powers* Walter Wink writes about the 'spirit' which occupies large corporations and shapes the mindset of its employees. He reflects upon how the oil company Shell is regarded in some of the developing nations as having a spirit of domination in their scant regard for the well-being of the communities among whom they site their refineries. In recognition of this issue corporate businesses are now presenting their products in the form of a story which projects the company image they wish to promote. The former Midland Bank portrayed itself as 'the listening bank', the Co-Operative Bank spoke of itself as a family business that would never invest its moneys in countries that oppress the poor, and British Telecom presented its communications network, through the imagery of ET, as a business which offers pastoral care within the family.

I am quite convinced that God's agenda for healing not only includes the individual's needs but also the community or group stories which have gone into the making of us and by which we shape the world in which we live. Consequently the pattern for healing wounded group stories is listening to history, discovering its repeating patterns and the locality in which they occur, discerning how these patterns still shape the present community, finding routines which bring healing to such wounded history and then deciding on how to develop a practical follow up for the benefit of that community. According to Nicholas Frayling, who went to Ireland to learn something of the story that binds both English and Irish in an ongoing dynamic of hostility and violence, principally located in what the Republican group story describes as the 'occupied territory' of Northern Ireland, the route to healing lies in listening to wounded history. He says that we (the British people) cannot live in the past, but unless we find a way of owning past deeds, unless we can discover some corporate sense of responsibility based on our common humanity, as well as nationality, then we shall be led, as successive British Governments have been led, into tinkering with consequences instead of addressing causes.[12] I realise that there is much more to the story of Northern Ireland than this, and that there is an equivalent and alternative Unionist group story which needs to be heard and appreciated. However, reconciliation is not possible until we learn to listen accurately to the multi-layers of such group stories as these and discover the repeated patterns of wounding which help us to locate where the energy and the power of healing needs to be directed.

We are living at a time when wounded history and its recycled stories are being taken seriously all around the world. At a conference in 1993, held in Richmond, Virginia, entitled 'Healing the Heart of America', the organisers felt that the issues of unacknowledged history and unhealed memories were powerful contributory factors in engendering present-day conflicts, prejudices and bitternesses. The conference concluded that there is a continuing agony within the American nation and that it stems from two peoples, Native and African Americans, who were denied the freedom and dignity that the founding fathers of that country claimed to cherish. Such White denial and guilt, and the reciprocal Black anger, combined to produce a time-bomb of colliding emotions which was easily triggered.[13] John Dawson, a long-term resident of Los Angeles, graphically describes the police beating of Rodney King, which was shown on prime time television and which sparked off the riots of March 1991 that claimed the lives of 59 people and caused millions of dollars worth of damage to properties and spread from city to city across America.[14] He goes on to say that the reason behind such a quick outpouring of rage and anger is because, alongside of that nation's legacy of wrongdoing against its indigenous peoples, American cities, by the fact that they are now the greatest gathering of ethnic and cultural diversity in the world, have inherited the wounds of the world.

We also need to appreciate the fact that we are actually handling a number of such group stories and that they overlap to some degree. Our family group story can colour how we see our place in the community. A brief survey of some urban council estates well illustrates the fact that the majority of families were uprooted from long-established communities and placed in new housing miles away. Many share a sense of rootlessness and isolation which can become oppressive and leave such families feeling hopeless about their future. The children of these families focus their frustration and vandalism on the property which represents the uncaring policies of a faceless council. There are cities which have quite different identities, as a comparison between the stories of Liverpool and Chester, some fifteen miles apart, can testify. These factors are very important when considering a strategy of mission and witness. Recently I was asked to lead a day conference in preparation for an evangelistic mission to the city of Warwick. The organisers wanted an opportunity to reflect upon the story of their city, to understand its strengths and weaknesses and, if possible, to locate segments of this story in their geographical location. Also they wanted to explore the story of the churches in relationship to this community, whether they had become part of the solution or part of the problem of the city's needs. This would help them decide how they presented the Gospel to the people in those localities who were differently affected by the story of the place and the church in which they lived. It is not enough to trot out the gospel formula and hope that everyone will understand. We must recognise that such witness has to pass through the filter of people's experience of life, their personal and group stories, which will colour how they perceive what we are saying in our mission. If we can learn and understand their stories with all their conclusions and consequences, then we can present the good news in such a way that it fits into their story and become more effective. The church leaders in Warwick, in the light of their research, felt that their mission must begin with a service of apology and reconciliation between the churches for their failure to care for each other, for harbouring resentments down the years which the community had become aware of, and as an opportunity for committing themselves to a new era of respect and partnership.

We can therefore conclude from our studies into the importance and power of memories that they play an important role in their potential to bless or wound both individuals and groups. Our commission as Christians is to carry the good news of healing and reconciliation to the whole world and this means paying serious attention to unhealed history. The core of such healing is confession and reconciliation. However, before engaging with such a commission we now need to understand something of the powers which shape wounded history.

Lord, come and heal our land.
Let there be light in our darkened, soulless cities;
Let there be green in our wasted, industrial sites;
Let there be letting go of our wrangled, unhealed memories;
Let there be gardens in the ghettos of our church's story;
Let there be loving for the soil from which we came;
Let there be a neighbour in me for the nations of the world;
Lord, come and heal our land.

(Russ Parker[15])

4 THE POWERS THAT SHAPE GROUP STORIES

History repeats itself,
it has to,
because nobody listens.

(Steve Turner[1])

Like many others I was appalled at the accounts of ethnic cleansing in Bosnia Hercegovina where thousands of innocent Muslims were burnt out of their homes, tortured, raped and killed and thrown in mass graves around the country. We looked on with disbelief as we learnt of how neighbours who had lived together fairly amicably for generations suddenly turned on each other with a ferocity that could scarcely be believed. It was hard to understand until we listened to history from a Serbian point of view. They cite German atrocities against the (Orthodox) Serbs during the Second World War which were carried out with (Catholic) Croat participation, Serbian marginalisation under the Croat Tito's communist regime and, most important of all, the defeat of the Orthodox Serbian army by a Muslim army on the plains of Kosovo in 1389. In fact Kosovo holds some of the sites and shrines claimed as sacred to Serbian church and national history. Slobodan Milosevic, the former Serbian President, justified the fighting in Kosovo in language that was tantamount to a holy war to undo the defeat which had been an abiding national shame upon his country. None of this justifies the horrors of the Milosevic regime but it does remind us of how unhealed history can exert a powerful influence in people's lives in the present, and until we learn to heal history, we will go on repeating it into the future. However, in order to go down the road of healing we must know something of the powers, both spiritual and natural, which keep these wounded group stories locked in place. Once we have discovered something of the network and interaction of these powers, we shall have a true opportunity to pray and engage upon a strategy of healing which will disarm all these powers and see captive groups go free from the destructive, repeating patterns of their wounded history. Under the heading of the natural powers we will look at the nature of storytelling, and the reinforcing of history through symbol and ritual. We will then consider our sinful nature in relation to the spiritual powers, and finally the issues surrounding spiritual warfare on a strategic level.

The natural powers

The nature of storytelling

We have already looked at the rhythm of memories and the role which storytelling has upon them. The telling of stories is actually a natural part of our existence and we share them because we want people to understand us and 'get the point' of what we are saying. Jesus did this all the time; he told parables. I well remember a conversation I had with my former professor of theology at Manchester University, Frederick F. Bruce, when he said that a parable was a story with a kick like a mule! What he meant was that in telling stories, real or fabricated, Jesus was trying to make a point, and we miss the value of the parable if we do not get the message. An example of this is the telling of the story of the Good Samaritan. We must be careful not to get lost in the details of the story and go hunting for significance in every reference to all the characters so that we miss the punchline at the end. In this case it is found in the telling question, 'Which of these three do you think was a neighbour?' (Luke 10:36).

Similarly, when we are telling stories, particularly group stories about our families, churches, communities or nations, we are trying to make an important point. We are either wanting to share something that our listener will celebrate and affirm, or to offer something that is still waiting to be healed. I have no doubt that we have all had moments when we have been sharing something only to be interrupted with the response, 'I know just what you feel.' The effect of this remark is to puncture our story and minimise its importance. We feel angry and frustrated. We do not want cheap agreements, but for others to understand the importance of our story – only then begins the journey into healing. Michael Mitton once told me a true story of some American missionaries being asked by a group of Innuit people if they were willing to hear their story and need for healing. The missionaries said 'Of course.' They sat down to listen and five days later the story had been told!

This is not the place to investigate all the ways in which we frustrate the inbuilt need to tell our story with our eagerness to help, heal or deliver from evil. There will be times when we will feel defensive or have another point of view to offer and be tempted to interrupt. This is the time to listen first and share our stories next.[2] I once led a day conference on healing a nation's wounds and asked a Protestant representative what he thought Gerry Adams thought of the Orange marches. The man in question thought it was a needless question because the answer was obvious: Adams was against them. However, Gerry Adams is on record as recognising that Orange marches are a shared part of the story of Northern Ireland. Although he objected that they were focused (for him) on largely Catholic housing areas, he would nonetheless fight for the Orangemen's right to have them.[3] When I asked the representative why he had got it wrong, he said that he had been listening to his prejudices rather than to the person.

It is important that we listen accurately and to all the stories. This is in fact the most important issue in the emerging discipline of 'narrative ethics' and pastoral care. There are three issues to bear in mind when listening to group stories if we are going to see any kind of healing and renewal in the groups concerned. First, there is the quality of relationships between the one telling the story and the one listening. Are we telling our stories to wound, to bless or to signal a need? We can gauge the answers to these questions by looking at the effect they have upon the hearers. This will also give some clues as to the nature of the relationship and the focus for healing needed between them. If we feel threatened or have a need to justify our story in the light of the one told, or feel we have been misrepresented, then our story must be told and put alongside the first.

Second, there is the quality of accuracy and content in the telling of the story. It is imperative that we get the facts. We may colour the story with the pain or hurt that that story carries. I was fascinated to listen to Gerry Adams when he was interviewed to give his comments on the situation in Northern Ireland, especially following a bombing or a killing of someone. This was in the days when John Major was Prime Minister and a prime mover in initiating the present peace accord. However, when Adams spoke of Major's political motives and objectives he often described him in the language of a modern-day Cromwell seeking to deny the Irish people their homeland and culture. Whatever may be thought of the politics of John Major, it is undeniable that he acted throughout with integrity, tolerance and an openness that has yet to be fully appreciated. It told me how much Adams was still repeating the wounded story of his people and it coloured how he listened. It also suggested something of the way in which we all demonise those who have hurt us, in order to justify our actions of hate towards them. We are rightly outraged when the terrorist bombs, murders and maims innocent women and children as at the Omagh bombing. However, the terrorist sees it as a war against the evil oppressor who would destroy and steal their land and heritage. He does not allow himself to really see; his focus is on the threat to his people's survival and it is OK to fight back. If we are going to be channels of healing and reconciliation, we must see both of these group stories and truly appreciate them before we can act.

Being charismatic, I do not question the present use and validity of the spiritual gifts of the Holy Spirit, but I would want to check out some alleged prophecies that seem to be based on personal intuition but do not seem to connect with the facts. I have read with concern of extended times of prayer warfare in some part of town where it has been prophesied that a certain demonic power is located. However, upon further inspection, I have found that there has been no discipline of research and the gathering of facts upon which to pray and discern what God is saying. It is purely subjective and unverifiable. This is why in the accompanying course to this book, we stress so much the need for research before action. It is going to be the human group story which will offer insights and clues to the nature of spiritual warfare in a community; it will not be gained just by claiming to discern and decide what the spiritual superpowers in any given place are. We must not fight on the wrong battlefronts.

We must also listen to more than one representative of a group story. In working for the healing of wounded churches I have found people who will say that they were really blessed through the ministers of that church and others who will say that they were abused by them. The danger is to cancel out one story with the other.

I will say more about this later, but for now I will say that we need to do this because we are seeking two important elements in every group story, something to celebrate and something to heal.

Finally, there is the quality of response we make to hearing a group story that affects me one way or another. It is here that the ministry of healing and reconciliation is to be found. For example, if I have been listening to a man sharing his grievance against the English because he is descended from slavery and still finds prejudice against his people in my country, what is my response to be? I may well make apology as a representative of my people though not a perpetrator of its crimes. However, I need to follow this through with a penitential lifestyle that illustrates my apology in my daily life. Consequently, I will not make a slave of others in whatever form this happens, whether it is by manipulation, denying others their gifts and opportunities to serve because of their age, sex or race, or enforcing my beliefs upon someone else. We conclude that one of the powers that shape group stories is the basic need to be heard in order to be celebrated or healed.

Reinforcing history through symbol and ritual

In 1996 there took place the first conference of the World Christian Gathering of Indigenous Peoples at Rotorua in New Zealand. I watched a video of this event while attending an international gathering of church leaders in Singapore, who had come together to look at the issues of reconciling wounded tribes and nations. The video gave a taste of the gathering of two thousand people representing thirty countries. There was sharing of hurts and afflictions from representatives of each tribal group. Each day the tribes presented their celebration of Jesus with their own songs and dances, wearing their own costume and regalia. For example, Maori men did the haka, a dance originally for the summoning up the spirits of war, but now they performed it to celebrate the triumph of Jesus over evil through his death and resurrection. It was a wonderful blending of tribal identity with the praises of Jesus. When the video finished, all of us in the conference in Singapore fell silent for a moment. Then, quite spontaneously, the English people there began to weep and we fell on our knees to ask God for forgiveness for our nation's bad track record of stamping out tribal culture and identity wherever we planted the

British Empire. I was weeping for some other reasons as well: the fact that these tribes knew who they were, their identities have been maintained through their language and culture, and that I sense the English do not know who they are because we have become such a divided country.

Among the powers that shape group stories are the public rituals and symbols which keep those stories alive. They are a visual replay of the identity of such people-groups. Who can forget the spectacular opening ceremony of the Sydney Olympics in September 2000? It was an international stage on which the people of Australia told their nation's story. At the heart of the whole story was the need for reconciliation between the settlers, who carried the baggage of being the criminal and unwanted peoples of a Great Britain who had cast them out, and the aboriginals, who had suffered at the hands of these incoming whites. All through the unravelling of the story was the graphic picture of the aboriginal dancer and the young white singer who walked, danced and sang together Australia's history and the need to accept and celebrate their differences. It was Australia's way of saying sorry and demonstrating their need to heal the past in order to enjoy a better future together. This core belief about its nation's story was given a sensational demonstration when the aboriginal sprinter, Cathy Freeman, won the gold medal in the 400-metre race. Whatever level of meaningfulness this may have had, the fact of the public ritual of the Olympic Games was a way of telling the story and giving a voice to the needs for healing and unity in that nation. It fed the public desire to celebrate who they were and put into practice the hopes and aspirations of the ritual and symbols it had used. Oliver Holt, writing in the *Times* newspaper, described Freeman's victory as a nation coming together, shedding its guilt and voicing its hope for a better future. Despite the refusal of John Howard, the Australian Prime Minister, to apologise to the Aboriginal people for the mistreatment of the past, the rest of the country appeared to be saying sorry.[4] Interestingly enough, the Aboriginal Affairs Minister, John Herron, was applauding the significance of the occasion at Palm Island, a former penal colony for 'troublesome' aboriginals, where his own grandparents had disappeared.

Perhaps the issue of the importance of public symbols and rituals is nowhere more forcibly demonstrated than in Northern Ireland. Who can forget the stand-offs between members of the Orange Order, the police and the Catholics at Drumcree? Tom Hennessey and Robin Wilson point out that such cultural or group-story conflicts can have every bit as much, or even more impact on society than the detonation of the IRA bomb in Canary Wharf.[5] They understand such public demonstrations as being a sign of the growing importance of 'recognition politics' where tribal identity, being under threat, is taken to the streets in the form of ritual and symbolic re-enactment. Stephen Baker said that just as the marches which enforced victory on the people centuries ago were the determining factor in the necessary elimination of hope, so now the annual remembrance makes real in the present those events of long ago. That is why it is so important that the marches progress through the places of the minority community; if they did not do so, only the victors would remember and they are not the ones who need to be reminded.[6] He sees the marches as a powerful liturgical tool to maintain a certain social reality. The issue of flags and emblems in Northern Ireland has also highlighted the deep divisions over national identity and allegiance. Republicans see their flag as representing the longed-for dream of one Ireland whereas the Unionists see it as a rebellious affront. The proposal to change the name of the police from 'Royal Ulster Constabulary' is deeply felt by Unionists as an attempt to dilute if not remove the Britishness of Northern Ireland. Even culture is seen as a weapon to cry out the unhealed story and the need for identity. Ian Paisley Junior, of the Ulster Democratic Party, is on record as saying that he was uncomfortable with Gaelic language and culture and felt that it had been politically hijacked even by those who did not speak it. He felt that the language was hostile to him.[7]

Of course, the story of Northern Ireland is a very complex one and, although I do not pretend to know or understand it all, the issue of marches, flags and emblems is a very powerful vehicle for reliving and representing the tribal stories waiting to be heard and healed in that land. The same process can be seen at work in National Front demonstrations where the Union Jack is carried as a reminder of the national story perceived to be under threat from incoming ethnic groups. The Palestinian wears his familiar headdress as a visual statement of a people without a land; the Amish in North America wear their distinctive clothing as a way of silently telling the story of their origins and purity of life. The list is endless, but they are all in one way or another sacramental actions telling the group story. In

Christian terms we say that a sacrament is an outward action of an inward change as in the examples of baptism and communion. Rituals and symbols are outward actions telling the group story kept alive in the hearts of its representatives. It is a way of getting in touch with the spirit of a group and giving it breathing space. This is not to say that it is demonic or occultic, but it is a way of locating the human spirit that has been invested in a group story and seeing something of how it is affected for good or ill. Consequently, as servants of the living God who longs to bring healing to people-groups, we need to learn the people's stories and their localities and find ways to identify publicly with these stories. It is this truth which lies behind the growing phenomenon of Christians going to sites of great hurt, such as battlegrounds like Verdun and Gettysburg; or to locations which still speak of damage done to peoples, like the sites of the Scottish clearances, Sydney harbour, and Hobart in Tasmania where countless minor offenders were exiled in imprisonment. At such places the task of reconciliation has been identified and offered by those representing the perpetrating nations as a start towards healing wounded history and reconciling peoples.

The spiritual powers

Our sinful nature

We may find it quite acceptable to think of personal sin and the repercussions we experience from our sinful actions and even the long-term effect they can have upon us when they are not confessed and forgiven. However, we also need to accept that behind much of the social strife we see in our world is the problem of unconfessed and consequently undealt-with corporate sin. Stanley Banks, my old Bible college principal, said that by the grace of God we can choose not to sin, but we cannot choose not to have the consequences of our sin; this is also true for people-groups. God has written into his constitution for relating to humanity, at both individual and group level, the spiritual principle that we reap what we sow. Therefore we cannot disregard the sins committed by our governments or by our nation or by our church and family leaders as not concerning us, just because we ourselves did not commit such acts. We are accountable. It is surely this principle which lies behind the dialogue between

Abraham and God for the survival of the cities of Sodom and Gomorah (Gen. 18:20–33). God had announced that the sin of these cities was now too great to ignore and he was about to judge it. Abraham was shattered that God would destroy the righteous along with the wicked in the city of Sodom, and pleaded for God to spare the place if there were any righteous inhabitants at all. God agreed to this act of representation but unfortunately there were no righteous people in the city and it was destroyed.

Rudy and Marny Pohl give a telling illustration of how we are tempted to look at a nation's sins more as political necessities, crimes of the times or unfortunate circumstances, but rarely as sins which need confessing and forgiving. Referring to the history of their homeland of Canada they write:

> When one of our provincial governments or our federal government violates a treaty with a Native group, we don't call that sin. When pulp and paper companies and mining companies, with tacit government approval, knowingly continue to pollute rivers which Native peoples depend on for drinking water, causing disease and premature death, we don't call that sin . . . When constitutionally guaranteed French language and Catholic education rights were illegally revoked by the newly-arrived English-speaking majority, we did not call that sin. When the province of British Columbia, with widespread support of the Canadian people, dispossessed Japanese Canadian citizens in the 1940's and sent them to internment and illegally sold their properties and possessions, we didn't call that sin.[8]

If we are to see healing of nations, then it must begin with a spiritual awakening to the sins of the nation and the need to come before God in humility and repentance in the firm hope and expectation that God will hear and forgive and heal. It is no longer acceptable for us to plead ignorance. Albert Speer, the former minister for armament production, was the only Nazi minister to admit the guilt of the sins of his nation's leaders. He said:

> Things that would have shocked and horrified me in 1934, such as assassination of opposition leaders, the persecution of the Jews, the incarceration and torture of innocent men in

> concentration camps, I tolerated as unfortunate excesses in 1935: and things I couldn't have stomached in 1935 were palatable a few years later. If I did not see, it was because I did not want to see![9]

Contrast this with the confession by F. W. de Klerk when responding to a question from the floor in the Royal Albert Hall following his lecture as a recipient of the Nobel Peace Prize. He was asked whether it was international sanctions which had brought about the end of apartheid. De Klerk replied, 'It was not the sanctions, but a deep self-analysis on our knees before God.'[10] I am sure that we are living in days when God is raising the voice of the prophets in our land to challenge and call us back into awareness and response-ability for the sins of our nations, our communities, our churches and our families.

From Genesis to Revelation, God calls all people-groups to live righteously with each other and before him. Jonah was sent to challenge the city of Nineveh to repent and be saved, and it was. Jesus lamented Jerusalem's constant refusal of the living word of God in its midst and its stoning of the prophets (Luke 13:34–5). Isaiah, Jeremiah and Ezekiel all challenged their own people, other nations and cities to turn to God or face the consequences of unforgiven corporate sins (Isa. 13—23; Jer. 46—51; Ezek. 25—32). Jesus rebuked the cities of Bethsaida, Capernaum and Korazin, the focus of his ministry and miracles, because they did not repent of their sins and so would reap the consequences (Luke 10:13–15). In his visions on Patmos John sees the wrath of God outpoured on the city of Babylon and contrasts this with the healing of God poured out in a renewed Jerusalem where the presence of God abides for ever (Rev. 17—18; 21:1–2).

If these group sins are not healed then they will have destructive consequences, which if left unchecked will damage people-groups continually as a repeated pattern of pain and ultimate judgement. John Dawson writes of such unhealed histories:

> Paradoxically, the greatest wounds in human history . . . have not happened through the acts of some individual perpetrator; rather through institutions, systems, philosophies, cultures, religions and governments of humankind. Because of this, we as individuals are tempted to absolve ourselves of all individual responsibility. However, unless someone chooses to identify themselves with corporate entities, such as the nation of our

> citizenship, or the subculture of our ancestors, the act of honest confession will never take place. This leaves us in a world of injury and offence in which no corporate sin is ever acknowledged, reconciliation never begins and old hatreds deepen.[11]

The consequences are roots of bitterness which are carried in the group story and can range from anger, alienation, bitterness, hatred, unforgivingness, revenge and, in certain circumstances, violent reprisals on the perceived perpetrator group. The devastating wars in Bosnia, Rwanda and Sudan are but a few terrible examples. In considering this theme of corporate sin we must briefly look at two other issues it raises, that of blessings and curses and the judgement of God down the generations.

Blessings and curses

'Any moment may be taken in two ways: a blessing for growth or curse that cripples.'[12] The book of Deuteronomy sets out a clear mandate for the relationship between God and the new nation of Israel based on his covenant commitment to them and theirs to him. On the one hand they would be blessed if they kept God's commands (Deut. 28:2ff). However, if they disobeyed God then the nation would be overrun with curses (Deut. 28:15–68). The blessings would bring health and prosperity to cities, families and the ground itself. The curses would bring famine and ultimate expulsion from their homeland. Of course this is a covenant agreement between God and the people of Israel, and some may say that it does not apply in a general sense to any other group or nation. This does not follow, however, because scripture makes it quite clear that God challenges and judges the other nations precisely because they have not lived in righteous relationship with Israel in particular, nor with himself. This is because he is not only the God of the Israelites but also the God of the universe. The prophet Amos challenged the smug apathy of Israel who rested on their sense of being a special people above all the nations:

> Are you not as the sons of Ethiopia to me, O sons of Israel? declares the Lord. Have I not brought up Israel from the land of Egypt, and the Philistines from Caphtor and the Arameans from Kir? (Amos 9:7 NASB)

Here God compares Israel's Exodus with those he has brought about for other nations. It must have shattered their pride to hear the court prophet Isaiah prophesying how God had plans to make their former enemy states into a partnership of equal blessing with Israel:

> In that day Israel will be a third party with Egypt and Assyria, a blessing in the midst of the earth, whom the Lord of hosts has blessed saying, 'Blessed is Egypt my people, and Assyria the work of my hands, and Israel my inheritance.'
>
> (Isaiah 19:24–25 NASB)

Whereas there may not be a covenant relationship between God and the other nations, there is certainly an expectancy that they will be held accountable to God for their actions. This theme is followed through into the New Testament where John boldly declares that God so loved the world that he gave his only begotten Son for the world's salvation (John 3:16). We must learn to understand this text as an appeal, not only to individuals but to whole peoples, to believe in God and be saved. The Apostle Paul takes up this issue in his preaching in Athens when he declares that God made from one person every nation, 'that they should inhabit the whole earth; and he determined the times set for them and the exact places where they should live' (Acts 17:26).

We can conclude from this brief survey that God holds nations and people-groups responsible for their conduct, and likewise offers them the possibility of blessings or the judgement of curses. In his book *Healing the Nations* John Sandford describes this as *inherited* curses, and distinguishes them from *pronounced* curses which are said either knowingly, and with intent, by those who wish to do us harm, or unknowingly by those who do not realise the impact their words could have.[13] Those who deliberately utter curses may be involved in various levels of magic or witchcraft, and devise and perform their curses with ritual and prayers. Such curses can also be uttered by those we have hurt or offended who quite literally wish to visit on us or our descendants the pain we have inflicted upon them. Examples of pronounced curses which are said unwittingly can be statements such as 'You will never do anything right', or 'Things just never go well for us in this family'. These become scripts which repeat themselves within families, churches and nations down the years until they are recognised, challenged, repented of and broken, through the power of Jesus Christ. In order to bring healing at a group level (as well as for individuals) it is necessary to research the histories behind curses, the injuries, misunderstandings, betrayals and woundings which we carry, for it is here that the power of on-going sickness is to be located. Once we have discovered this, we can own them in confession and a lifestyle of repentance, looking to Jesus for his authority to set us free from the power of curses and their repetitive and destructive effects among us.

Exactly the same process is required in the case of inherited curses where the power of God is at work. This time the core focus is the consequences of our breaking God's laws and principles. What is common to both is the spiritual principle of law that God has established between himself and peoples as well as individuals. It is the law of sowing and reaping which can only be altered through confession and repentance. As we shall see shortly, interacting and capitalising upon this law are the spiritual powers of darkness with whom we do battle.

The judgement of God down the generations

As distasteful as it may seem to us in the twenty-first century, it appears, disturbingly, that God visits the sins of one generation upon descendants irrespective of the innocence or otherwise of those succeeding generations. Here we are considering not the law of sowing and reaping but the power of God to punish those not guilty of the original crimes. It seems grossly unfair! The scriptures which illustrate this fact are as follows:

> Then the Lord passed by in front of Moses and proclaimed, 'The Lord, the Lord God, compassionate and gracious, slow to anger and abounding in lovingkindness and truth; who keeps lovingkindness for thousands, who forgives iniquity, transgression and sin: yet He will by no means leave the guilty unpunished, visiting the iniquity of fathers on children and on the grandchildren to the third and fourth generations.'
> (Exodus 34:6–7 NASB; cf. also Num. 14:18; Deut. 5:9)

This seems not only unfair but completely in conflict with our conception of God being loving and forgiving. Sandford points out that there is a difference between God's pardon and his forgiveness.[14] Forgiveness clears away guilt and restores us to fellowship with our

Father but it does not do away with discipline or punishment. He uses the illustration of being forgiven by a person for offences and crimes committed against that person, but nonetheless having to go to prison to satisfy the demands of the law. However, this is all about the descendants, not the perpetrator, being punished for something they did not do. Sandford appreciates this and suggests that God instituted the law of sowing and reaping with the intention of blessing but with the introduction of sin into the world, it is sadly inevitable that instead of blessings being sown and reaped in subsequent generations, it is sin and destruction. In keeping with the theme of God being Lord of the universe, the scripture presents the law of sowing and reaping in terms of God being in control of it. As if to emphasise this point, the scriptures also point out that as far as God's disposition is concerned, he judges each person according to their own choices. This is the meaning of the twice-quoted proverb, 'The fathers have eaten sour grapes, and the children's teeth are set on edge' (Jer. 31:29; Ezek. 18:2). Both prophets are challenging the belief that sons will automatically inherit the sins of their fathers and are proclaiming that God will judge each person according to their own choices. Jeremiah points out that this is to be the basis of the new covenant that God will make with all people, and Christians say that this was fulfilled in the life, death and resurrection of Jesus. We therefore need to make a careful distinction between *intention* and *consequence*. It is not God's intention to punish sins down through the generations but such unconfessed and unhealed stories will reap a consequential lifestyle among us. In healing wounded history it is imperative that we discover these repeated patterns, and if they relate to our own group stories they must be owned in confession and offered to God for healing. Sometimes, however, these group stories are further complicated by the fact that to some degree the powers of evil have gained hold of them and, for them to be healed, we must wage warfare against our spiritual enemies.

Strategic level spiritual warfare

> 'Do not be afraid, Daniel. Since the first day . . . your words were heard, and I have come in response to them. But the prince of the Persian kingdom resisted me twenty-one days. Then Michael, one of the chief princes, came to help me.
>
> (Daniel 10:12–13)

> For our struggle is not against flesh and blood, but against the rulers, against the authorities, against the powers of this dark world and against the spiritual forces of evil in the heavenly realms. (Ephesians 6:12)

Spiritual warfare, unfortunately, is a part of our everyday experience as Christians. We struggle with temptations and sins of commission as well as of omission: we do the things we ought not to do and we do not do the things we should. We find it hard to walk the narrow way of holiness and love but by the grace of God we keep going. There are times when we feel powerless and dwarfed by the size of corruption in our industries and in the corridors of political power. Also we read of the struggles which Jesus had in being tempted personally by Satan in the wilderness, and we rejoice in his ability to cast out demons and the triumph of the cross by which Jesus made an open show of the limitations of demonic power (Col. 2:15). However, we also have to take seriously the commission of Jesus to be his witnesses which included, alongside the command to proclaim the Gospel and pray for healing, the exhortation to cast out demons. We may find that this does not sit easily with our modernistic world-views, and be tempted to reinterpret demonisation exclusively as an old-fashioned way of talking about psychiatric disturbances. I am quite sure that there will be similarities in behaviour, but even the writer of Matthew's Gospel knew the difference between spiritual and psychological disturbance, however primitively understood. In describing the range of those who came to Jesus to receive their healing Matthew includes those who were lunatic (disturbed by the moon: *seleniazomenous*) and those who were spiritually bothered (*daimonizomenous*) (Matt. 4:24). There is not space in this book to examine the nature of spiritual warfare in great depth as I am concerned to focus on the role of the demonic in affecting wounded group stories and therefore to find ways to combat these effects as part of our commitment to bringing healing and reconciliation. However, it may help us to clarify the different forms of spiritual warfare before proceeding. First, there is the

personal level which is individually focused, and comes about largely through varying degrees of temptation and oppression. Next

there is the occult level of spiritual warfare, which has at its core a rejection and opposition to Christian values. Finally, there is strategic

level spiritual warfare, which concerns the relationship between

spiritual powers and how they affect group stories and their localities. This last category has seen a big upsurge in interest since the 1980s when the focus of spiritual warfare was lifted from the individual and personal level to the corporate and group level. Since then it has developed into a worldwide explosion of prophetic prayer encounters whereby the intercessors come to a community to discern and pray against any spiritual superpowers which are hindering evangelism and revival there. The objective is to bind such powers and oust them in the hope of releasing more fruitful witness within that community. The major exponents of this ministry are C. Peter Wagner, George Otis Junior (from whom we originally got the term 'spiritual mapping'), Cindy Jacobs, John Dawson, Tom White and Ed Silvoso, collectively described as the founders of the 'prayer-track movement'. In this last section we will ask the following questions:

- What are these principalities and powers?
- What is spiritual mapping?
- What are strongholds?
- How do we combat these powers?

What are these principalities and powers?

This is not so easy a question to answer as it seems. The standard Evangelical and charismatic view is that they are evil or demonic superpowers and this is why we are exhorted to wrestle against them for their defeat and expulsion from human affairs. Walter Wink takes a broader view of the subject and says that principalities and powers form the 'inner' and 'outer' realities of any given manifestation of power. He is not demythologising the subject but seeking to give coherence to the wide range of references to them in the New Testament. By 'inner' he means the spirituality of institutions or corporate structures and systems, and by 'outer' he means the actual political systems, appointed officials, representatives of those structures, in short, the tangible manifestations which power takes.[15] For Wink, the problems begin when the principalities become idolatrous and place themselves above God's purposes and hence become demonic. He maintains that as the powers are ordained by God (Rom. 13:1) they must have originally been good and there does seem to be some allusion in scripture to reconciling such powers

(Col. 1:20). Elsewhere we read of the devil and his angels being cast into eternal fire (Matt. 25:41). Consequently, at a basic level we must accept that there is some difference between the demons cast out of people and these principalities and powers. Similarly we are told that the church is to make known the manifold wisdom of God to these powers (Eph.3:10), and the context suggests something of completion rather than deliverance. Andii Bowsher points out that this is very different from the examples in the gospels where the demons clearly knew who Jesus was.[16] Another interesting comparison is the apparent necessity for demons to occupy a body (Mark 5:12), and the entire lack of reference to the principalities and powers being cast out of anything. Let us then look at the terms used in the New Testament to describe these powers and see if this helps our enquiry.

Colossians 1:14–16 mentions *thrones*, *powers*, *rulers* and *authorities*. Of these, 'thrones' refer to the institution of power in a state, city or economic body. The throne of Paul's day was a literal chair of authority on a raised dais, symbolising the seat of authority. This word is used of the throne of grace (Heb. 4:16), the throne of Christ (Heb. 1:8) and the throne of Satan (Rev. 2:13).

The word used here for 'powers' (or 'lords'), *kyriotētes*, is rarely used to describe spiritual powers, but seems to refer to the realm or dominion over which a ruler reigns. It is the sphere of formal influence of that structure of power.

In the case of 'rulers' the word used is *archai*; it (or the related *archōn/archontes*) can be used of actual rulers (Luke 12:11), Jewish leaders (Matt. 9:18), the jurisdiction of a governor (Luke 20:20), the prince of demons (Matt. 9:34), holy angels (Eph. 3:10), evil powers (Col. 2:15) and the Jewish authorities (Luke 8:41; 11:58 (magistrate); Titus 3:1). In the New Testament these words are used 17 times of divine powers and 24 times of human rulers. Consequently the word can indicate the ruler's office, the ruler himself and the structure of power exerted by that ruler. It is sometimes translated as 'principalities'.

The main use of the word translated 'authorities' is to denote delegated rights of government in one form or another (cf. Acts 1:7; Luke 12:5). Though used to describe the sphere of influence of a power (Col. 1:16) the word was not used at all before the New Testament to describe angels or demons.

We can see at a glance from our survey that these principalities and powers are a mixture of celestial and earthly, spiritual and political, invisible and structural. There does not seem to be much evidence, if any at all, for a hierarchy of demons, as the interchangeability of the terms is too unsystematic. However, we must not be reductionist and think that there is no such thing as a spiritual power at work. The powers turn out to be human institutions, structures and organisations. The writers of the New Testament acknowledge the reality of spiritual powers working within these systems but they do not always demonise them, and neither should we. As Andii Bowsher says, 'Each human institution has a temporal-social identity and it also has a spiritual identity which is its reality as it intrudes into and relates to the heavenly realms.'[17] He goes on to explain that the spiritual world affects and is affected by the social and ethical climate of the human community. Much of the evil by which these powers may well be bound is of the same order as human evil: a perversion of the good that humans are created to effect which in some circumstances has become a means of access for demonic beings.

In the light of this, it now appears that the nature of the confrontation with the principalities and powers needs to be broadened. Apart from the reference in Daniel quoted at the beginning of this section, there does not seem to be any other biblical reference to direct engagement of spiritual superpowers in the conflict of spiritual warfare. Rather, there does seem to be some reference to addressing spiritual powers, but with the motive of renewal and healing. I am thinking principally of the angel of the churches mentioned seven times in the book of Revelation. I shall say more about this when we come to look at healing the church's wounded group story, but for now let us record that Jesus seems to view the angel as the carrier of the church's story for good or ill, who is affected by this story. Consequently the congregation of the church is presented with a summary of its story and relationship to its community through this spiritual power. This is actually an example of discerning the nature of the spiritual power, how it relates to a collection of group stories, church and community. This brings us to spiritual mapping.

What is spiritual mapping?

Cindy Jacobs defines spiritual mapping as 'backing prayer with diligent research to discern connections between the physical history of a land and the spiritual issues to be prayed for'.[18] Through prayer God reveals the spiritual condition of a group and place; this goes beyond the natural senses and is dependent upon the Holy Spirit's gifts to us. There needs to be caution here that the spiritual is confirmed, if possible, by the research that is undertaken, to make sure it coheres with the group story. Far too much so-called prayer warfare has been entirely subjective and uncorroborated, and leaves open to question the value of the whole enterprise, especially if it is not backed up with a penitential and repentant lifestyle on the part of those involved in their communities. It is certainly important to keep the spiritual and the personal issues in balance and in connection with each other when doing this kind of exercise. The real task of mapping or understanding a group story and its location is research which enables us to identify the repeating patterns of that group and where they are sited. This gives us the group story and its twin ingredients: that of blessing, which we want to keep and increase, and that needing healing and release so that there may be no ongoing hurt or destructive patterns. It is this information which makes informed  prayer and action possible. Peter Wagner offers a very good and comprehensive research programme for gathering information on a city before engaging in what he calls prayer warfare.[19] He examines three criteria, the historical, the physical (where he pays attention to the spiritual values invested in buildings and places and their geographical location within the city), and the spiritual (by which he means the religious – Christian or otherwise – values prominent in the life of the community). Once this information is secured, prayer is then focused on a number of targets which affect the life of that community. The city's redemptive gifts are identified, the strongholds of Satan are located, the territorial spirits over the city are revealed and the corporate sins of that community are realised. All this activity of prayer should then give some guidance as to a plan of response for attacking the powers which dominate and shape that city. As we shall see in later chapters, research is certainly the cornerstone for any ministry  taken to bring healing to any wounded group story. This issue is followed through carefully in the workbook that accompanies this book so that you will have the resources needed to engage in the work of reconciliation and healing for each of the group stories we shall be examining. However, Peter Wagner and those mentioned who have pioneered this approach to corporate story focus largely on the spiritual powers which stand behind the human story, and in particular the identifying of spiritual strongholds which, they suggest, are the barrier to the advance of God's kingdom.

What are spiritual strongholds?

In the majority of examples of spiritual mapping the focus is largely upon recognising where and how the demonic powers have infiltrated a group, and breaking such strongholds. They present some very good research questions for gaining an understanding of how certain cities or communities were established, but the *raison-d'être* for this labour is to engage in spiritual combat with the forces of darkness over the city in order to see evangelism released with a new power. Strongholds are mentioned in the New Testament and Paul writes about demolishing them through divine power (2 Cor. 10:4–6). Cindy Jacobs describes a stronghold as 'a fortified place that Satan builds to exalt himself against the knowledge and plans of God'.[20] What is meant by this is that spiritual powers gain an access into the life of a city or a tribe. In order to gain a real harvest of converts for God, these powers must first be bound and their captives set free. Jacobs goes on to list a number of different strongholds that need to be confronted. They are personal, territorial, mental, social, ideological, occultic, sectarian and where the church has failed to live up to its care of the community.

Ed Silvoso sees strongholds as being located 'in the heavenlies', and the focus of spiritual warfare is to do battle there. By the 'heavenlies', he means the 'spiritual realm' where thoughts and deeds are engaged in a struggle between demonic powers that would seduce us and the Spirit of God who would guide us into holiness of life.[21] Silvoso goes on to advocate an aggressive policy of prayer warfare to break down the control these kinds of strongholds exercise over the minds of a city's population and to prepare them for being more open to receive the good news of the Gospel of Christ. An outline of his strategy is as follows:

1. Establish God's perimeter: the faithful remnant of Christians establish a beachhead of godliness and unity between the churches who are free to utilise the spiritual gifts available.
2. Securing the perimeter: meeting for deeper understanding of the Bible and strengthening of pastoral leadership in the churches.
3. Expanding God's perimeter: establishing the model of repentance

for the sins of the church and the community. Such renewal prepares the church to launch out in mission.
4. Infiltrating Satan's perimeter: establishing a network of prayer cells and targeting the community street by street.
5. Destroying Satan's perimeter: a combination of practical caring and prophetic proclamation of the Gospel, bearing in mind the kind of spiritual climate that has been discerned as characterising the community.
6. Establishing God's perimeter: an increased commitment to evangelism and healing the church's sins and being wary of any spiritual counterattack.[22]

George Otis Jr says that the reference to the Prince of Persia in Daniel 10 is a clear reference to a territorial spirit and stronghold with clear boundaries.[23] This, coupled with the reference to world rulers in the list of spiritual powers in Ephesians 6:12, makes a convincing case to take seriously the fact of territorial powers. Be this as it may, in the passage quoted from 2 Corinthians 10, it is clear that the context is the discipleship of the individual who wages war against those who would set themselves up against the rule of Christ. It is at least a personal stronghold that is in mind here. This does not mean that it cannot refer to a group context like a city but it must be remembered that all the issues mentioned are those found in the human story – arguments, pretensions, thoughts and acts of disobedience – and not the attributes of spiritual powers which are never really described in any personal detail in scripture. Yet it is clear from scripture that the powers of darkness, however we understand them, wage war against the human race and in particular target our weaknesses, our unhealed wounds and our unforgiven stories – our strongholds which oppose or neglect the will of God.

How do we combat these spiritual powers?

While I do not wish to undermine or deny the importance of prayer warfare in the healing of wounded group stories, I think it is a far more effective strategy to focus on the human story rather than merely to use this information to target particular powers and engage in spiritual combat with them. It is important that our warfare also includes lifestyle issues, corporate action which is social and political if necessary. I think the real battle is in the area of healing need. This may appear reductionist but it is apparent that demonic powers operate on one simple principle and that is *only by the right of access* to the group story in question. What gives such powers, however we conceive them, this right? It is that which is unhealed or still waiting to be forgiven. The last piece of teaching Jesus gave his disciples was that if there were sins which had not been forgiven by God or the persons or peoples who suffered by our actions, then these sins were still waiting to be forgiven (John 20:23). This being the case, they could become the roots by which the demonic powers gain access to lives and stories. Only here does the unhealed wound go on recycling its poison within the systems of our group stories. In all other circumstances, where the forgiveness and healing love of God have been applied, whether for cure or care, the powers of darkness do not have a right to tempt or oppress or have any level of influence. This is because the resurrection life and power of Christ have been applied, which is tantamount to a fresh disarming of the powers at the foot of the cross (Col. 2:15). This does not mean that all spiritual warfare will suddenly end, as the struggles of Jesus with Satan in the wilderness illustrate. However, such a knowledge will change our response to such warfare. If the powers of darkness have no right of access then we can confidently, through the authority of Jesus, break such attempts to gain a foothold within our lives. Of course this has to be backed up with a walk of disciplined holiness but it does mean we need not be fooled into thinking that the powers of darkness can do just what they like. It also means that the focus of our research for the city and the peoples is to find out what needs healing and forgiving and, by so ministering to this, to deny the enemy any right of further access or hold. Consequently, in the healing of wounded history and the places where it is located, the more strategic step is not just to do battle with the powers, but to be a channel for the reconciling power of forgiveness to take effect on land and within people-groups. It is this outpouring of mercy from God which can transform wounded history and release new possibilities of healing grace for families, churches, communities, tribes and nations. As we shall see, our ability to do this successfully and powerfully also turns on our right of access to group stories in which we had no direct part because they belong to history. This will be the subject of our next chapter, because it is at the heart of all successful warfare.

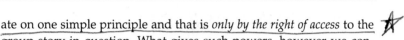

5 THE ROLE OF RECONCILIATION

Human societies could not exist without forgiveness and the public acts of contrition and confession that make reconciliation possible.

(Hannah Arendt[1])

So far in this book we have examined the dynamics of corporate or group identity and the importance of land, the prime place affected by these group stories. We have studied how these stories carry conclusions and consequences which are lived out in repeated patterns of life and bring either blessing or wounding to individuals and groups alike. In addition, we have looked at the powers which shape those stories. I have concluded that the most appropriate response to make to wounded group stories is one of healing rather than spiritual warfare, although the latter certainly does have a supportive role to play. The form of healing that is required is that of reconciliation and at the heart of this is the core ministry of representational confession.

Before we examine the dynamics of reconciliation, consider the following testimony to reconciling tribal stories. Dr Rhiannon Lloyd, a former paediatrician from Rhyl in North Wales, conducted a three-day trauma recovery programme for both Hutu and Tutsi survivors of the Rwanda genocide. The first step was to encourage the damaged and wounded to write down on a piece of paper the worst experience they had had. Following on from this, the people gathered together in small groups and told each other their stories. As John Dawson rightly says of this episode, 'this is often the first trembling step towards trusting other people again.'[2] Rhiannon tells how she encouraged people from different ethnic groups and denominations to get together and learn how to listen not just to facts but to the pain in everyone's heart.[3] Next, their stories and the atrocities linked to them were listed on a large sheet of paper for all to see and they were then asked, 'What does God feel about this?' A big red cross was drawn through the line of listed hurts symbolising the fact that in his death on the cross, Jesus carried all our sins and hurts. In the light of what Jesus had done for them, each person was encouraged to stand and tell God their story and not to hold back their anger and any other emotions. Naturally this could not be hurried, and in the course of time people opened their hearts of grief to God and poured out their sobbings and sharings. Rhiannon is well aquainted with the culture of these people and knows that it is one where the showing of grief is difficult because it is regarded as a sign of weakness. It is for this reason she gave them time to share and focused the sharing on the death of Jesus for all their sins and sorrows. However, discovering Jesus as pain-bearer as well as saviour and healer acted as a catharsis for the pouring out of the horrific stories.

At the end of this time of storytelling, a big, rough wooden cross was placed on the floor and everyone nailed their piece of paper with its appalling stories to this cross. The sound of hammering echoed throughout the day. It is a graphic symbol of how Jesus most truly identified with and represented our sinful stories and their results to our Father in heaven. It is only when this statement of faith has been made that the power of grief and the lust for revenge is broken and talk and acts of forgiveness begin to flow. Because many could now identify with how Jesus died and forgave them their sins, Rhiannon now challenged them with whether they could forgive the perpetrators of crimes against them if they too repented. This is not easily done of course but Dr Lloyd testifies that many did just this. Over a period of two years she has returned to Rwanda to find that these acts of forgiveness are being backed up with a determination to rebuild community with the help of God. Now national leaders, both Catholic and Protestant, are leading these workshops which are being actively encouraged by the political leadership in the country, because they work.

A significant feature of Dr Lloyd's work, perhaps the most important resource she offers, is her personal repentance and confession of her own tribal prejudices. She tells people how God disarmed her of her own resentment towards the English (remember she is Welsh) when some English Christians repented on behalf of their forebears for what they had done towards her own people. This helped her to connect with the sins of the white Europeans against the Africans and she soon found herself repenting for these actions. 'This often became the catalyst for heart change in them, opening up a whole new dimension in working towards reconciliation.'[4]

The main focus of this tremendous work has been the individual's need to be healed and reconciled and I call this the first reconciliation step. The next step is reconciling at group and inter-group level. At the heart of the Rwandan nightmare of genocide has been the repeating cycle of inter-tribal conflict which hooks the individual into re-enacting this corporate story. The focus now becomes not so much the wrongs which the individual may have done, but the wrongs done by the group of which I may be a member, which I need to own and confess as a step to healing and reconciliation at group level. This is the hard but rewarding work of *representational confession*. But let us look first at the content and context of the ministry of reconciliation: at the model of Christ as reconciler; the divine commission to be reconcilers; and the dynamics of reconciliation and the penitential lifestyle.

The model of Christ as reconciler

Surprisingly the word reconciliation does not occur frequently in scriptures, being mentioned specifically only 16 times in the New Testament. The vast majority of these references point to Jesus: he is the true and only reconciler offered to us in the pages of scripture. However, these references do offer a powerful and comprehensive vision of what God has determined to do through Jesus to bring healing to the world of broken relationships. There are six different but related words used to describe reconciliation; W. E. Vine summarises their meanings into two aspects:

- to change from enmity to friendship;
- a change on the part of one party, induced by an action on the part of another.[5]

It is quite clear from the Bible that the party offering the possibility of reconciliation is God investing this process in the sacrificial death of his son Jesus Christ on the cross. On closer inspection of Christ as reconciler we can see that there is a wide and wonderful scope to this ministry of reconciliation. There is the *personal* or *christological* level, the *ecclesiological* level (where the goal is tribal unity between Jew and Gentile within the body of Christ), and the *cosmic* level where Jesus reconciles all the powers in heaven and on earth.[6]

Personal reconciliation with God does not occur in the same process as that between human beings. It is clear that reconciliation is the work of God whose goal is to restore our relationship with him, a relationship which we have broken and which he is determined to heal. It is not a human work, therefore, but is achieved and accomplished by God. The challenge and invitation for us is to respond to and receive this offer through recognition of our need and repentance for our sins.

> For if, when we were God's enemies, we were reconciled to him through the death of his Son, how much more, having been reconciled, shall we be saved through his life! (Romans 5:10)

> God was reconciling the world to himself in Christ, not counting men's sins against them. (2 Corinthians 5:19)

These scriptures imply an enormous agenda which will have a serious impact on every life. Consider, for example, the verses before the one quoted above from Romans which gives us the clue to God's motivation and the prospects for those who respond and those who do not. 'But God demonstrates his own love for us in this: While we were still sinners, Christ died for us. Since we have now been justified by his blood, how much more will we be saved from God's wrath through him!' (Rom. 5:8–9). It is the love of God which energises the whole offer of reconciliation so that we can cease to be enemies and become his friends. Refusal of reconciliation mans that we continue to choose the role of enemy and struggle with the powers of wrath and anger. To be reconciled we must listen to and remember the pain of such a broken relationship, its continuing consequences for those separated, and choose to respond to love and receive new life. The personal reconciliation to God suggests serious principles for the reconciliation needed for healing broken relationships between people and people-groups. We will look more closely at this when we discuss our commission to be reconcilers.

Ecclesiological reconciliation in scripture is principally focused on bringing Jew and Gentile together within the body of Christ. This is not a vision of amalgamating the different cultures of Jew and Gentile into a homogeneous new nation where separate identities are merged into a new, monochrome society. It is rather the weaving together of the variety of ethnic diversities into a cohesive, multicultural and multilingual people united under the Lordship of Jesus Christ. In order to do this, God reconciles the past and present histories of the nations along with the particular covenants given to the Jewish people.

> Remember that at that time you were separate from Christ, excluded from citizenship in Israel and foreigners to the covenants of the promise, without hope and without God in the world. But now in Christ Jesus you who were once far away have been brought near through the blood of Christ. For he himself is our peace, who has made the two one and has destroyed the barrier, the dividing wall of hostility, by abolishing in his flesh the law with its commandments and regulations. His purpose was to create in himself one new man out of the two, thus making peace, and in this one body to reconcile both of them to God through the cross, by which he put to death their hostility. (Ephesians 2:12–16)

> I am talking to you Gentiles . . . For if their [the Jewish nation's] rejection is the reconciliation of the world, what will their acceptance be but life from the dead? (Romans 11:13, 15)

In these passages the Apostle Paul is summarising the story of the nations: the chosen nation of the Jewish people has been temporarily rejected by God because of their disobedience to the covenants made with them. During this time the good news has now gone out to the Gentile peoples who are responding to the new covenant of reconciliation and peace with God through the death and resurrection of Jesus Christ. However, Paul sees a day coming when the Jewish believers will be re-grafted into this new body of Christ and so fulfil their calling to be a light to the nations of the love of God. It will be through the gift of reconciliation whereby the hostility between the nations and between those nations and God will be healed. Consequently Paul throws out a challenge to us today: he builds on the back of our reconciliation with God the divine impulsion to mend broken relationships between the nations of which we are members and representatives.[7]

Cosmic reconciliation gives us a visionary glimpse into the ultimate healing purposes of God when not only people, but earth and the heavens themselves will be reconciled to God through him. Once again we are told that it is only achieved through the power of the cross. 'For God was pleased to have all his fullness dwell in him, and through him to reconcile to himself all things, whether things on earth or things in heaven, by making peace through his blood, shed on the cross' (Col. 1:19–20; cf. also Eph. 1:9–10). As we have noted earlier, this is exactly the picture of the consummation of the ages which John paints in the closing chapters of his Apocalypse where he sees a new heaven and a new earth and a redeemed community of saints which he calls the new Jerusalem (Rev. 21:1–2). It is the final healing in God's redemptive purposes and it links land, people-groups and the heavens. In addition, this reference to earth and heavens also implies that there will be a final reconciliation within the spirit world, however we understand this concept. The Hebrew world-view imagined a heaven filled with angels and an earth stalked by demons.[8] The Hellenistic, or Greek, world-view saw the earth surrounded by layer upon layer of spirits which blocked earth's access to God. This cosmic reconciliation implies an end to spiritual warfare and an ultimate reconciliation of the enmity between the 'powers' and God. This helps to explain and make clear that behind the ongoing enmity between people-groups is the influence of the spiritual powers which to some degree have gained a hold over the repeating process of wounded group stories. It also underlines the fact that not all the powers are evil, because they are to be reconciled. The reference to 'all things' also suggests the dimension of the past and the dead. 'Present alienation and evil feed on unresolved conflicts running back into the past and upon weaknesses and vulnerabilities borne from earlier experiences of oppression, violence and failure.'[9] However, on the last day God will triumph over all things and will restore creation to its rightful healing and the dead in Christ will be reunited with those still living (cf. 1 Thess. 4:16–18).

We can see therefore that the range of Christ's ministry of reconciliation extends far beyond the individual's need to be saved. It reaches to the heavens and also to all the human stories and creation itself. The marvel as well as the mystery of all this is that on the basis of this model of Christ the reconciler, we, as his disciples, are given this selfsame calling of reconciliation.

The divine commission to be reconcilers

> All this is from God, who reconciled us to himself through Christ and gave us the ministry of reconciliation . . . We are therefore Christ's ambassadors, as though God were making his appeal through us. We implore you on Christ's behalf: Be reconciled to God. (2 Corinthians 5:18, 20)

Paul is careful to remind us that it is not the church which reconciles but God through Christ, and the first relationship to be healed is that between each person and God. As Robert Schreiter comments in his book,

> We are not in a position, either as victims or oppressors, to create new narratives of sufficient power to overcome completely the damage that has been done by situations of violence and oppression. While we may overcome these situations, we seem never to be liberated completely; a residue of that violence and oppression has seeped into our bones . . . We are indeed invited (by God) to cooperate in the process of reconciliation.[10]

Our high calling is to be a resource for the grace of God which is offered to individuals to find their way back to God; to be a part of bringing healing to broken relationships between people-groups and through our witness and testimony to reveal these reconciling purposes to the principalities and powers in the heavenly places (cf. Eph. 1:18–23; 3:10–11).

However, while the church certainly has this ambassadorial commission from God to be a channel for reconciliation, it is a fact of history that we have often forfeited this right because we have become part of the problem rather than part of the solution. Far too often the church has been seen as part of the establishment and as a result has been identified with the oppressors. Who can forget the telling pictures of the dramatic flight for safety of the Archbishop of Port-au-Prince in Haiti in January 1991, when mobs of angry poor burnt down the old cathedral in violent protest at that church's indifference to decades of corruption and oppression? In the aftermath of the genocide in Rwanda there has been the numbing revelation that church leaders took part in the slaughter. The Roman

Catholic Church in the Republic of Ireland is fighting for its survival in the aftermath of child sex scandals on an unprecedented scale. As a result of such stories, many church leaders are giving a bold and daring lead in acknowledging their church's failure to stand for the victims of suffering by offering repentance and confession on behalf of their churches.

At a meeting of the Synod of the Nippon Sei Ko Kai, the Anglican Church of Japan, the leaders present offered an unequivocal apology for the behaviour of the Japanese nation during the Second World War. This was in direct contrast to its political leaders who would not acknowledge, let alone admit, any atrocities committed. The statement was so bold and far reaching that I think it worth quoting some extracts from it:

> The Nippon Seo Ko Kai, after 50 years since the end of World War II, admits its responsibility and confesses its sin for having supported and allowed, before and during the war, the colonial rule and war of aggression by the State of Japan.
>
> The church had chosen to comply with the government policy and had forgotten its mission . . . we have been a closed church whose main concern is the expansion of the membership and the retention of the institution, thus being *unable* to serve as the salt for the earth as indicated in the Gospel. The Nippon Sei Ko Kai confesses to God and apologizes to the people in Asia and the Pacific that we did not admit our fault immediately after the war, were unaware of our responsibility for the past 50 years, and have not actively called for reconciliation and compensation until today. The Nippon Sei Ko Kai confesses that, even after the war, it has yet to get rid of discriminatory attitudes. We pray that we will be changed to recognize our mission to do justice as the people of God, and, as the vessels of peace, to listen to the voices of division, pains, cries and sufferings of the world.
>
> As a sign of repentance, we the people of the Nippon Seo Ko Kai will do the following:
>
> 1. To share the confession of our war responsibility among all of the parishes.
> 2. To convey an apology to the Churches in the countries which Japan invaded.

3. To start and continue a programme in each Diocese and Parish, to review the historical facts and to deepen our understanding of the Gospel.

(49th Regular Synod, Resolution No 34, May 1996)

Similar confessional risks have been taken by other church leaders. In the United States of America, the Christian composer Jimmy Owens has written a musical called *Heal the Land*. Part of the programme calls for church leaders in various cities to come together to repent of their disunity and apologise to each other for being such an obstacle to the kingdom of God and for failure in their calling to be witnesses of the love of God. This programme has given birth to a national movement of reconciliation and healing between churches. In the wake of these meetings the churches have begun to adopt shared policies to bring about urban renewal and justice for the poor and marginalised in their cities. The Archbishop of Canterbury, the Most Revd George Carey, and Metropolitan Athanasios of the Ecumenical Patriarchate both responded to the invitation of Pope John Paul II to join him and other church leaders in pushing open a Holy Door into the basilica of St Paul's without the Walls as a symbolic act of repentance as well as a plea for reconciliation for 'the sins committed against Christian unity during the last millennium'.[11] The year 2000 also saw the first visit of a reigning pope to Israel where he spoke at Yad Vashem, Israel's memorial to the Holocaust victims and all victims of suffering. Pope John Paul II expressed deep sadness over the fact of Christian anti-Semitism. However, Rabbi Shalom Gold, who was taking part in the event, said that the Pope had shown great courage but what he had said was not enough to eliminate 2,000 years of hatred and distrust. He was in fact hoping for something more substantial, an apology for the Roman Catholic Church's complicity with the Nazi regime in the actions of Pope Pius XII who was thought to have ties with Hitler and was a known anti-Semite. Incidentally, we must not undervalue the bravery of Pope John Paul II, because even within his own church he was criticised for what some considered to be an excessive penitence and self-questioning which would undermine faith in Christianity and its institutions.[12] It is just as well that we are aware that confession can be dangerous because it exposes us and makes us vulnerable before others. It may feel as if our solid ground is shaking beneath us and the temptation is to run and hide within our institutions. Another example of the church fulfilling its call to be a channel of reconciliation is in Chile where, as the Pinochet regime was beginning to crumble and fall, the church established 'houses of reconciliation' where survivors of torture and persecution would come and tell their story, because it was important for the truth to be heard and not glossed over, trivialised or denied. The church was determined not to forget on behalf of its community, and had earned the right to do this because it had stood by the people during the times of persecution and had suffered for its witness. This is also one of the ministries of the Corrymeela Community in Northern Ireland where those who have suffered in 'the troubles' are given safe and shared spaces to grieve, scream and hope. It is also important to realise that the church will invariably carry within its own community the selfsame divisions as the society it serves. The question is, what will the church do in order to keep its integrity? For the church, to be a resource for reconciliation is like taking up the cross of Christ as it cares for the victims of injustice and persecution. As we have seen, reconciliation is a demanding process and involves a number of essential ingredients if it is to be productive.

The dynamics of reconciliation

We must not heal the wounds of history lightly. Reconciliation is not an attempt to gloss over the wrongs committed by perpetrators by reducing it to a conflict resolution – a bargaining over what each side gives up in order to end hostilities – important as this may be. This tends to be managed by the professionals in an operation which is highly technical and skilled, but which often means that the victims' stories are not properly heard or acknowledged. Godly reconciliation does not settle for an uneasy peace where the parties in dispute find ways to coexist; the Christian understanding of reconciliation is to bring healing of relationships through the grace of God in Christ. The following are some of the essential elements if true reconciliation is to be possible:

- remembering
- lament
- confession
- repentance: the penitential lifestyle
- forgiveness

Remembering

It is so important that we are given room to tell our story. To be denied this right is to be extinguished, forgotten and relegated to the league of the denied. This is why we must beware of cheap healing, of a form of reconciliation that all too hastily calls upon the victims to forgive and move on with their lives. 'To trivialise and ignore memory is to trivialise and ignore human identity, and to ignore and trivialise human identity is to trivialise and ignore human dignity.'[13] As Archbishop Sean Brady said in his sermon in the Anglican Cathedral in Portsmouth, 'Forgetting the past can bring no understanding of the present . . . A sort of healing the memories is needed so that past evils will not come back again.' It is vital that we listen accurately so that the factors of suffering are uncovered from the victim's story and perspective. If we fail here then the vicious cycle of history is not really breached. Yet it continues to amaze me how we automatically assume that we know how to listen and do not bother to learn. In the Acorn Christian Foundation we have developed a threefold approach to our vision of caring: listening, healing and reconciliation. Reconciliation turns on the hinges of meaningful dialogue and no dialogue is possible unless we can listen to others and to God and also to ourselves. What we hear will be uncomfortable, and we will be tempted to reinterpret it in order to manage it more comfortably. I would strongly recommend therefore that all church leaders go on a listening training course. I remember seeing an advertisement in *The Times* for a sophisticated form of communications systems. It consisted of a photograph of a cleaner washing out the ears of the giant statue of Abraham Lincoln at the Lincoln Memorial in Washington DC. The caption underneath the picture said 'Good listeners make the best leaders!'

If we fail to listen then the perpetrators of the suffering are not really facing up to their responsibilities and so true forgiveness from the victims will not be possible. There is indeed a place for forgiveness but it must never be hurried or engaged with until the sufferer has been truly heard. The truth must be told and as fully as possible. A very public example of remembering is the Truth and Reconciliation Commission in South Africa. John Hughes points out that one sentence often remembered by the victims of torture in the former apartheid regime was 'Go ahead and scream as much as you like – nobody can hear you, nobody cares about you, no one will ever know.'[14] He goes on to say that one of the benefits of the Commission was that it exposed the lie of silence and restored the plank of human dignity to victims who could now articulate their story to a listening public who were shaken by what they were hearing. He sees this as a time of catharsis and healing for victim and perpetrator alike. Ruth Slovo, whose mother was killed by a letter bomb sent by government authorities (her father was leader of the Communist Party in South Africa and a member of the ANC), stated in an interview on Radio 4 in October 2000 that she felt a sense of intimacy binding herself to those who had confessed to this atrocity. She did not believe for one moment that the truth was really being told by those who were confessing but nonetheless acknowledged the value of her mother's story being publicly told at last. This also underlines the fact that the process of reconciliation most truly begins with the victim: the perpetrator cannot set the pace for his or her own forgiveness.

Remembering is a challenge to step into the light and come to terms with the consequences either of our own actions or those of the people groups of which we are a part. Remembering is that disturbing discipline by which we unmask the dark ways in which we have lived in denial of what we or our people have inflicted upon others. It similarly deconstructs the way that victims have tried to rationalise why they have suffered. An obvious example of this is how some abuse survivors believe that they invited their suffering because they deserved it, because they were inferior or sent out the wrong signals. Stanley Hauerwas reports that the United States exemplifies the attempt to have time blot out past wrongs through forgetfulness. He mentions in particular the issue of slavery and says that its continuing effect is a wound so deep in the American soul that 'we prefer, both black and white, to ignore its continuing presence in our lives. Yet every denial of history haunts us, frightening us with the reality so that we feel helpless before this ghost of our past.'[15] He goes on to quote the experience of Wendell Berry whose forebears owned slaves: 'Once you begin to awaken to the realities of what you know, you are subject to staggering recognitions of your complicity in history and in the events in your own life . . . a historical wound, prepared centuries ago to come alive in me at my birth like a hereditary disease and to be augmented and deepened in my life.' The first step on the journey of reconciliation is the cathartic and challenging act of remembering.

Lament

Scripture is full of lament, of crying to God by giving a voice to the pain, injustice and outrage of suffering. It is not necessarily the search for answers, but the need for others to recognise the wrongness of the acts perpetrated against us. The Psalmist screams out his pain when he says 'Out of the depths I cry to you, O Lord' (Ps. 130:1). A similar lament is found in Psalms 22, 73 and 88. This is a recurring theme for the oppressed tribes in captivity in Egypt (cf. Deut. 26:5–11). Perhaps the two most poignant examples of lament are found in the book of Job and the Lamentations of Jeremiah. Job is hideously disfigured and pestered by counsellors who see his cry to God as a betrayal of trust in God's providence. Consequently there is hardly any room for him to lament as every painful complaint he utters is smothered in exhortations to do better. Jeremiah describes the sad cycle of the city of Jerusalem which throughout its history had rebelled against God and was now on the eve of its own destruction. In the New Testament we find lament on the lips of the dying Christ who in the darkness of his suffering shouts out: 'Why have you forsaken me?' He, like us, gets no answer to his question at the time he asks for one. The point of lament is to know we have been heard and especially by God who we hope will act to save us. Claus Westermann says that in essence lament is the language of suffering and its function is to appeal to God's compassion.[16] Lament is not an isolated groaning or bemoaning of the facts, it is a public outcry and the real importance of the church's role in reconciliation is to provide a context for this shared recognition of the wounded story – this is its primary contribution to the healing of relationships. However, this shared awareness between victim and perpetrator can be quite a bumpy ride. Very often the victim is not satisfied with a recognition or an apology for wrongs committed. He or she is looking for justice and a change to the structures which perpetuate the injustices.

Confession

The core dynamic of confession is ownership of the story in question. It may be sins I or my people-group have committed. It can also refer to the gifts and callings of God upon us. John the Baptist was not shy in confessing that he was not the Christ but that he was like a voice crying in the wilderness in order to prepare for the coming of the Christ (John 1:19–23). The risk of owning that we have done wrong is that the victims of our wrongs may demand justice and a change in our relationship so that we work together for a better future. Our apology is not enough, and yet even if it is not accepted it is not valueless, because it has helped to begin the process of healing. We may well have further demands made upon us by those who suffered at our hands, but even if our confession appears to be a small degree of healing, the victim sees that we have begun to own our part in their suffering. We can only go forward from this point if we have a heart and a will to do it. A common criticism I hear from some participants in public meetings of reconciliation, where the focus is upon healing wounded group stories, is the dissatisfaction with too much emotion at the expense of working together for real structural change. At one multicultural gathering of church leaders in Ruistenberg in South Africa in 1991, one comment that was heard was, 'I don't want nice apologies so white people can feel good. What I want is whites to join us in the struggle to dismantle apartheid and create justice.'[17] Walter Wink says that it is necessary to distinguish here between the need for societal reconciliation which awaits justice, and personal forgiveness which individuals are capable of achieving.[18] Of course, as Christians we will say that this confession is made both to God and to the victim as we call on the grace of God to empower us to own, acknowledge and work to repair the damage we or our people have done to others. However, there are a number of scriptural references where confession is made not just for personal transgressions but on behalf of the nation, as in the case of Ezra, Nehemiah and Daniel. The remarkable factor in all of these examples is that the confessor is not personally a perpetrator of the nation's sins. This will be the focus of the next chapter where we shall explore more fully the role and the effects of representational confession.

Repentance: the penitential lifestyle

This is essentially a personal response by the individual with respect to their own sinful agenda. It is a decision to change direction from the old pattern of sinful rebellion and destructiveness toward others as well as myself and to walk in newness of life. As such it is the core of the gospel message of Jesus (cf. Mark 1:15; Matt. 4:17; Luke 13:3, 5;

15:10; Acts 20:21). The churches too are challenged to repent and renew their life in the spirit (Rev. 2:5, 16, 22; 3:19). The church's witness is challenged in the form of a corporate story which needs to be radically changed and healed. It is not too clear whether this is an appeal to the church en masse, or to the leaders or individual members of the congregations to awaken to the renewing presence of the Lord. What is not happening here is that the angel or another representative of the church is being asked to repent on behalf of the church. It is clear, however, that the expectation is that the whole church will be touched by God and respond as a group. This does, however, open the way to asking whether repentance can be offered on behalf of others. I think the clear answer is no, but what we can do is to identify with the sins and crimes of our people-group by personal repentance backed up with a penitential lifestyle. This is in fact the work of intercession which is prayer on behalf of others, whereas supplication is prayer on behalf of myself. An example of intercession is the prayer of Moses that God would not destroy the people for making the golden calf. There is no confession or repentance on behalf of the sins of the people, just a plea that God would not destroy them but have mercy upon them (Exod. 32:11–14). However, it has to be acknowledged that what followed the prayer was a time of judgement on the people as even Moses is angry at their sins. The next time he appears before God he asks the Lord to forgive their sins and Yahweh only frees the nation from his wrath by punishing the sins of those who had rebelled (Exod. 32:27–8, 30–5).

John Dawson rightly points out that the true intercessor finds that prayer of this sort has a double edge. He writes,

> When we ask God's mercy on others, we should never say, 'How could they do such a thing?' We know exactly how they could do it, because the potential for the worst evil lies within each one of us, apart from God's saving grace and the life of Christ within us.[19]

He sees the struggle to pray for another to be released from the bondage of sin to be the stirring impetus for ourselves to come to terms with our own personal sin. Like the Psalmist, we too must cry out 'Search me O God, and know my heart, try me and know my thoughts; and see if there is any wicked way in me, and lead me in the way everlasting' (Ps. 139:23–4 NASB). It is from this crucible of recognition of the need for our own cleansing that we are made ready to engage in the redeeming work of reconciliation.

However, there are examples in scripture of individuals confessing the sins of their people and yet they are plainly innocent of the crimes in question. Such a form of national confession is a different category of prayer from the ordinary forms of intercession and needs to be recovered within the prayer life of the church.

The action of repentance is to demonstrate the genuineness of confession by walking in newness of life. In her work in Rwanda Rhiannon Lloyd points out that the real power which lies behind the ability to forgive others for the damage they have done to us is to become deeply aware of how God has forgiven us. This is what it means to walk in newness of life. It is not a condition we lay upon others before we forgive them. Rather, it is a showing forth that we know we have been forgiven and the only way we can show it is to live a new life. This can be extended to group story material as well. If I have confessed the sins of slavery within my nation, then for me to walk in the penitential lifestyle of repentance is not to entertain the roots of slavery in my life. I will not lust for power; I will not disrespect the dignity of other people by ignoring them or demonising them; I will not make people dependent or beholden to me as a means of getting what I want; I will not keep people on the poverty line by paying them improper and low wages. The list could go on, but the principle is clear: we need to look at the root ingredients of a major group sin and be determined not to repeat them in our own lives. John Dawson does a similar exercise when he looks at the act of abortion within his nation. He identifies abortion's root sins as lust, the love of comfort, the love of money, rejection and unbelief.[20]

Forgiveness

Essentially forgiveness is the act of letting go or of giving up some grievance one person has against another who is seen to offend or damage him or her.[21] The first forgiver is God who does not hold our sins against us but who offers us forgiveness; in order to benefit from this offer it is we who must repent. As John writes in his epistle, 'If we confess our sins, he is faithful and just and will forgive us our sins and purify us from all unrighteousness' (1 John 1:9). It is important to realise that the offer of forgiveness is made even before we come to the place of repentance and receiving it and therefore benefiting from it. God is not waiting for us to repent before he makes this offer; it is often the offer of forgiveness which prompts in us the conviction to repent. From our perspective it is quite appropriate therefore for us to forgive others even when they show no sign of being interested in receiving forgiveness. It is always good to remember that the first beneficiary of the offer of forgiveness is the one who offers it and not the one who receives it. This is why someone like Gordon Wilson could forgive the IRA bombers who killed his daughter in the explosion at Enniskillen even before the perpetrators showed any sign of remorse. He has as his model Jesus, who, without a repenting perpetrator in sight, nonetheless said 'Father, forgive them, for they do not know what they are doing' (Luke 23:4). To forgive someone is a choice not to go on with life wanting revenge against the other.

Of course, such forgiveness can easily be misunderstood. We do not forgive and forget. To forget is to deny the offence and trivialise our own pain. Actually, to forgive is to speak of a great grace and a great judgement. It is a great grace because we are saying that with the help of the love and power of God we are not pursuing revenge but rather wanting to free the perpetrator from continuing in their destructive pattern of life. It is a great judgement because we are pointing out that what was done was very wrong and that they must face up to the consequences and implications of what they have done: it is the impetus to live a penitential lifestyle. What actually happens is that we remember the evil or the damage others have done and, in the light of our being forgiven by God for our sins, we dare to forgive also. It is in this way that forgiveness is a resource for reconciliation and as we have already mentioned, rightly begins with the victim.

Forgiveness is not saying 'It does not matter'. If it does not matter then it does not need forgiveness. However, our story is important to us and we do not minimise this when we forgive: we actually state its importance when we do so. This is why forgiveness must not be hurried up or offered cheaply because it is the story of our life that we are sharing.

Forgiveness is not saying 'You did not mean to do it.' This is also to deny the perpetrator a real opportunity to own their deeds and change their ways for the better. We must not collude with denial and embrace what Schreiter has described as 'the narrative of the lie'.[22] He points out that on an individual and group level it has often been by acts of violence that others have tried to destroy the stories which give us our identities and replace them with their own narratives. This is why we must not diminish ourselves for the sake of a shallow peace. Such collusion will always threaten and undermine reconciliation, because the story that divides perpetrator and victim has not been brought into the light and worked through for a true healing of relationships.

Forgiveness is not a replacement for justice. We may well forgive those who have committed crimes against us but who must still face the law for their crimes. When Gordon Wilson forgave the IRA for the killing of his daughter Marie, he was not asking that they should not be brought to justice, as this would be to condone their actions and cheapen the life of his daughter. There is no inconsistency in this, as we choose a future without revenge and hopefully the perpetrators mend their ways. This separation of matters is not so simple when we come to the issue of wounded group stories. In South Africa, The Truth and Reconciliation Commission have now heard in the region of 20,000 statements of gross violation of human rights. For many, the focus of the debate on the subject has been the level of amnesty offered. Should it be blanket amnesty (as it is in the majority of cases) or a full exposure with limited prosecutions?

According to John Hughes, his investigations revealed that the important item for the victims was that the truth be told in as much detail as possible. However, he goes on to say that the hoped for outcome of this commission was an outworking of restorative justice in which the goal is not punishment for punishment's sake, but to bring the perpetrator and victim to work together to build a new future.[23] He goes on to say,

> South Africans have done something extraordinary by expecting and hoping for so much: they have risked a commitment to restorative rather than a retributive justice; they have allowed and even required that as much truth be told as possible; they have offered forgiveness in the hope that restorative justice provides a vision of reconciliation, and of a future which is not bound by the destructiveness of the past.

This determination to tell the truth and overcome the narrative of the lie has witnessed some remarkable confessions about the apartheid system, ranging from the leadership of the Dutch Reformed Church for its failure to protest properly against the system to the confession of Melanie Verwoerd, the great-granddaughter-in-law of H. F. Verwoerd, one of the makers of the apartheid system. She said, 'We owe it to ourselves, our descendants and our fellow man . . . to rid ourselves of the stigma of apartheid and not attempt any longer to disguise the darkness of our collective past with the tempting light of well-intentioned separate development.'[24]

It is to the group level of reconciliation that we must now turn our attention and particularly look at the unique form of prayer called *representational confession* which forms the heart of healing wounded history.

6 REPRESENTATIONAL CONFESSION: THE RIGHT TO RECONCILE

O Lord . . . we have sinned and done wrong.

(Daniel 9:5)

More things are wrought by prayer
Than this world dreams of.

(Tennyson)

At the heart of healing wounded history and its ongoing consequences is the unique form of corporate intercession which I have called *representational confession*. This is a form of prayer which is aimed specifically at a group level and is never used by the individual for himself or herself or offered just for the individual. Daniel and Ezra pray for the remnant nation of Israel (Dan. 9:4–19; Ezra 9:5–15); Moses prays for the fledgling nation which was still more or less a confederation of tribes (Exod. 34:8–9); Nehemiah prays for the restoration of his captive nation and the rebuilding of the ruined city of Jerusalem (Neh. 1:5–10); and Jesus takes decisive action for the salvation of the human race by dying on the cross and rising from the dead, which the Apostle Paul describes as a representational act of identification: 'God made him who had no sin to be sin for us, so that in him we might become the righteousness of God' (2 Cor. 5:21). It is doubly interesting that this last text forms the climax of teaching on reconciliation and the church's commission as Christ's ambassadors to apply this healing to a broken world. All these forms of prayer have a similar pattern of ingredients and to understand them we will look more closely at the example of Daniel's prayer for the captive people of Israel.

Personal conviction and repentance

> I, Daniel, understood from the Scriptures, according to the word of the Lord given to Jeremiah the prophet, that the desolation of Jerusalem would last seventy years. So I turned to the Lord God and pleaded with him in prayer and petition, in fasting, and in sackcloth and ashes. (Daniel 9:2–3)

Daniel's intercession for Israel is not a cold application of techniques to a problem but is in response to the conviction of God's word and spirit in his life. Like all intercession it is prophetic in character, because he is seized by the prophecy of Jeremiah who had spoken of seventy years of captivity. Daniel was caught by the conviction that this was the time to hold God to his promise to release the captive nation. Also the seriousness of the condition of his people and the destructive power of disobedience to God's will struck his heart, which is revealed in his fasting and wearing sackcloth and ashes as a sign of mourning and personal repentance. It is important to point out that there are two principal issues in this form of praying (if not in all prayers of intercession) and they are *the facts* and the *working of the Holy Spirit*. It is essential that these two work together whenever possible.

We have already discovered that working with wounded group stories reveals that they operate on a number of levels. The winners of a war will always remember the event from the perspective of success whilst the losers will see it as a failure, and both perspectives will colour the way we relate to each other. Kenneth Milne, a Church of Ireland minister, underlines this when he speaks of the relative ease of sitting on a commitee to compile a new history of Europe for readers in several EU countries (France, Germany, England and Italy), compared with being a member of a working party trying to understand sectarianism in Ireland. It was far easier to have a wide range of European scholars agree on the causes and effects of the two World Wars than to know the causes, symptoms and treatment of sectarianism. He concluded that the reason for the Irish experience being more difficult to understand was that the European historians were dealing with matters on which the books had been closed, while the Irish situation was grappling with a situation where the question of winners and losers had yet to be settled.[1]

Consequently this form of praying must include as much as possible of the facts and consequences from all sides so that no one story is allowed to cover up or deny the other. This will become more vital to healing when we look at the work of group confession. In engaging in this kind of ministry I have always been grateful for the work of our historical researchers who in some way prophetically chart for us the pathway of our prayers and intercessions. This is not to undermine the intuitive and revelatory element of prayer, but I believe that such 'revelations' wherever possible should be checked by the facts. It is interesting to note that in the episode where Jesus was delivering a disturbed boy from demonisation, although he already knew what kind of spirit needed to be cast out, Jesus nonetheless checked out his discernment by asking the boy's father questions such as 'How long as he been like this?' (Mark 9:21). Why is this? I believe it is because discernment corroborated by the facts releases authority to act. We would do well to follow the example of Jesus.

I had the honour of taking part in a gathering of Gentile and Jewish Christians who had come together to pray about the original wound in the Christian community, the schism which had divided our two peoples from being one family under the headship of Jesus. It is our belief that this first wound became a repeated pattern of sickness within the body of Christ and has not been properly recognised or confronted. However, before we met together, the Towards Jerusalem Council II had been commissioned by the International Reconciliation Coalition to research this issue and had come up with the salient facts for us to act upon. Consequently Daniel Juster and Father Peter Hocken provided us with a detailed account of the sorry story which troubled and convicted us to the core and gave us some real guidance of what and where we should go to pray.[2] Among the many facts they uncovered was that it was at the Ecumenical Councils of the church at Nicaea that the main discriminations against the Jewish faith and culture were agreed. These included the forbidding of Jewish Christians to celebrate Passover or practise their dietary laws, and the changing of the date of Easter from its Jewish Passover context to a Roman calendar – to name but a few. In the light of the facts we felt it only right that we returned to the actual site in Northern Turkey and hold our service of apology and reconciliation there. It proved to be a powerful time of healing for all involved and renewed our commitment to work together for the healing of the body of Christ and in particular to find ways to honour the Jewish nation and give them their due recognition as God's chosen people. The Holy Spirit also gave us a prophetic prayer as one of our number prayed the prayer of apology before the Jewish Christian representatives there and pointed out that just as the Christian church sought to silence the Jewish Christians in this part of the Middle East, so it was reaping what it had sown, because its own witness had similarly been silenced. We all deeply repented of our complicity in this and asked God to teach us new ways to belong to each other. The researching of facts can be tools in the hands of the Holy Spirit to give us guidance and conviction in our praying for healing and reconciliation.

However, we do need to accept that there are times when we may not be able to get the facts, because we are dealing with a history which may not be accessible to us through books. Yet it is always important to act on the basis of 'informed intercession'[3] and a way of evaluating the intuitions that people may receive is to examine the repeating patterns of the wounded group story and where they are located, and to compare this with the revelations given in the hope that they offer corroboration. I think it was the late Dr Martyn Lloyd Jones who said that theology was no other than 'logic on fire'. The same is true for intercession. We do not merely gather facts, analyse them and decide how to act in prayer. We surrender the facts to God and ask that the Holy Spirit set our hearts on fire with his convictions and broken heart for his people. It is this divine energy that is the fuel of true repentance and intercession. We need to be a people moved and troubled by God. Daniel was moved to humble himself and repent; Ezra was so upset at what God showed him about the sins and woeful condition of his nation that he tore his tunic, pulled out his hair and beard and sat down appalled at the situation (Ezra 9:3). Jesus was moved with compassion and healing care for the lost because they were like sheep without a shepherd (Mark 6:34). All these are examples of the impact of the Holy Spirit upon the individual as God made them aware of the sins of the people and their consequences. This is not to give licence or carte-blanche approval to all the extraordinary behaviour of intercessors, but it should at least caution us to consider what God is doing through such activities. It is not to the individual practitioner that we should give our attention, but to the seriousness of the condition which God challenges us with.

Finally, the combining of facts and the Holy Spirit is to emphasise our personal need to repent and be reconciled if we wish to stand in the gap where healing is brought to wounded group stories. It is precisely here that I feel most fraudulent in this work. I am only too aware of my failings and sins and how hard I sometimes find it to confront them properly. Yet it is as wounded healers and wounded intercessors that we are called. If God were to wait until all our sins and problems have been sorted out before we intercede for others, we would be doing very little for the kingdom. But let us be challenged by the Daniels and Ezras of this world to come under the weight of the Holy Spirit, and be people who know how to repent personally, for ourselves and for what God shows us are the sins of our wounded group stories.

Confession and rights of access

> I prayed to the Lord my God and confessed: . . . 'we have sinned and done wrong. We have been wicked and have rebelled; we have turned away from your commands and laws'
> (Daniel 9:4–5; cf. Ezra 9:6; Neh. 1:6–7)

From a personal and individual act of repentance Daniel now moves on to a confession of his nation's sins, the results of which were the long captivity in Babylon. What is so remarkable and unique about this prayer of representational confession is that, although innocent of the crimes of his nation, Daniel nonethless prays from the perspective of the guilty. This is also true of Ezra and Nehemiah and, I would suggest, is implicit in the very act of Jesus becoming our sin-bearer upon the cross. What is the point of this and by what authority can they do it? Before answering these questions it is necessary that we understand the process of confession before we discuss how Daniel and others apply this ministry to the group story of their nation.

In the Old Testament the predominant word for confession is *yādāh* and it is usually translated as praise or thanksgiving. It is used six times for confession and largely in this context of offering the sins and problems of a corporate story rather than being focused upon individuals (cf. Neh. 9:3; 1 Kings 8:35). As such, confession carries the idea of recognition of a truth that is publicly admitted. In the New Testament there are only two words for confession, and they are *homologeō* and *exomologeō*. As in the Old Testament, the focus is not exclusively on sins. When John the Baptist is asked to state who he is and what his mission was it is recorded in John's gospel that 'He did not fail to confess, but confessed freely, "I am not the Christ"' (John 1:20). The obvious theme here is one of acknowledging a truth or telling plainly the truth of a matter. This use of confession is used by the writer to the Hebrews to exhort Christians to own Christ as Lord: 'Therefore, holy brothers, who share in the heavenly calling, fix your thoughts on Jesus, the apostle and high priest whom we confess' (Heb. 3:1). And again he writes, 'Through Jesus, therefore, let us continually offer to God a sacrifice of praise – the fruit of lips that confess his name' (Heb. 13:15). Alongside of this is the confession of sins, such as the passage in the first letter of John where he writes, 'If we confess our sins, he is faithful and just to forgive us our sins and cleanse us from all unrighteousness' (1 John 1:9; cf. Jas. 5:16). In all of these examples there is the common thread of confession involving a costly admission or acknowledgement of something that God has laid upon the heart. Jim W. Goll says that confession of sin goes far beyond a mere verbalising or admitting of wrong. 'It is a deep acknowledgement of guilt, a profession of responsibility from a convicted heart which is a heart absolutely convinced of the reality and horror of sin. I believe that this is a revelatory act that comes only through the working of the Holy Spirit.'[4]

From this we can see that confession contains two fundamental acts of faith which are those of *ownership* and *offering*. We cannot confess what is not ours. As a preliminary step towards healing and recovery we need to own what belongs to us before we can do anything about it. This is where the convicting power of the Holy Spirit is absolutely necessary, as we are often in the place of denial or transference where we blame others for our problems. How often have we heard people say something like, 'It is not my fault really – if only I had had a better home and upbringing I would not be like I am.' It is true that we are shaped for good or ill by the influence of others, but God will hold us responsible for our reactions to what is done to us. Confession also involves offering to God what we have been enabled to own as ours. We cannot save ourselves or try and carry around within us the unacknowledged sins and wounds of our lives. If we try to do this we usually end up damaging ourselves, sometimes beyond repair.

Offering is the necessary step towards God to ask for his powerful intervention to bring deliverance or blessing to our story. In keeping with what we have learned about confession, offering is also an opportunity to give to God what is worth celebrating about our lives in order for God to bring his blessing and anointing to our situations. If we do not celebrate the good then it will shrink through lack of affirmation. This becomes even more important when we apply it to wounded group stories. We must be careful that we do not concentrate so much on what we feel is wrong with our world that we overlook the strength of the blessings that God has given us and neglect them and become overfocused on what is wrong or on the power of the demonic. Part of the agenda for healing wounded history is to offer to God what still speaks of his presence among us and ask for his anointing and blessing upon it so that its effects may grow. Consequently, when we research group stories we are looking for two issues: that which goes on wounding and that which still has the power to bless. We are to own both items and offer them to God either for his healing and deliverance so that we can be set free from them, or for his blessing so that their capacity to enrich may grow.

What is unique about the prayer of representational confession is that the intercessor, though innnocent of the particular sins of the group story in question, nonetheless includes himself in with these sins. We need to ask what right of access do Daniel and Ezra and Nehemiah and Jesus have in carrying the sins of a whole nation or people in this way?

Representation

The first reason links us back with corporate or group story. We have noted the examples in scripture of how various groups were judged or blessed on the actions of individual members of that group. For the covetousness of Aachan, and his rebellion against the express orders of God to devote all booty to the Lord, he and his family came under judgement. We also saw that the blessings given to faithful Abraham would be also passed on to his descendants because they were literally carried within Abraham's genes. There is also the example of Jesus being the one person who can carry the needs of all people in his actions on the cross of redemption and atonement. At the heart of this ability to act on behalf of the group story is the right to represent. The simple reason why Daniel and others own and offer to God a story for which they are not personally responsible is because they belong to that group, they are its living representatives. There is nowhere in scripture where such representational confession is made by one person for a people not their own. I cannot represent and confess the sins of the Japanese or American peoples because they are literally not my people. I can intercede for them, bless them and honour and respect them all, but I cannot represent them. However, when I understand the group stories of which I am a part, then I have a God-given mandate to represent my people before the throne of God. It is my hope and prayer that we rediscover this prayer ministry of reconciling group stories which so gripped Daniel and Ezra and Nehemiah. So then, because I am a member, I can carry my family story, my church story, my community and tribal story before the living God, so that the patterns of wounded history may be healed and my people freed from their damaging repetitious cycle. I can also bless the good because it reflects that God is still among us and so can increase their capacity to bless and lead to a knowledge of God. This is not fanciful, it is the challenge of God for us to find who our people are and be an effective intercessor for them.

When we are involved in public confession and reconciliation of sins and wounds which stand between tribes or churches and communities we need to do our best to make the representation at the highest and most comprehensive level. For example, when certain Japanese politicians regretted the unfortunate actions of their nation during the Second World War against British prisoners of war, it was considered inadequate. This was because for the survivors nothing less than an apology backed up with compensation would do. However, they insisted that the apology came from the Emperor Akihito, although he was only a boy at the time of the war. The level of representation was not enough for them. Therefore we saw their dignified and silent protest to this effect when they lined the Mall in London when the Emperor drove by on his first state visit to the United Kingdom. We must try and ensure that our public ministries involve the fullest and most satisfactory representatives of the group story in question. Another example of this is the apology given by Archbishop George Carey in Dublin and Limerick. Many other representatives of the English church and people had extended apologies and they had been warmly received and welcomed as a step in the right direction towards reconciliation. However, when Carey apologised for the English invasion and occupation of Ireland, saying that England had no rights to Ireland, it set off a wave of deep emotion among the people, who felt that the wrongness of seven hundred years of English occupation was at last being recognised at a level it truly deserved. It conveyed honour and respect for the Irish people and culture and undoubtedly helped the peace accord develop to the extent of the present ceasefire and determination for honourable coexistence in Northern Ireland. Interestingly enough, not long afterwards, the Republic of Ireland held a referendum on whether that nation should maintain, as part of its official policy, the integration of Northern Ireland into the Republic. Over 90 per cent voted to give up that demand, so as to release Northern Ireland to settle its own destiny.

Despite what I have just said about levels of representation it is important to point out that it is the calling of all Christians to be ambassadors for reconciliation of our wounded group stories. We may not be able to gather all the people we would ideally desire and so we are tempted to doubt the worth of doing this work. We should be encouraged by the fact that in the cases given in scripture it was individuals who stood alone for their people and often out of the public eye. Besides all this we should remind ourselves that one of the principal truths of scripture is the effectiveness of the faithful remnant who keep alive the hopes and needs of their people despite whatever disasters have occurred (cf. Gen. 45:7; 2 Kings 19:30–31; Isa. 10:20–21; Zeph. 2:7). Our confidence in our right to reconcile is the call of God who challenges us to recognise the group stories of which we are a part and a representative.

Identification

When Daniel prayed he said, 'O Lord, we have sinned and done wrong', when he could just as accurately have prayed, 'O Lord, they have sinned.' Why? Because he chose, by the conviction of the Spirit in his life, to identify with the sins of his nation. We have already noted the emotional impact this revelation can have: Ezra describes his response as self-abasement (Ezra 9:5). There is a complete absence of self-righteousness in him and Daniel alike. Neither man condemns or accuses the people as sinners, or describes himself as the faithful one. Rather, they take up a lament for the fallen nation and the ravages of sin and unhealed history upon the land. Perhaps the discovery is long overdue that at the core of true intercession stands a weeper rather than a warrior. This should challenge us to beware of subtly disguising our accusations of others' failings as intercessions. How often have we said that if only the other had not sinned against us we would be much better people than we are! I have heard such prayers as 'Our church would be much better off if we had not had that liberal minister who didn't preach the word.' This kind of prayer actually distances us from the ones in need of healing. It is a way of saying that I do not belong to the problem. True representation involves an *identification with* as opposed to *a standing apart* from the problem. A Daniel would have prayed, 'O Lord, we have sinned, we are a church where we have not preached your word. Forgive us and heal us.' We do need to repent of our arrogance and get back to owning our group stories as ours and confessing them as such. We must not think that the work of representational confession is a mere playing with words where we use collective terminology (we, us, ours) to demonstrate a new style in praying. Neither is it a simple matter of our choosing who or what to identify with simply because we see a truth or our conscience is disturbed. Jim W. Goll writes that Daniel entered into deep identification with his people and the horrifying condition of their sin because he was gripped by the spirit of revelation which was wedded to the spirit of conviction.[5] It was this encounter with the Spirit of God which transformed Daniel from a righteous witness to his faith and culture when in captivity, to the powerful representative of his nation before the throne of God in prayer. Nehemiah, also in captivity, was serving as a cupbearer to the king when he heard the news of the ruin and desolation of the city of Jerusalem. He was overcome with grief and had to sit down because of the weight of his weeping (Neh. 1:3–4). What followed was the prayer of confession: 'I confess the sins we Israelites, including myself and my father's house, have committed against you' (Neh. 1:6). Ezra was a priest commissioned with the task of helping to rebuild the temple in Jerusalem. Upon arrival in the city he discovered that many of the people, including priests and civic leaders, had intermarried with some of the pagan people in the region. Although innocent of this breaking of the Mosaic Law himself, Ezra nonetheless was so disturbed by what he saw that he confessed the sins of his nation as his own: 'O my God, I am too ashamed and disgraced to lift my face to you, my God, because our sins are higher than our heads and our guilt has reached to the heavens' (Ezra. 9:6). The power and authority to identify with comes from without, it comes from God, who disturbs us with the unhealed wounds of our group story and challenges us to take up our God-given right to represent in the power of the Spirit.

Identificational repentance

John Dawson, a pioneer in this field, wrote that

> unless somebody identifies themselves with corporate entities, such as the nation of our citizenship, or the subculture of our ancestors, the act of honest confession will never take place . . . The followers of Jesus are to step into this impasse as agents of healing. Within our ranks are representatives of every category of humanity. Trembling in our heavenly Father's presence, we see clearly the sins of humankind and have no inclination to cover them up. Thus, we are called to live out the biblical practice of identificational repentance, a neglected truth that opens the floodgates of revival and brings healing to the nations.[6]

There has been much debate about John Dawson's terminology of 'identificational repentance', which has become the standard term within the prayer-track movement for describing this form of praying for corporate stories.[7] There is the objection that it is not possible to repent on behalf of another, let alone those who are long since dead. It is quite true that our repentance will not be accepted by God for another so that the other does not need to repent for themselves. Our repentance cannot be a proxy vote to replace the actions of another and relieve them of their own responsibilities to repent. However, this is not what practitioners of identificational repentance are advocating. Gary Greig, Associate Professor of Old Testament at Regent University in Canada, says that God's people can seek and receive God's forgiveness on a corporate level for the sins of others in order to release God's grace for them to repent individually.[8] He cites the case of Moses' prayer for Israel after their sin with the golden calf as an example (Exod. 32:9–14). Yet in this prayer, Moses does not use the language of inclusion and identification with the sins of his people as do Ezra and Daniel. He does elsewhere when he once again prays for the rebellious people (Exod. 34:8–9). A further clue to the connection between repentance and identification is the exhortation in Leviticus to confess generational iniquity. 'But if they will confess their sins and the sins of their fathers . . . then when their uncircumcised hearts are humbled and they pay for their sin, I will remember my covenant with Jacob . . . and I will remember the land' (Lev. 26:40–2). There is no question here that those who died on the journey out of Egypt and who perished in the desert are the ones to be restored to God's covenant. The whole focus is on the living who are carrying the burden of the consequences of their ancestors' sins, from which they need to be delivered. Consequently identification and repentance from the living representatives of the nation's group story set the living free from the effects of damaged and repeating patterns of their corporate story. Brian Mills and Roger Mitchell affirm this position when they write that identifying with the sins of a nation and confessing them will lead to the revoking of God's judgement over that land. This will make it easier for individuals to respond to the voice of God because what is being tackled by this ministry is a breaking of the darkness which is preventing individual people from seeing the light and preventing the leaders of a nation from leading it in the way it should go.[9]

Some attention should be given to the use of the term 'vicarious repentance' which was popularised by Ray Mayhew when he studied the theories of the atonement in the work of J. McLeod Campbell.[10] This is modelled on the example of Jesus as High Priest, who bears all our sins in himself upon the cross and for our atonement. Mayhew is quite clear that only Jesus can make vicarious atonement for the forgiveness of sins as he was innocent and holy. As such Jesus literally carried our infirmities and diseases (Matt. 8:17). As believers we are part of a royal priesthood and we are committed to adopting the model of Jesus' priesthood which is that of burden-bearer (cf. Rom. 15:1; Gal. 6:2). However, in both of the texts cited the issues in focus are not the as yet unforgiven sins of others but the struggles and battles we experience, which without the support of fellowship would crush us. However, this does not rule out our call to restore the fallen and remind the sinful that there is forgiveness through Jesus. The term 'vicarious repentance' is used exclusively for the carrying of generational sins of nations and other groups. While Jim Goll does say that we cannot add anything to what Christ has done, but can only model what he did,[11] he nonetheless goes on to say that God is searching for people who will take on the burden of corporate and generational sins and not simply carry them but carry them away like the scapegoat in the wilderness.[12] I think this exceeds the brief of identification and betrays some of the ideas taught by Rees Howells, a mighty intercessor, whom Goll has acknowledged as one of his mentors. Cindy Jacobs, one of the leading pioneers in this work of identification with the sins of the nations, rightly sounds the alarm over Howells' teaching that the intercessor is to enter into the sufferings of others by carrying such afflictions personally in order to bring healing.[13] She says that to say we bear someone's sickness physically in intercession is a false fellowship of suffering. We may certainly feel the depth and power of group sins as we pray and intercede and this may cause us some disturbance but we must not make the mistake of rashly concluding that we are carrying these sins in a vicarious manner in order for them to be forgiven and healed. Only Jesus can do that. We are, however, applying the finished work of Christ at a group level through the vehicle of identification and this is always recognised and responded to by our Father in heaven. Consequently I find the use of the word 'vicarious' confusing and unhelpful, and it detracts from the power and purpose of identificational prayer.

A final few words need to be said about the debate as to whether repentance or confession is the right word to describe these core actions of indentificational prayer. To some degree this is a superfluous argument about semantics, as all the practitioners engage in very similar ministries and are supportive of each other and honour each other's costly sacrifice to this much needed work. Chris Seaton sees confession as something that can be seen simply as a verbal acknowledgement rather than something profoundly transforming.[14] He is absolutely correct to stress the need for transformation, but I think he undermines the fact that confession in the Bible is a commitment to be radically changed. The same thought is found in the book *Sins of the Fathers*, where there is an anxiety that confession may be used as an excuse to mask a proud unwillingness to identify with the sins of others.[15] I think that from reviewing some of the writers in this field it becomes obvious that confession and repentance are inseparably linked and it is not a case of either/or. The biblical intercessors we have studied along with Daniel are all said to have confessed the sins of their nation, but they individually adopted a penitential lifestyle, not only as demanded by their confession but also as a determination not to repeat the sins of history in their own lives.

Legal obligations of guilt

A final right of access to group story and generational sin is that of the legal demands which God makes upon a people for their sins. Karl Jaspers wrote that the individual members of a nation are judged collectively by God on the basis of how they treated 'the least of these' (Matt. 25:31–2).[16] It is certainly true that scripture is packed with references to God challenging his people to repent and turn from their wicked ways, or they will reap the bitter harvest of their guilt. One has only to look through the major prophetic books of the Old Testament to see that one of their functions was to warn and challenge the nation to return to the ways of the Lord. Roger Mitchell and Brian Mills identify three levels of involvement in corporate guilt in the Bible. First is *associated guilt* where we, though innocent, are implicated because the perpetrators belong to us through ancestry. Next is *actual guilt* where groups are directly involved, such as the immorality in the church at Corinth where the whole church is challenged to put it right (1 Cor. 5:6–7). Finally there is *vicarious guilt* which refers to the unique carrying of all our guilt and sins by Jesus.[17] This is very similar in approach to that of Jasper, who suggests four levels of guilt, but he is thinking primarily of state offences against its own membership:

- criminal guilt, which applies to perpetrators of violent acts;
- political guilt, which extends beyond perpetrators to include those who were silent and failed to protest at the wrongs done by their society;
- moral guilt, which is the personal or spiritual side of political complacency and extends to everyone who allowed themselves to be intoxicated, seduced or was bought by personal advantages;
- metaphysical guilt, which refers to corporate guilt in which we all share by virtue of our common humanity.[18]

If God challenges us about the sins of the nation then we can approach his throne for the healing of our nation or any other group story of which we are a part. There is also an expectation from the victims that representatives will own and apologise for the sins of their people. No dialogue or process of reconciliation will begin without it. The missiologist David Bosch said that confessing our guilt in itself is a supreme blessing and a sign of grace. It opens up the fountains of new life and cleanses us.[19] Bishop Eric Pike, the diocesan bishop of Port Elizabeth in South Africa, felt that he should use Lent to go on an eight-day pilgrimage march to highlight his own and his church's deep concern regarding the unacceptably high rate of violent crime in the country and in the Eastern Cape in particular. He wanted to focus attention on the church's failure to protest against the apartheid system and to identify with the victims of violence. Bill held services of cleansing whereby he sought to lance the boil, the hurts of apartheid. Many saw this pilgrimage as the beginnings of the church coming out of its apartheid ghetto into a new birth for the healing of the land.

Confessing generational sins

> We have not listened to your servants the prophets, who spoke in your name to our kings, our princes and our fathers, and to all the people of the land. (Daniel 9:6)

In praying for his people to be set free from their present captivity, Daniel looks back down the generations because he sees that the root of the present problem lies in the past. He goes back at least seventy years to the days when the nation still had kings and princes to rule them. He is thinking of the last reigning monarch, Zedekiah, who was blinded, but not before he had seen all his sons slaughtered along with the leading elders of the nation. Then he too was led off to captivity in Babylon and disappears from the pages of history – an ignoble and calamitous end to the monarchy that could boast ancestors such as Solomon and David. Daniel in fact goes back beyond the seventy years of captivity and mentions the now defunct Northern kingdom of Israel and sees that the nation's present peril is also a result of Israel's unfaithfulnesses (Dan. 9:7). Ezra similarly scans the history of the nation back to his forefathers and sees the consequences of their sins and disobedience resulting in the pillaging and captivity of the nation (Ezra 9:7).

Representational confession involves identifying the generational sins of whatever group story we are working with by observing the repeating patterns of those sins. It is being able to apply the spiritual law of cause and effect, of sowing and reaping, to our group story. This gives us clarity on just what it is that needs to be confessed and offered to God for his forgiveness and release from spiritual bondage. Once again I would underline the importance of research as a spiritual exercise in the pursuit of healing and reconciliation. The International Reconciliation Coalition has produced a document called *What Christians Should Know about Reconciliation*. It is a very useful resource for looking at history with discernment as a means of preparing for a healing and reconciling of the history of your family, church, community or nation.

Locating wounded history

> Our sins and the iniquities of our fathers have made Jerusalem and your people an object of scorn to all those around us . . . O Lord, look with favour on your desolate sanctuary.
>
> (Daniel 9:16–17)

Daniel not only identified with a people, he also identified with a place – in his case Jerusalem, the city which was once so full of promise and the presence of God but which had now been reduced to a heap of rubble and its temple destroyed. As we have already discussed, land is the place where the effects of actions are seen, and sometimes for the healing to take root among the people we need to go to the very site in question. The wounded or sinful story is felt most powerfully on the site where the things first went wrong. Consequently Daniel focuses on the city of Jerusalem where the kings and priests so rebelled against God; the city held the story and certain buildings (such as the temple and the royal palace) held the sharper focus or fine tuning of these stories. We have already referred to the example of the horrors of the Jamie Bulger story in Liverpool. Imagine my shock when I was told by a student researching for a Master's degree on this story that a similar murder had happened in the same city almost a century earlier. Following on from their research it was discovered that Liverpool has in fact a sorry story of dumping bodies in the city. There was the infamous slave trade during which many died of diseases caused by being cramped in unsanitary conditions, and their bodies were buried without church ceremony. Napoleonic prisoners of war were similarly housed in pest-ridden conditions and suffered a similar fate. Latterly there came the massive influx of Irish immigrants following the ravages of the potato famine in the 1840s. It seems that the story of that part of the city was one of having bodies dumped upon it. We should not be surprised that Jamie Bulger was murdered in such a place. Interestingly enough, the people of Liverpool held a service of apology and reconciliation in November 2000 for Liverpool's part in the slave trade, in the hope of improving the image of the city.

It is important that we do pray on the sites of wounded story as a resource for bringing healing to the people-group connected with the location. During Bishop Eric Pike's pilgrimage walk in his diocese he visited places where violent crimes had taken place, to meet with the bereaved and local communities and to pray for and cleanse those sites so that they should not go on being a focus for more violence. In response to this awareness there has been more and more praying and services of apology on wounded sites all around the world (see the beginning of Chapter 2 above). There have been prayers on battle sites such as Culloden near Inverness in Scotland, the Boyne and Aughrim in the Republic of Ireland. The Reconciliation Prayer-Walk ministry led by John and Yvonne Presdee have walked down the whole route of the First World War battle-front in Europe, stopping at various places to apologise for the senseless killing of millions of young people. There have been prayers at sites of massacres such as Auschswitz, Wounded Knee in South Dakota and Hiroshima and Nagasaki in Japan. Many have held prayer vigils at the sites of political importance in the city to try and identify the ruling spiritual values of its founding fathers. Some have gone further and have focused a work of healing and confession on these sites, such as the peace park in Nagasaki. A similar peace park is to be opened some time in 2001 at Aughrim in County Galway in the Republic of Ireland. Trees are to be planted by representatives of the Protestant community in memory of Catholics who died in the battle and representatives of the Catholic community are planting trees in memory of Protestant dead. This is an act of apology and recognition of both peoples' right to life and respect in Ireland on a site that has been a focus for continuing the old animosities. In 1997, on the fourteen hundredth anniversary of the death of Columba on Iona and the arrival of Augustine on the Kentish shores of England, a national pilgrimage was held which walked throughout the British Isles visiting sites of Celtic witness in an effort to celebrate Celtic and Catholic Christianity. I suggested to the organisers that without displacing the focus of this event they should not disregard some of the wounds of history which separated Celtic and Catholic and which were still smouldering in the minds of many. An example is Whitby where in the seventh century a synod was held which effectively outlawed the Celtic way of being Catholic and reversed the policy of encouraging women to share in the leadership structures of the church. Hilda was abbess of a double monastery for men and women – such examples were quickly discouraged. Something which was not altered for thirteen centuries! Consequently I was asked to write a liturgy called 'Heal the Land' which was a service of apology and confession, healing and reconciliation and was used on these sites as a way of recognising the unhealed story attached to the place.[20]

Prayer-walking on land is of course quite an old practice because it has its roots in scripture. Joshua is an early example: he and the tribes walked around the city of Jericho as an integral part of the battle between the two communities (Josh. 6:1–21). The Psalmist encourages the inhabitants of Jerusalem to pray for the peace of the city and in particular focuses on its walls and the gates (Ps. 122:2, 6–7). He encourages them to go about the city and know the story of each building, to keep it alive so that it can be passed on to the next generation (Ps. 48:12f).

When we prayer-walk the location there may be a variety of reasons for doing this. We may be wanting to learn its story so that we can intercede effectively and relevantly; we may be wanting to find out why it is that certain parts of a community are more resistant to the witness of the church than others; we may want to go and bless the good places so that something of the presence of God continues to be linked with these sites.[21] I think we need to bless places of worship such as cathedrals which, because they are the longest-used buildings within communities, carry the story of those communities more than any other place. We should give thanks for parks and gardens and open places which offer us rest and reflection and time to be still and know God. The phenomenal growth of the Marches for Jesus around the world is an example of how Christians want to go about their cities and simply proclaim that Jesus is Lord of the community. This is done in the belief that it shakes the hold of the powers of darkness over the city and releases its inhabitants to become more aware of the presence of Christ among them. As Jesus went about the city, the message he picked up was that the people were like lost sheep in need of a shepherd. So he encouraged his disciples to pray to the Lord of the harvest to send out workers to gather in the lost (Matt. 9:35–8). It is interesting to note, by the way, that even the style of approach commended by Jesus is to be a healing one; it is to cohere with the spiritual and psychological condition of the group in question. They are like lost sheep and the evangelists are to adopt the style of farm-workers and shepherds. If Jerusalem is the beleaguered city which has seen many military attacks upon its walls, can you imagine which memories a march for Jesus may connect with? If we use the language of military conquest, even in the name of Jesus, for such a group story, it is more likely that we would remind them of siege rather than salvation. It is better perhaps in such circumstances, if we have taken the time to discover the story of the group and its location, to adopt styles of witness which do not recreate problems but actually meet the unhealed needs.

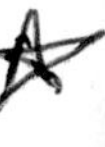

We need urgently to recover this ability of Jesus to walk the city and discern its story and therefore to pray more effectively. We need to rediscover the prophetic capacity of listening with the ears of Christ so that we may be empowered to speak the word of God to people as well as the places in which they live. We need to listen not only to discover the story of today, but the generational story which has given rise to the present-day group story.

The impact of representational confession

> While I was still in prayer, Gabriel . . . came to me and said, 'As soon as you began to pray, an answer was given, which I have come to tell you . . . Seventy sevens are decreed for your people and your holy city to finish transgression, to put an end to sin, to atone for wickedness, to bring in everlasting righteousness, to seal up vision and prophecy and to anoint the most holy.'
>
> (Daniel 9:21, 23–4)

This is the only time in scripture that we are explicitly told that angels are dispatched in response to prayer. It is amazing to realise that

Gabriel tells Daniel that his prayer of representational confession drew an immediate response from heaven. The sheer range of prophetic insight that this prayer solicits is breathtaking. Daniel is told that the captive people will go free and soon; that God would keep his promise given through Jeremiah that the captivity in exile would last only seventy years. Gabriel announces that the ruined city will be rebuilt and even goes on to describe something of the layout of its streets and trenches (Dan. 9:25). In other words, the consequences for the nation of its generational sins are interrupted and the people are freed to resume their identity as a nation. However, the prayer response moves far beyond the immediate ending of the exile. Daniel is given a glimpse of what is to come, which is very disturbing. He is shown how the city in a future time is going to be the arena for a climactic battle between God's anointed one and a ruler who will set about destroying city and temple and anointed one alike. Then finally will come the time of resurrection and restoration when righteousness will triumph for ever. The implication is that the nation's group story will always connect with the welfare or otherwise of the city of Jerusalem. The repeating patterns, for good or ill, of the Jewish nation will be especially and particularly focused on their holy city. The final part of the story will be when the anointed one returns to the city to restore it for ever.

Some have made a direct connection between Daniel's prayer and the revelation of strategic level spiritual warfare involving some spiritual power identified as the prince of the Persian kingdom (Dan. 10:12–14). Some have seen this as a reference to a principality or demonic overlord which exercises control over people's lives in that geographic area or over the tribal peoples living in that locality. Daniel's prayer is seen as the radical resource to mobilise the armies of heaven and dislodge the rights of demonic powers over people and places. Whatever the truth of this suggestion, we should first note that according to Daniel this further insight into the battle is given at a much later date than the time of his prayer of confession. According to Keil and Delitzsch it could have been five years later, as the prayer was made during the first reign of Darius the Mede and the revelation of battle over the Persian kingdom came in the third year of King Cyrus.[22] Also, Daniel is told that this second time, the angel Gabriel came as a response to his determination to gain understanding and to humble himself before God (Dan. 10:12). However, it does refer to the fact that God had 'heard his words' (v. 12) and this seems to imply that Daniel was indeed praying. It is also quite likely that by the time that Daniel had this vision the return from exile was already under way, as we are told elsewhere that it began in the first year of the reign of Cyrus (2 Chron. 36:22; Isa. 44:28; Ezra 1:1). It is much more true to scripture to say that as a result of following through the response to the original prayer of representational confession and the freedom from captivity that was its immediate result, Daniel was given deeper insight to what God would build on the foundation of this prayer. It would literally shake the heavens.

Gabriel tells Daniel that now the people were going free and returning to their homeland, warfare had been unleashed in the heavenlies over the dominating power at work in the nation of Persia. The warrior angel Michael is called to join battle and it rages for twenty-one days before Gabriel is free to inform Daniel of the unfolding events for the Jewish nation. Michael is mentioned only five times in the Bible and always in connection with battle (Dan. 10:13, 21; 12:1; Jude 1:9; Rev. 12:7). At no time is this angel described as fighting against people, if we accept that the reference to the prince and king of the Persian kingdom are references to spiritual powers animating the rulers of the Persian people. This would make sense if we see it as the backcloth to the battle among the rulers of Persia to support or oppose the return of the captive peoples to their homeland. It is interesting to note that Michael is described as the prince over the Jewish people (Dan. 10:21) and it is quite likely that we are to understand the prince over the Persian kingdom in a similar way. However we understand these princes over kingdoms, it does at least tell us that one of the long-term consequences of representational confession is to shake the heavens as the nation's group story is healed and the people are set free to move forward into newness of life.

The consequence of Ezra's prayers of confession was a deep conviction of sin which gripped the community. There was a wave of repentance that swept through the people as they confessed that they had indeed done wrong in intermarrying outside of their faith and culture. What followed was national regeneration as the people renewed their commitment to the covenant with God, and this took the form of public confession before the leaders of the community (Ezra 10:1–17). Following Nehemiah's anguished prayer for the city of

Jerusalem, God brought his anxiety to the attention of the king, which resulted in Nehemiah sharing his concern for the city. What followed was the complete rebuilding of a city, constantly inspired and encouraged by this one man who was gripped by God's hand to see the burden of his prayers through to full realisation.

We can conclude, therefore, that the prayer of representational confession is specifically invoked for the healing and renewal of wounded group stories. It is a very effective way of praying, if these biblical accounts are anything to go by. I believe that God is calling his people to rediscover this way of praying and to let the Holy Spirit of God grip us with its importance and apply such intercession to our wounded group stories, be they those of family, church, community, tribe or nation. Next we shall look at these four group stories and discover how the work of representational confession can bring healing and renewal to them. This book is accompanied by a workbook which will help you process the material you have been reading and learn to apply it to your own circumstances. Before we do this, however, we need to explore what the New Testament has to say about healing group stories and whether it is part of the ministry of Jesus.

7 JESUS, THE TRUE REPRESENTATIONAL CONFESSOR

Something wonderfully creative is to be seen here, it is 'for us'. (Donald Coggan)

It is quite true to say that in the New Testament there is no explicit reference to Jesus or any of the apostles praying prayers of representational confession. This does not mean to say that the concept of praying for and bringing healing to group stories is absent, however. We have already noted that the power of atonement to some degree rests on the principle that one person can represent his people group for good or ill. Consequently Paul compares and contrasts the effects upon humanity of Adam and Jesus: 'For if the many died by the trespass of the one man, how much more did God's grace and the gift that came by the grace of the one man Jesus Christ, overflow to the many!' (Rom. 5:15). Elsewhere we read of Jesus addressing the story of seven churches in Asia through the single focus of the angel who presides over the group story of each church (Rev. 2—3). There are numerous references to Jesus challenging various groups of people to beware of the judgement of God hovering over them if they do not change their ways. Consider how he pronounces woe over the corporate stories of the scribes and Pharisees (Matt. 23:15), the rich (Luke 6:24), the lawyers (Luke 11:46) and towns such as Korazin and Bethsaida (Luke 10:13–14). Luke the Evangelist ends his gospel account with Jesus himself summarising the essence of what the Old Testament scriptures taught about his ministry. 'This is what is written: The Christ will suffer and rise from the dead on the third day, and repentance and forgiveness of sins will be preached in his name to all nations, beginning at Jerusalem' (Luke 24:46–7). Of course it is a matter of debate if this is a reference to nations repenting or individuals in those nations. Bearing in mind what we have learnt of the Hebrew idea of corporate identity and of how the prophets challenged nations and cities to repent, it is quite acceptable to interpret this passage as a references to nations turning to God. In fact the first reference of this passage must be to the whole nation first and, only because this is so, it can then be applied to the individual members of those nations (cf. Isa. 10:5–19 regarding Assyria; Isa. 13, 14:1–21 regarding Babylon; Isa. 15 and 16 regarding Moab; Jer. 49:1–6 regarding Ammon; Jer. 49:7–22 regarding Edom).

There are three particular ways in which Jesus models for us in the New Testament his high priestly role as a resource for healing wounded group stories:

- representational prayer;
- proclamatory and prophetic prayer;
- vicarious sacrifice.

Representational prayer

It is significant that Jesus only gave his disciples one specific format or style of prayer to use and it is collective and inclusive throughout. This is of course what we now know as the Lord's Prayer (Matt. 6:9–13; Luke 11:1–4). It is first and foremost a model of corporate prayer. As Jim W. Goll says, 'This is really a priestly prayer . . . we are to enter into the place of confession, petition and intercession not just for ourselves alone, but for every member of whatever group we are carrying in our hearts.'[1] In language similar to Daniel, Ezra and Nehemiah, Jesus encourages us to use words such as *we* and *our* instead of *me* and *mine*.

> *Our* Father in heaven,
> hallowed be your name,
> your kingdom come,
> your will be done
> on earth as it is in heaven.
> Give *us* today *our* daily bread.
> Forgive *us our* debts,
> as *we* also have forgiven *our* debtors.
> And lead *us* not into temptation,
> but deliver *us* from the evil one.

It is apparent that this prayer was never intended for personal and private use, as this limits the horizons which Jesus has set for it. It is a prayer which the representatives of a particular group are to share in, rather than its general and rather tame use as a vehicle for individual reflection within a church liturgical setting. Its potency lies in the fact that it has a double application: first for the group story in question and derivatively for personal reflection. Consequently the request 'give us our daily bread' is not so much an appeal for personal sustenance but an intercession for renewal or revival of (possibly) a church, a family, a community or a nation. Our own need is therefore to be seen as a signal representation of the need of the group. This applies also to the core request of this prayer which is 'Forgive us our debts as we also have forgiven our debtors.' The examples of representational confession we have explored have itemised the corporate sins which concerned them most. This Lord's Prayer offers a template upon which we are invited to place the particular issues which wound our group stories and for which confession and forgiveness are the doorways through which healing is made possible. The word for debts and debtors comes from the same Greek word, which is *opheilēma*. It carries the sense of 'that which is legally due', and the implication in this context is of that which has failed to be given to another and has therefore caused injury and offence.[2] The challenge of this way of praying is to face up to the fact that if we do not forgive those who have offended us, then God will not forgive us our sins. We have always taken this to be a reference to the individual's need of healing, and this is at least the case. However, if this corporate focus is to be maintained throughout the prayer then we are faced with the fact that if a group of people holds an unforgiving attitude towards another group, then God will not forgive the sins of that group. In other words, the Lord's Prayer is an exhortation to reconciliation between wounded groups who will otherwise go on repeating the damaged story and its consequences which bind them together.

There is a further reference to inclusive prayer in the episode of Jesus' cleansing of the temple in Jerusalem. Following his confrontation with the money changers he began teaching, and in particular quoted the prophecy of Isaiah by saying, 'It is written: "My house shall be called a house of prayer for all nations"' (Mark 11:17; Isa. 56:7). The context in Isaiah is a vision of the day when the ministry at the altar in Jerusalem would reach out to the nations who would eventually come and share in its power and effect. It is also a reminder that one of the main purposes of the Jewish nation was to be a blessing to all the other tribes and nations. Paul picks up this theme as he develops his thoughts on justification and salvation for everyone. He links the journey of Abraham with the grace and blessings available, through his faith, for nations. Abraham is called the father of nations and Sarah is similarly described as mother (Rom. 4:17–18; Gen.17:5, 16). Therefore, when Jesus cleansed the temple, he was calling the nation back to its role of intercessory prayer and healing for other tribes, for upon its actions, to a great degree, depended the welfare of the Gentile peoples.

Proclamatory and prophetic prayer

As we shall see in further detail in the chapter on 'Community Group Story' (Chapter 8), Jesus had a particular concern for the holy city of Jerusalem, and occasionally addressed the entire city in a style of prayer that was both proclamatory and prophetic. One such example of this is his triumphal entry into the city riding on a donkey. He was aware of the mixture of responses he received: from those who believed in him, acclamation and praise, but from some of the Pharisees, rejection. They implored him to prevent his disciples from praising him (Luke 19:37–9). However, as he got close to the city 'He wept over it and said, "If you, even you, had only known on this day what would bring you peace – but now it is hidden from your eyes"' (Luke 19:41). Jesus looks prophetically forward into the future and sees that one of the consequences to the city of rejecting him was going to be collapse and destruction at the hands of its enemies. Like the prophets of old, he sees through the individual and immediate circumstance to the story of the nation which will unfold as a direct result. Consider, for example, how Isaiah in confronting the vacillating king Ahaz, who is reluctant to put his trust in God at a time of political instability, sees the story of the Jewish nation as being wrapped up in the king's actions. The king is even addressed as the House of David, as if to underline the fact that in the choices of the man lies the fate of the nation group he represents (Isa. 7:10–17). The prophetic word was that the child Immanuel would be born and, before he became a man, the nations troubling

Israel would have vanished and the greater threat of Assyria would have appeared. So Jesus, gazing at the reception before him as he entered the gates of the city of Jerusalem, saw a prophetic window through which he addressed the whole city as if present before him. If this is our model, then we too should be open to God to listen to the story of our community and where appropriate pray the proclamatory and prophetic prayer which will stir all to follow the Lord.

Vicarious sacrifice

The fullest and most profound example of Jesus' healing ministry and his intercessory lifestyle is his death upon the cross, and his resurrection which authenticates and makes effective his offering of himself, once and one for all, upon the cross. All four gospel Evangelists devote almost a third of their material to this one event. However, Jesus spoke of his death and the necessity for it long before the final conflict at Calvary. One of the earliest hints comes during a routine question about fasting and the failure of Jesus' disciples to observe this practice properly. Jesus answers his critics by saying, 'But the days will come when the bridegroom shall be taken away from them, and they will fast in that day' (Mark 2:20). By the time he came to Caesarea Philippi and taught them who he was, the Messiah, 'death was no longer a possibility, or even a probability, but a certainty'.[3] He linked the calling of the Messiah and suffering, which he prophetically foresaw, as necessary ingredients and not accidental (Mark 8:31).

As we trace the rest of his teachings on the sufferings to come, Jesus describes them in a variety of ways: as a *baptism of death* to be  confronted and wrestled with ('There is a terrible baptism ahead of me, and I am under a heavy burden until it is accomplished' (Luke 12:50 NLT)); as the *cup of God's punishment against sin* which Jesus must  drink instead of others ('Are you able to drink from the bitter cup of sorrow I am about to drink?' Jesus asks his ambitious disciples (Mark 10:28 NLT)). Not long afterwards in the garden of Gethsemane, Jesus cried in agony to be delivered from his cup of suffering if it were possible (Mark 14:36). Hunter points out that in the Old Testament, out of twenty metaphorical uses of the word 'cup', seventeen cases describe it as a divinely appointed suffering or punishment by God for human sin.[4] This then was the cup of Jesus, the mingled sins of all humanity. So closely had Jesus associated himself with those he came to save that he had betrothed himself to the human race for better or worse, and he tasted in all its naked horror the wrath of God against the sin of humanity.

Jesus also talks about his sufferings and death *as a ransom*: 'The Son of Man did not come to be served but to serve, and to give his life as a ransom for many' (Mark 10:45). He foresaw his death as a price to be paid. There has been much debate about this passage and whether the price was paid to God or to Satan, who allegedly held unsaved souls captive. This is not the subject of this book, save only to underline that it at least implies that humanity is doomed because of its sin and that Jesus himself paid the price 'for the many' because we clearly could not save ourselves. This immediately reminds us of the language of the suffering servant of Isaiah 53, and Jesus no doubt knew the connections he was making when he uttered these words. The death of the holy one would exempt the guilty. The final de-

scription of his sufferings is in terms of *a new covenant*. In the upper room as they met for their final meal before his arrest, Jesus took the Passover cup and said, 'This is my blood, poured out for many, sealing the covenant between God and his people' (Mark 14:24 NLT). This seems to be a reference to the new covenant in Jeremiah's prophecy between God and the house of Israel where the focus was forgiveness and God's intention to remember particular sins no more (Jer. 31:31–4). It is also a reference to the Servant of Isaiah who would be the mediator of that covenant, but this time between God and all people, the many (Isa 52:13—53:12). The reference to the blood is not just a reminder of the blood of the animals killed in sacrifice but also to the times when blood was sprinkled on the people to ratify their covenant with Yahweh (Exod. 24:8). Without the shedding of blood, there is no forgiveness of sins, and no one other than Jesus, holy or innocent, has shed his blood for our salvation (Heb. 9:22).[5]

Having looked at Jesus' own descriptions of his sufferings and death we have seen that at the core is the belief that he is the only sufficient sacrifice for our sins and salvation. All of these examples have illustrated that the one (holy and sinless Messiah) acted on behalf of the many. As we explore this further we can see that we discover language very similar to that of representational confession, especially when we look at the sufferings of the servant and lamb in the prophecies of Isaiah.

> *He* suffered and endured great pain for *us*,
> but *we* thought *his* suffering was punishment from God.
> *He* was wounded and crushed because of *our* sins:
> by taking *our* punishment, *he* made *us* completely well.
> All of *us* were like sheep that wandered off.
> *We* had each gone *our* own way,
> but the Lord gave *him* the punishment *we* deserved . . . *He* was silent like a lamb being led to the butcher,
> as quiet as a sheep having its wool cut off.
>
> (Isaiah 53:4–7 CEV)

Here is Jesus, the truest representational confessor of the sins and wounds of all wounded nations and groups. Like Daniel, Ezra and Nehemiah before him, he is innocent of the sins in question. Like them before him, his once-for-all offering of himself as sacrifice for the sins of the whole world is his way of saying 'We have sinned, father forgive us!' However, there is one essential difference between Jesus and our heroes from the Old Testament and that is that he is holy and divine as well as being innocent. This single fact means that the confession of Jesus is not a hopeful, earnest prayer for others but the very means for the many to be ransomed, healed, restored, forgiven and transformed! Unlike the examples before him, Jesus alone is qualified, in his supreme act of representation of all humanity, to actually carry sins in himself, 'not negatively but positively and redemptively. Something wonderfully creative is to be seen here – it is "for us", and by his wounds we are healed (Isa. 53:5). Vicarious suffering has immense restorative power.'[6] One of the profoundest interpreters of the cross in the early years of the twentieth century was P. T. Forsyth. One day he was gazing at Holman Hunt's painting, *The Scapegoat*, which depicted the animal at the heart of the Day of Atonement sacrifice which symbolically carried away to God in the desert the sins of the Israelite nation which were confessed over its head with the laying on of hands (Lev. 16:7–10, 21–2). Forsyth was profoundly disturbed by the picture and the message it conveyed of Christ as the true sin-bearer and he wrote:

> The goat went out loaded, not with individual guilt, but with the curse of a nation's sin, just as Christ went out bearing, not the guilt, but the mysterious curse and load of sin as it presses upon the whole world . . . The Christian thought is that Christ carried the horror and the curse of the sin, amid fearful loneliness and agony, into the presence of God by confession full and complete . . . Mind after mind, in the solemnized exercise of spiritual imagination, has tried to pierce with sympathy the darkness of Gethsemane, to gauge with amazement the nature of the Saviour's woe . . . It is a task too great for human power. Fully to gauge these sorrows is to fully bear them. Fully to express them would be fully to confess them; the thing no man could do, else the God-Man had not come to do it on our behalf.[7]

So we have seen that Jesus actually pushes the boundaries of representational confession further by using it as a vehicle for vicarious suffering, delivering forgiveness and healing as a direct result. For Christians, therefore, he is the model of high priestly intercession, representation and identification. Consequently we are called to be a royal priesthood and a holy nation and bear into God's presence the needs, the stories, the pains and sorrows that damage group stories (1 Pet. 2:9; Rom. 15:1; Gal. 6:2). However, we are not called to suffer instead of others, or to carry their wounds and sicknesses for them, or to carry the guilt of others. There is only one vicarious sufferer and that is Jesus Christ. We are, however, called to carry, as representatives, the group stories of which we are a part and where there is the need, however old the material, to own it and offer it to God in confession in the deepest spirit of personal repentance. In representational confession we lift up the once-for-all sacrifice of his Son for the healing and forgiveness and renewal of our wounded group story. In confidence we hope that God will look upon his Son who carried it all, and see and forgive.

In the concluding chapters of this book we shall apply some of the insights we have learned to four particular group stories: those of family, church, community and tribe or nation. This will not be an in-depth treatment of these four groups, but an opportunity to understand something of how these stories affect us and how the work of representational confession can bring a measure of healing and renewal to ourselves and the group stories we carry within us. The workbook which accompanies this textbook will offer you practical guidance and some ministry opportunities to apply this teaching to your own circumstances.

8 THE FAMILY GROUP STORY

> The more an individual understands his or her past, the greater the possibility that he or she will be able to control what is passed on to the next generation.
>
> (Dave Carder[1])

> Everything we do affects the next seven generations.
>
> (Sioux Indian proverb)

Whether we are an only child, or come from a family with many brothers and sisters, we have all been shaped by our family group story. This is equally true if we have been adopted, fostered or grew up in an orphanage. Whichever one has been our experience, we will carry within us the mixed bag of good and bad memories, and they will go on shaping our responses to daily life. There will be some form or expression of the repeated patterns of our family group story which will impact upon us from time to time. As a simple example of this fact, let me share something of my own journey of self-exploration. As a genealogist I have researched my family tree in some detail. One of the noticeable patterns I have located within the Parker family story is that for at least five generations fathers hardly spoke to or had real dialogue and intimacy with their sons. Of course this whole theme has been well explored by such people as Robert Bly and his influential book *Iron John*. His thesis is that the malaise of modern man is that he has lost connection with his wildness and that this is principally because he has not been fathered.[2] As I researched my 'fathers' I discovered that they were not particularly villainous or unskilled in the art of communication; they were all in their own way popular with their friends and successful in their careers. However, for reasons of history, there was a breakdown of communication within one generation which seems to have been carried down through succeeding generations. Perhaps it is an oversimplification to say that we are usually unable to give to others what we have not received for ourselves. Be that as it may, I can nonetheless trace this breakdown in intimacy with sons through at least five fathers. In my own circumstance, I tried to get closer to my father – this was a result of my becoming a Christian and the inspiration I received from the father/son relationship between Jesus and his heavenly Father. My attempt failed. Yet my father was not hostile or even opposed to my attempts; he simply did not seem to know how to respond. I loved him and was frustrated by him.

As the years went by I would, from time to time, 'hook' this inner need I had to be fathered. This largely came through the medium of cinema when I would be watching a fairly normal relationship between father and son. For example, I remember seeing the film *Billy Elliot*, which is about a thirteen-year-old boy, growing up in the harsh realities of a mining community facing the hardships of a strike. Billy is determined to be a dancer, which at first his hardworking and tough father thinks is effeminate. However, Billy's determination wins over his father, who becomes his biggest supporter. The final scenes of the film show a now mature Billy Elliot waiting in the wings of the Royal Court Theatre, ready to make his entrance for his part in Tchaikovsky's *Swan Lake*. Sitting in the stalls of the theatre Billy's father is weeping with pride and anticipation, waiting for his son to leap upon the stage. When the moment came, my eyes filled with tears and the little boy part of me simply wanted his father to love him too. I have learned to recognise what is happening at these times, and find ways to channel the love of my heavenly Father into the little boy who waits to be embraced once more. At first I was ashamed of such feelings in a grown man, but I have now come to recognise part of the Parker story, and to offer them to God for his healing touch. It also made me more determined that I would not pass on to my son this repeated pattern of our family story. The way to healing, I found, was not to demonise my father and the fathers before him, but to own his story as my story and, in confessing it to God, offer it to him for healing. Consequently, the prayer I prayed was 'We (Parkers) are a family where fathers do not speak to their sons. Forgive us, heavenly Father, and help us to change and learn how to love our sons and not repeat the patterns of our family.' I am happy to report that my son and I have a very good relationship where touch and love are commonplace.

There is no doubt that the family is under siege and in danger of disintegrating in our modern society. According to a recent survey 750,000 British children have no contact with their fathers following the breakdown of marital relationships.[3] The reasons are many and varied and comprise radical changes in morals, lifestyle, poverty and spirituality. Dennis Wrigley of the Maranatha Community helped launch in the Houses of Parliament a 'Call to the Nation' to wake up to the crumbling of family values; he challenges us to tackle the decline in Christian values in the nation. He wrote:

> We are deliberately putting our interests and rights as adults before . . . the children. We are failing to recognise their vulnerability and the truth that vast numbers of them live in fear and loneliness and are deeply damaged. We are depriving them of love and security. We are polluting their minds and teaching them vulgarity in language and lifestyle. We are desensitizing them to violence. We are poisoning them with squalid and degrading sexual images. We are implanting into our children wrong standards – lust, greed, violence, dirtiness, bad manners, lack of consideration for others and lack of respect for themselves.[4]

The fragmentation of the family in modern society and its destructive effects on the cohesion of community has been the subject of intense research, and many theories and solutions abound. Both the current Labour government and the Conservatives before them put the subject of family values in their manifestos. Solutions such as better policing, the introduction of curfews for 10 to 16-year-olds, the provision of more youth clubs, better housing and the demolition of multistorey deck-access blocks of flats, and the disciplining of parents who fail to supervise their children properly have all been advocated. Occasionally there has been the clarion cry, 'Why isn't the church doing its job properly?' It is not in the remit of this book to offer an analysis of the problems and cures of family breakdown, save only to recognise that there is need to understand the *macro story* of our society and to be committed, as the church of Christ, to be a healing resource for our wounded world. However, we do need to recognise that every family has its story and that as its living representatives we must know it, and be a channel for bringing healing and transformation to the repeating patterns which still damage and hurt us.

Whatever the status of our family story, it is beyond question that it has a repeated pattern for good or ill. Dave Carder would go further and say, 'The truth is that due to the fallen nature of all parents (and children), all families are flawed and therefore dysfunctional to a certain degree. Addictive and compulsive behaviours (food, sex, work and so on) are extremely common in even "the best of families".'[5] Like many other observers of human behaviour, Carder knows that we are shaped by the first journey of our lives which is the one where we travel through the family story and its terrain. On the way its values and patterns are sown in us and later reaped in the way we live our adult lives. Sometimes these patterns are like secrets which we keep out of sight and not for discussion within the family itself. These secrets do not have to be extraordinary in order to be powerful. They only have to remain secret and undiscussed. These secrets can be common everyday affairs such as the mother going to work and the child who feels abandoned; parents who get divorced and the child who wrestles with divided loyalties as a consequence; or a father who is emotionally or physically absent resulting in a child who feels unwanted or unworthy of love. The tragedy is that such patterns, sown in one generation, are reaped and repeated in the lifestyle of the next and so on down the generations unless they are recognised, owned and offered for healing and transformation. A classic example of family repeated patterns can be found in the family of Abraham in the Bible.

The Abrahamic family story

This is a family group story where the repeating patterns run through at least three generations to include the families of Isaac and Jacob. It is fascinating to watch the story unfold and to note that the patterns repeat themselves even though God is intimately involved in the family. Indeed, in order to feel the full impact of this family story we must try and suspend our knowledge of how God worked through the stories of the individuals involved. This is because it is all too easy to concentrate on what God does and not fully focus on the human story.

Abraham: the first generation (Genesis 16:1–16; 17:15–22; 21:21; 22:2)

The object of this study is to pick out the core features of the story and to explore how they are repeated down the generations of this family group. The first thing to notice is that the birth of the older son Ishmael is against the backcloth of rivalry between would-be mothers, Hagar and Sarai. Sarai is unable to have children and, in accordance with standard practice in the culture of the time, agrees to her husband having a child by the family slave. When Hagar conceives and becomes pregnant she begins to despise her mistress who is barren (Gen. 16:4f). It was common belief in this society that children were a sign of God's blessing and barrenness was a sign of his disfavour. Hagar may well have thought that her son would inherit and this tempted her to arrogance. Sarai in her turn mistreated Hagar, who ran away but was induced to return with a promise from God that her unborn son would be the father of many descendants (16:6–11). However, her dreams that her son would be Abraham's heir were shattered when it was announced that Sarai (now to be called Sarah) was to have a son and that the inheritance and covenant with God would be made through him and not through the older son Ishmael. There is some indication in the text that Abraham agonised over the future of Ishmael whom he surely loved, when he pleaded with God that Ishmael too would have a share in the covenant (Gen. 17:15–22). However, Isaac is the chosen and favoured son and Ishmael has to take second place. This forms the first ingredient in the repeating pattern of this family group story and it is *favouritism*. It is Sarah who, for very selfish and understandable reasons, favours her own son Isaac. In that culture her identity would have been bound up with being the mother of a son and this may well have sown the seeds of possessiveness and a codependency between her son and herself. Ishmael is equally Abraham's son, and no matter how much his father loved him, he nonetheless gave way not only to God's choice of Isaac, but also to the bitter prejudices of his wife. None of this undermines the gracious purposes of God in establishing his covenant with the family of Abraham nor their faithfulness in believing and trusting in God. However, they too were the products of their own families of origin and no doubt struggled regularly with their emotions and personal relationships. It is a salutary reminder that God does choose the weak and the broken through whom to demonstrate his wonder and his purposes. Consequently, we must not be distracted from the true human story by glossing over it with God triumphant.

With the birth of Isaac and the almost smothering love of his mother Sarah, the family story takes on a new twist of conflict. The new baby boy is celebrated and feasted quite publicly, unlike the birth of Ishmael which was greeted with hostility and fear from Sarah and no celebration feast. It is apparent that Sarah uses the occasion to appease her insecurity and to establish her identity as a woman of substance in the community: 'God has brought me laughter and everyone who hears about this will laugh with me . . . Who would have said to Abraham that Sarah would nurse children? Yet I have borne him a son in his old age' (Gen. 21:6–7). The matter could not have been helped by the fact that twice Isaac is addressed as Abraham's only son (Gen. 22:2, 16). It is true that this is how God understands Isaac in so far as he has established his covenant with this son only, but it should not be taken as a disregard for Ishmael. However, it cannot have gone unnoticed by Ishmael and Hagar, who would interpret the expression as one of exclusion and disinheritance for themselves. This triggered the next ingredient in the repeating pattern of this family story and that is *sibling rivalry*. Ishmael, who was by this time fourteen years old and who had enjoyed the undivided love of his father hitherto, now faced the prospect of being overlooked and marginalised within the family. He no doubt felt angry and hurt and rejected and transferred his bitterness towards his half-brother Isaac. When he saw the party given for Isaac's birth he began to mock the new son and despise him (Gen. 21:9).

The history books are littered with stories of wounded siblings who felt that they were not equally loved, and whose lives and relationships are complicated and distorted as a consequence. No amount of achievement or success can eradicate the need for people to be loved, and very often the drive for success has been fuelled by the attempt to achieve acceptance from the parent who never loved them enough. In talking with the minister of a very large church which boasted a membership of several thousand and a budget which ran into millions, I said that he must feel very blessed in his work. His reply was instructive: he said that no matter how much the church grew and prospered, he still heard a voice inside of him which said that it wasn't enough and he had to try harder. He later identified the voice of that of his father who in earlier life had told him he was an underachiever. This minister had been pushing himself and his church to reach the place where he could earn the 'Well done!' of his father – it never came. Others have responded by hating their more favoured brothers and sisters and moving away from the family, or they have rebelled and drifted into a drug-dependency lifestyle in order to disguise or deny the pain they are feeling. They often find it extremely difficult to trust themselves or others and are more suspicious about opening up to others. All this seems to have characterised the life of Ishmael and resulted in the third ingredient of this family story and that is *a child leaving the family home*.

It is Sarah who is determined to get rid of the rival son and her mother because she fears that Ishmael will claim his right of inheritance as a son. Abraham is caught once again between the love for his older son and the determination of his wife. It is only when God promises to look after Ishmael that Abraham gives in to his wife's demands (Gen. 21:10–13). This has been the pattern of things for Ishmael ever since he was born, that his father has not stood by him enough in times of dispute; now he is going into exile. This would have seriously damaged his sense of self-worth and poisoned his future relationships with his father and brother Isaac. Ishmael's name recurs down through the generations until today where Palestinians (who, through their Islamic faith, trace their roots to Abraham through Ishmael) and Jews are still fighting over inheritance and land. We read that Ishmael had sons who, even after his death, lived in hostility with the sons of Isaac (Gen. 25:13–18). Esau, who also fell foul of the family story, in rebellion and to taunt his parents, marries a daughter of Ishmael who is now described as a Canaanite (Gen. 28:9; 36:3). The divided family is still in conflict in a further generation when Joseph is sold into slavery through the Ishmaelites who buy him from his brothers (Gen. 37:25–7).

To summarise, from the first generation of the Abrahamic family group story, among all the issues that shaped this family, there emerge the three core dynamics of *parental favouritism*, *sibling rivalry* and *a child leaving the family home*. What we will now examine is the ways in which these three core dynamics are repeated in at least two more generations.

Isaac: the second generation

It is interesting to note that as with Sarah, so with Isaac's wife Rebekah, there was a long period before she gave birth to children. In Rebekah's case it was twenty years, and so the relief at becoming pregnant must have been immense. She gives birth to twins, Esau and Jacob, and early into their childhood we see the repeating pattern begin to emerge: 'Isaac, who had a taste for wild game, loved Esau, but Rebekah loved Jacob' (Gen. 25:28). Here is *parental favouritism*. Isaac even goes against the divine prophecy which said that Jacob was the chosen son to inherit (Gen. 25:23). Whatever the reasons, whether it was pride in his son's achievements which got out of hand or whether he was rebelling against the 'favoured son' routine which had so dogged his own life, Isaac was determined to promote Esau. The consequences were to throw Jacob under the obsessional influence of his mother and so Isaac's history is repeated in Jacob. Once again we have divided parents and children bound to an almost smother-love relationship. Dave Carder sees this tendency to be one of despising what is important.

> Isaac gave up his wife just after Esau actually gave up his birthright. Isaac's abandonment of his wife provided the groundwork for her mistrust of him. She could see that she did not always count with her husband. When the chips were down, he would place his own security over hers. That concept, coupled with Isaac's attachment to Esau, pushed her later into taking matters into her own hands; if she could get the inheritance for her son Jacob, her future would be secure. Surely her boy Jacob would take care of her all of her life, even if her husband wouldn't.[6]

Under his mother's influence Jacob tries to fulfil the prophecy of his birthright by deceiving both Esau and his father in order to obtain it (Gen. 25:29–34; 27:1–41). It is tragic to see how the children have become pawns in the breakdown of parental relationships. Here the *sibling rivalry* is fought out over the matter of inheritance and promise once again. The family is deeply divided and torn apart as a result. Once again *a child leaves the family home* as Jacob flees in terror to his uncle Laban (Gen. 27:42–5) and Esau is angry and bitter, and nurses plans to murder Jacob (Gen. 27:41). Even though Jacob returns after twenty years having in the meantime acquired family and belongings, and is greeted, rather stiffly, by Esau, the two never live together again (Gen. 33:1, 13–20). History, unhealed and unacknowledged, repeats itself in the second generation and, as we shall see, in the third.

Jacob: the third generation (Gen. 35:16–29; 37:2–27)

Although the family scenario is somewhat different, the same dynamic emerges as in the two previous generations. Jacob's wife, Rachel, died shortly after giving birth to Benjamin, her second child. However, we are told in the story that Jacob loved Rachel but was tricked into first marrying her older and plainer sister Leah (Gen. 29:19, 31–2; 30:1–2). This triggered rivalry between the wives and friction between Rachel and Jacob; it was almost a repeat of the difficulties in the relationship between Abraham and Sarah. The consequence of his love for Rachel and his grief over her death is that Jacob favours Joseph, the first child he had by Rachel. There are already clues about the obsessional side of this *parental favouritism* in the way that Joseph indulged in destructive gossip about his brothers to his father (Gen. 37:2). Because his father spoiled him by giving Joseph a richly embroidered coat he not suprisingly had dreams of his own inflated importance compared with his brothers (Gen. 37:5–10). With hindsight we can see the hand of God on Joseph's life and that his dreams also had a deeper, more prophetic edge to them than anyone realised at the time. However, this does not disguise his obvious relish at being his father's favourite and his boasting of his importance to his brothers, who despised him for it.

A typically indulgent parent, Jacob did nothing to correct his son's excesses, although he rebuked him in private. We can only imagine that he might have been reliving his own childhood through his son and remembering the days when he was not celebrated and affirmed enough by his own father. It is a sad fact that the wounds of one generation become the indulgences of the next. Joseph's brothers soon come to despise and hate their spoilt brother whom they perceive as being loved more by their father than them (Gen. 37:4). Every family has its favourites but it becomes a problem when it is carried to obsessional lengths and to the detriment of the other children. This becomes the seedbed for *sibling rivalry* and the breakdown of relationships between Joseph and his brothers who now cannot speak even one kind word to him (Gen. 37:4). They were also jealous of his dreams of power because, for them, these did not speak of divine favour but of fatherly indulgence, something they all sorely missed (Gen. 37:11, 19–20). The result of this rivalry was a growing hatred and the spur-of-the-moment decision to kill him which was almost as quickly modified into selling Joseph into slavery. It was all covered up with a sham grief as they told their father that some wild animal had devoured his favourite son. Consequently another *child leaves the family home.* It would be cheap and easy to say that surely it is OK because God was in all of this, and used it to provide the Israelites with food and shelter when the future, colossal famine destroyed the surrounding area (Gen. 50:19–21). We must stay focused on the human story and realise that God's sovereignty in our affairs does not make wrong right, but can often become the opportunity to right wrongs and bring healing.

Conclusion

We have seen that for three generations in the family story of Abraham there was the repeating pattern of parental favouritism, sibling rivalry and a child leaving the family home. Earl Henslin goes so far as to examine the family dynamic of Jesus and offers some very useful insights into the damaging patterns that he had to confront and change in order to grow and fulfil his ministry.[7] There is also a case to be made from the fact that the core dynamics observed form a fundamental part of the psyche of the nation of Israel and that they surface in his fellow countrymen's conflict with Jesus. This is demonstrated in the Markan version of Jesus' return to his home town where he proclaims his calling and mission. The *parental favouritism* is focused on the fact that Jesus is illegitimate and not the son of Joseph ('Mary's son'), but that his brothers and sisters are (Mark 6:1–3). In their sight he is disqualified from his calling owing to his faulty parentage, even though everyone recognises his abilities. *Sibling rivalry* takes the form of rejection by his community who take offence in him rather in the manner in which Joseph's brothers hated him (Mark 6:3b–6). According to the Lucan account of this event *a child leaves the family home* in that Jesus was driven out of the synagogue where he was teaching and up to the cliff edge where he was almost thrown to his death (Luke 4:28–30). The final expulsion of this child of Israel is upon the cross, but his death and resurrection make possible the healing of all wounded stories. This confirms for us that we each have a family group story and that it contains repeating patterns for good or ill which are sown into us and, if not identified and worked with, will be repeated through us to the next generation.

Representing the family group story

Being a member as well as a representative of our family story gives us a right of access into this story for the purposes of bringing healing to it. As we carry within us this story and its repeating pattern, we need to discover this pattern and in a representational confessional approach bring it to God for healing, transformation and renewal. This is not to alter the destiny of the dead but it might be to change the legacy of sowing and reaping of hurt and pain which they have left upon the family. Practical suggestions for how we can go about this can be found in the workbook that accompanies this book. The first step to take in preparing for this prayer of ownership and offering of our family story is researching the story in order to discern what there is to celebrate and what there is to heal about our story. This may well lead to the need to back up the ministry of confession with personal counselling as we discover something of the reasons why we are shaped the way we are. It may also require the healing benefits of a requiem communion should we have discovered a need to respect and offer to God those ancestors whose lives were overlooked or not given a proper Christian funeral service. This may also include those who were stillborn, aborted or miscarried, and may well require the naming of these children if they have not been given a name before.[8]

The following are some questions for reflection which may help you build a picture of your family story and help determine what you need to own as yours and bring to God for blessing and healing. It would help the search enormously if you could involve other members of your family, as they would undoubtedly have insights that you do not.

Discovering your family group story: questions for reflection

- Who are the individuals who stand out in your family story, and why?
- What are the significant features of their story?
- Do any of these features still recur today?
  instability in marital relationships
  addictions of any kind
  family members marginalised and ultimately cut off from the family
  chronic illness
  stress-related illnesses such as allergies, chronic back pain, headaches, or gastro-intestinal difficulties
  depression, suicidal tendencies or hospitalisation for mental illness
  angry, mean and/or controlling behaviour
- How, if at all, were some of these issues handled or remedied?
- Is there any repetition of your past family pattern in your life today? If so make a list of the core dynamics that you have discovered.
- Finally, with as many of your family members as possible, begin to construct a prayer of representational confession of your family story, remembering to celebrate the good and confess for healing its destructive cycle. Rember to be inclusive and pray from the perspective of *we* and *our*. (Some examples of this can be found in the chapter on 'Church Group Story' in the workbook.) Ask the Holy Spirit to heal and renew what you carry of your family story so that you will find renewal for yourself and so that the family story can be transformed for the future benefit of its members.

9 THE CHURCH GROUP STORY

The church is a community on the way to healing.
(Charles Elliott)

Every church has its story of how it began, who founded it and why, and out of this it has developed its own identity which down the years has become a corporate story which shapes each generation of the church. As with all group stories, it will have its strengths and weaknesses and as such they are the core shape and pattern of church life repeated down the years, irrespective of the mixture of pastors and ministers who have come and gone. All kinds of ingredients go into the making of a group story; some are picked up unconsciously and some have well-remembered roots. Walter Wink mentions the story of an Anglican bishop who was having extreme difficulties in encouraging two churches in adjoining parishes to work together.[1] The bishop had tried repeatedly to merge the two congregations and appoint a single rector, but the people constantly refused. Finally he went to one of the churches and said, 'You have told me many reasons why you don't want to merge with the other congregation, but none of them seems very convincing. Now tell me – what is your real reason?' One older member of the church council eventually replied, 'Well, bishop, if you really want to know, they didn't tell us the Vikings were coming!' What the church member was referring to was the fact that the other church had a one-hundred-foot-high, round tower, built in the early part of the tenth century to serve as a lookout and warning post against approaching Viking marauders. One day the Vikings did come and the congregation with the round tower warned its own parishioners but, for reasons now lost in history, did not warn their neighbours, who suffered terribly. The church which had suffered had not forgotten the events of almost a thousand years and, what is more, they apparently had not forgiven either. What is fascinating was that even relatively new members of this latter congregation who had moved into the parish comparatively recently, nonetheless carried the same antipathy towards the other church even though they did not understand why.

On a similar scale, many church ministers report that upon becoming the pastor or priest of their church, they became a player in a play that they did not write. The collective story of the church projects an expected role onto its leader or minister, who invariably fails to live up to these hopes and aspirations. I well remember one expression used to me by my former churchwardens when they wanted to express disapproval or challenge the way I was leading the church: it was 'When the Canon was here . . .'! This was the minister who had led the church two generations before me and who had died some years earlier. He was no doubt a good pastor and did his job as well as any, but I found myself resenting him all the same. It is very hard to compete with or argue with the dead who have been idolised in the group memory of the church. The issues at work here were the group response to change brought in by the new minister and the sense of threat to that corporate memory and the subsequent fear of loss of group identity. It is the hope of the group that the new leader will become the protector and articulator of the group story of the church, and attempts to change it are seen, at a gut level, as a betrayal of role. There may well be thought-out discussion on the pros and cons of some disputed issue, but at a deeper, intuitive and group level, the energy of protest is coming from the need to preserve the group story intact, because it is this which gives a sense of belonging and permanence to the individual. This is also true of non-churchgoers, who will sign petitions and sometimes fight to get on the church councils in order to try and stop the demolition of church buildings because they convey a sense that everything is still as it should be with the world. We should not underestimate the importance of buildings and their connections with community memory. Cathedrals, as we have said, are often the oldest continuously used building within a particular community and, as such, hold within their history the story of that community.

Bruce Reed long ago examined these dynamics and said that one of the reasons why there is so much dispute over changes to liturgy and worship styles is because, for the individual, the ways they worship serve as anchors and reminders of where they belong, and to which group.[2] As such, they convey a sense of permanence and meaning in a threatening society full of dysfunction and change. Another way in which the church carries a group story is in the sense that it is to tell and present the story of Jesus: the community of faith not only experiences the gospel message but gives expression to that message in ways that are coloured by the community's own history. Charles Elliott describes this as acted memory or re-membering and re-presenting the story of Jesus through the life of the church group. He sees an intimate connection between the way in which the church lives communally and the presentation of the story of the living Jesus.[3] He describes the church as a theatre of memory where the story of Jesus and the particular church story come together in the celebration of the sacraments, the architecture of the building, the ornaments, the songs, the worship and the scenery and setting of the building. The church is to be renewed and transformed by the Jesus story and as such is to transform the society it serves. However, as Elliott points out, the church group story has its filters and its blind spots in which it refuses or is unable to hear the full Gospel of Christ.[4] He cites the example of the churches in some of the southern states of the United States of America where the psychological climate of racism is in the ascendant. When the message that all believers, irrespective of colour, creed and gender, are equal in Christ is preached, there swings into action this group denial and inability truly to hear this word. In other words, the church group story gets in the way of the story of Jesus and to some degree distorts it. Consequently, to be the vehicle of the love of Christ in all its fullness, we must know our church story and where necessary bring healing and release to it so we can truly live up to being the community of Christ. We have a model of this challenge to church story in the example of Jesus and his challenge to the churches of Asia, recorded in the book of Revelation.

Jesus challenges the church group story

In Chapters 2 and 3 of Revelation we have a highly structured format in which Jesus addresses the story and witness of seven particular churches: Ephesus, Smyrna, Pergamum, Thyatira, Sardis, Philadelphia and Laodicea. The structure of each passage is the same, even though five churches are exhorted to repent and two are commended for their faithfulness (Smyrna and Philadelphia). Standing at the heart of all these challenges is the fact that Jesus is dialoguing with the group story of each church and challenging it to change for the better. We shall examine this dialogue by looking particularly at Jesus' challenge to the Ephesian church. You might like to consult the chapter in the workbook on the church group story and use the exercises there to explore the other churches mentioned in Revelation or use it to explore your own church's story. The structure of each dialogue between Jesus and the church's group story is as follows:

- addressing the angel of the church;
- summarising the church's group story;
- challenges and consequences for the church;
- exhortation and promise.

Addressing the angel of the church

'To the angel of the church in Ephesus write . . .' (Rev. 2:1). Jesus' approach to the church is quite different from that of the apostle Paul who addressed his letters as 'to the church of God which is at Corinth' or 'to the church of the Thessalonians'. Jesus speaks to the angel of the church and before we can understand why, we do need to explore what or who is the angel of the church? As the Greek word used here is *aggelos* and it means 'messenger', some have concluded that it refers to the human leader of the church, perhaps the bishop. However, the word is used 75 times in Revelation alone and it usually refers to a heavenly being; it is hard to imagine that the term is used differently just for the references to these churches. The scriptures do mention angels of nations and individuals and so there is no reason to suppose that churches do not have angels also. We have already discussed how the archangel Michael seems to have a warrior and protective role in relation to the nation of Israel (Dan. 10). There is early church documentary evidence in the *Ascension of Isaiah* of some form of angelic protection for the church (3:15, 'the angel of the Christian church') and the *Shepherd of Hermas* speaks of Michael as 'the one who has power over this people (the church) and governs them' (Similitudes 8.3.3). This resonates with the passage in Revelation 12:7–9 where Michael once again comes to rescue the church from the grip of the dragon. We conclude therefore that every church has an angel connected with its story, and the question is, 'What are the functions of the angel of the church?'

It is interesting to note that although the angel is addressed, the dialogue then carries straight on to the entire congregation. Walter Wink says that it would appear that the angel is not something separate from the congregation but must somehow represent it as a totality.[5] It seems that the angel is the vehicle through which the group story of the church is addressed, the one through whom the many are presented as a single collective personality. Wink suggests that the angel is in fact the carrier of the spirituality of the church, representing the group story in a single entity.[6] As with his approach to all other spiritual powers and corporate identity, he suggests that the angel is the inner spirituality of the church's story whereas the congregation is the outer or incarnate life of that group story. Congregation and angel are inseparable. This certainly seems to be the case when we look more closely at the text in Revelation. In most cases when the word 'you' is used, it is invariably in the singular and refers therefore to the angel rather than the congregation itself. Consider, for example: 'I know your *(singular)* works; you *(singular)* have the name of being alive, and you *(singular)* are dead' (Rev. 3:1). This is repeated throughout the addresses to all seven churches. Consequently we can conclude that the angel is a type of representational confessor of the church's group story. However, it is up to us to listen to the church's story through the focus of the angel of the church. This is an invitation, not to step into introspection, but to be open to the reality of revelation and let God show us our angel just as he did to the Apostle John who recorded what he saw in the Apocalypse.

When David Runcorn was the minister of an Anglican church in Ealing in London he decided to try and listen to the angel of his church because he wanted to understand why his church functioned as it did. Alone in his church he prayed and committed the enterprise to God and then called on the angel of his church to speak to him and tell him the church's story. After a little while various impressions began to come to mind, such as that the angel felt unloved and neglected; this was because the church was built on a roundabout and all the traffic went around the building and made it difficult for people to get to the church in the first place. Other thoughts came to mind which helped David Runcorn to formulate with better clarity the dynamics which hurt or helped the church to be the church. This whole exercise can easily be dismissed as mere introspection, but listening to the angel of the church and entering into something of a dialogue helped David focus on what was troubling the church. (Some further suggestions for listening to the angel of the church are found in the workbook chapter on the church.) Based on the model of Jesus, it appears that the angel of the church provides us with a helpful window through which to see the congregational story in a richer light. 'The angel gathers up into a single whole all the aspirations and grudges, hopes and vendettas, fidelity and unfaithfulness of a given community of believers, and lays it all before God for judgment, correction and healing.'[7]

In the workbook there is a more detailed list of suggestions for discovering the essential features of our church's story but it is worth noting here some of the ways in which we can hear that story being spoken. To use the phraseology of Wink, the congregation and physical structures of the church life form the outer manifestation of inner spiritual reality or angel of the church. Consider the following:

Architecture and furniture

I have always been impressed by the fact that when the disciples had a wonderful impression of the temple buildings, Jesus had a totally different one: for him they spoke of the swift passing of humanity's attempt at fame and permanence (Matt. 24:1–2). The disciples saw the skill of human construction whereas Jesus listened to the story tied up with the building and learned a different message. I well remember Bishop Richard Hare comparing the shape of churches in Great Britain with those in Russia; the ones in Britain resemble fortresses and castles while those in Russia look like vegetables. The difference in messages is quite striking; the one speaks of power, entrenchment and defence while the other speaks of the garden and resourcing. Some churches still smack of the personality of their founder or those who gave money to perpetuate something of themselves for the succeeding generations. Some churches have been built with money from such dubious sources such as the slave trade and the tobacco industry. Some were built lavishly to the glory of the founder rather than that of God. All these buildings have their message and they sometimes get in the way of the Gospel and may well need to be repented of so that the building can be set free to be a living resource to the church of Christ.

Economics and history

It is important to know why a church was erected on the particular site it occupies. In many cases it was to destroy the influence and importance of pagan religion, or because the site was the most prominent in the community. Often it was because land was donated by the rich and affluent and to suit their own convenience, the church serving as the memorial to the family with privileged seating and private access to receiving communion. Quite a lot of churches were built from dual motives. With the development of new industries came the influx of working classes to work the railways and the coal-pits, and to labour in the factories. Churches were provided for them, literally on the other side of the tracks, so that they could be God-fearing, but do it separately from the wealthy who worshipped in the older, established church buildings in the city. Because they were not allowed to worship with the mother church congregation, many daughter churches were founded not just out of the desire to instil good faith in people but also out of a profound sense of rejection. Like all rejected people, often the daughter church's response is rebellion or excessive competitiveness; in both cases the motive is to gain recognition by the mother church and to claim that it is just as authentic as the one who seemingly rejects it. This is sometimes the reason why some daughter churches, if the mother church is central or catholic, goes out of its way to be evangelical or charismatic. This is not to fail in respect for these spiritualities but only to highlight some of the motivations embedded in the church story which often go unacknowledged or denied. The excessive reaction to these mother churches could be that the daughter church becomes more radically Catholic in its liturgy and style in order to shout out that it too is as important as the other. I was impressed recently when I listened to a leader of a very large new church in the south of the United Kingdom which had been formed when a group had left a Baptist church. He had discerned that part of the motivation for breaking away was to do with pride in being more dynamic and renewed than the rest of the original congregation. While he had not changed his mind about his beliefs and core values he realised that he and others had wounded the original church, and they went to meet with the current leaders and apologised for their pride and asked for forgiveness which was readily given. Now the two churches are growing in co-operation and witness in that town and it has proved an effective event to bring to faith in Christ people who had been cynical about Christian values. In healing our church's group story, we may well have to begin with owning and confessing the very motives that went into the foundation stones of its building and life.

Very often the church and its compulsory attendance were the means of keeping the new working classes in order and in work. Consequently, into the founding story of the daughter church or mission church go the twin motifs of the church being both their pastor and policeman. When I was the minister of a church in Coalville in Leicester I was constantly frustrated by the apathy and unbelief that characterised the spirituality of the congregation. However, when I researched the story of the church I discovered some factors which seemed to account for its condition and the moribund state of its angel. The church was only 160 years old and was founded on the fact that James Stevenson discovered new coal seams in Leicestershire, in an area where there was no existing community. As there was no history of mining in the area he forcibly removed a few hundred Durham miners and their families from their tied accommodation in the North East and brought them to the almost foreign land of the Midlands. In order to make sure that the miners worked hard and behaved themselves, he donated money for the erection of a church for them to worship in. It was also a well-known fact that in the mid-1980s Coalville had one of the highest rates of incest in Europe; it seems that the community had turned in upon itself. Something of the pain of being forcibly removed from their homeland seemed to linger within the church and was reflected by its suspicion of outsiders and its determination to stay an enclosed community. I felt that as minister I should own my church's story and represent the church and its past actions and so, during the Sunday morning notices, I apologised for the church's involvement in removing them from their homeland. I used such words as 'Please forgive us, the church, for aiding and abetting the forcible removal of your people from Durham to here when they did not want to leave their homes and families.' There was an instant rapport with many in the church, who felt something in themselves being moved and upset, as if some long-standing pain was being opened up for healing. I believe that the church began to grow from that moment onwards.

The family dynamics

Dave Carder has made an in-depth study of dysfunctional families, the way they shape us and the resultant patterns of life that are set up by them and passed on because of them. He also transferred his studies on to the church which he views as a family with all its interactive dynamics. He writes,

> One does not have to attend very many churches to realise that each has its own distinctive personality. By personality I mean the pattern the church uses to express itself to those outside, the way it conducts its business within, and the hierarchy of values it establishes for those who belong.[8]

He maintains that we look for family patterns in the life of the church that cohere (for good or ill) with the family patterns by which we were raised. For example, if we grew up in a home where the father was all-powerful and above contradiction, we might well look for a church where the pastor operates by the same principles. Certainly the handling of conflict is a good indicator of the spirituality and story of the church. Some of the patterns which emerge in some churches show that they almost seem to thrive on friction between some of the members and their leaders. In studying the life of one church I noticed that the average term of office for the minister was less that five years, and this had gone on for almost a century! Some of their ministers came from churches which had loved and nurtured them, but the moment they arrived at this new church, they came into the same stressful conflict. The results of one survey in the United States revealed that one out of every hundred churches, in four major Protestant denominations, each year dismissed their minister for reasons other than for immoral or unethical conduct. The primary reason was congregational conflict that existed before the minister arrived there.[9]

All these windows are helps for us to discern the church group story and the spiritual state of the angel of the church. It is our challenge and responsibility to bring healing and encouragement to both. Looking at the model of Jesus we can see one way in which he sought to challenge, encourage and exhort the angel of the church and the congregation to come to life in himself.

The revelation of Jesus for the renewal of the church and its angel

In each of the seven addresses to angels of the church, Jesus reveals something about himself in order to enhance the intimacy between himself, the angel of the church and the congregation's lifestyle and story. It is a form of shock therapy to galvanise the church into waking up to its group story and learning where it needs healing and how to change and be transformed. To the Ephesian church Jesus reveals himself particularly as 'These are the words of him who holds the seven stars in his right hand and walks among the seven golden lampstands' (Rev. 2:1; cf. his self-revelation to the angel of the church of Smyrna: 'These are the words of him who is the First and the Last, who died and came to life again' Rev. 2:8). Each self-revelation fits into the church group story which is being challenged or encouraged. In the case of the Ephesian church story, Jesus is challenging its failure to be a loving witness as opposed to being merely hard-working and doctrinally correct. The stars are thought to be the light of the church life and the candlestick is usually interpreted as the witness of that church. Consequently the Ephesian church is to make sure that its candlestick is not taken away, that its witness to being in love with God is not lost (Rev. 2:6). The church in Smyrna is undergoing persecution and some will lose their lives; so the word about Jesus being the one who came to life again comes as a powerful incentive to stand firm for the faith.[10]

This self-revelation of Jesus to the angel of the church and the congregation itself is also an act of love for the church. Paul writes in his letter to the Ephesian church that 'Christ loved the church and gave himself up for her to make her holy, cleansing her by the washing with water through the word, and to present her to himself as a radiant church without stain or wrinkle or any other blemish, but holy and blameless' (Eph. 5:25–6). It is only Jesus, by the power of the Holy Spirit, who can transform and renew the church's story and witness; it does not come by the direct assault of a strategic programme imposed from without. There is a dire need for the church and its angel to regain its intimacy with Jesus and to be set ablaze with the vision of what he is really like for them. On our part, we need to begin with accepting and loving the wounded angel of our church and we do this in part by owning the church's story as our own and bringing it to God for healing. The next element in the model of how Jesus connects with the church's group story is the stark reminder of the core issues of our group story.

Summarising the church's group story

> 'I *know* your deeds, your hard work and your perseverance. I *know* that you cannot tolerate wicked men, that you have tested those who claim to be apostles but are not, and you have found them false. You have persevered and have endured hardships for my name, and have not grown weary. Yet I hold this against you: You have forsaken your first love. Remember the height from which you have fallen!'
>
> (Revelation 2:2–5a, italics mine)

It is a simple but startling fact that Jesus does know the story of every church: how it began and how it has carried the witness of the Gospel or not; whether it is part of the solution or part of the problem of the community it is called to serve. The challenge for us is to ask ourselves whether we know the story of our church, and if not, why not? In addressing all seven churches Jesus does not give an extensive history of each one but picks out its core features and links it to how it relates in mission to its community. The assumption, indeed implication, of this comparison, is that the church is there to be the healer of community, but unfortunately the church is wounded and needs to apply healing to itself first and foremost. The Ephesian church seems to be hard working and is enduring hardships of various kinds, presumably some form of persecution. It is a church which is hot on morals and correct doctrine but it has somehow become hard and harsh in its pursuit of correctness. It is a church which has forgotten how to love and this alone is sufficient to endanger its life and witness. I cannot help but remember some of the Protestant churches I frequented on Merseyside during the 1960s when so much passion was taken up in denouncing the so-called heresies of the Anglican and Catholic denominations. Public rallies and protest marches against the dangers of the ecumenical movement were staged and nights of prayer imploring God to keep the church pure and holy (meaning, keep it safe from the teachings of liberals and Catholics). Others used well-rehearsed tactics of interruption at united services to prevent bishops and archbishops from preaching. We thought we were fighting the last battle for the purity of the Gospel. While I do not deny the need for gospel truth, I was challenged by an increasing awareness that we did not know how to love those with whom we disagreed, and the legacy we gave to the person in the street was that we liked nothing more than arguing with each other. Somehow, Jesus was lost from view in all of this. It may be an overstatement, but I heard one church leader say that when we put our principles before the needs of other people, it is usually other people who end up getting hurt. It was in response to this attitude among intolerant Christians that the comedian, Lenny Bruce, was provoked into saying, 'People are leaving church in their thousands in order to try and find God!'

In summarising the church's story, Jesus is singling out its strengths and weaknesses, its pattern of behaviour, and challenging it to change so that its mission calling may not be frustrated. I suggest that this is what we also need to do as we encourage the church to grow into wholeness of life and mission. It is no use simply giving the church new ideas and concepts to witness and grow if we do not attend to the repeating pattern of our church group story. So some of the key servants to renewal of church life can be those spirit-led researchers who take the time and the energy to uncover the church's story, from its origin if possible, and present it with its core dynamics. Then the church needs to accept this story as its own in the form of representational confession, which is one of the steps on the road to renewal and fresh release in witness.

Challenges and consequences for the church

> 'Repent and do the things you did at first. If you do not repent, I will come to you and remove your lampstand from its place. But you have this in your favour: You hate the practices of the Nicolaitans, which I also hate.' (Revelation 2:5b–6)

Once again we have Jesus encouraging corporate representation. He does not single out the good or the bad in the congregation but challenges the church collectively to repent of the sins of its group story. The church cannot do this unless it first owns, through confession, the whole story of its group life that has been brought to light by the Lord for his healing and cleansing. It does not help to victimise or demonise those in the church's history who may well have been the individuals through whom damage and destruction was brought into the church. We have to learn to own our history as ours and then we are in a place, like Daniel, Ezra, Nehemiah, Moses and Jesus, to offer it to God in confession and personal repentance in the hope and desire that God will accept our confession and bring healing to our wounded group story.

Exhortation and promise

> 'He who has an ear, let him hear what the Spirit says to the churches. To him who overcomes, I will give the right to eat from the tree of life, which is in the paradise of God.'
>
> (Revelation 2:7)

It seems that the main task for the church is to listen to what the Holy Spirit of God is saying. If the church listens to what God reveals and overcomes all the temptations to turn in upon itself, then the Lord of the church gives the church a promise of blessing which is its destiny. In the case of the Ephesian church, it is to have access to the tree of life, to return to the land from which the children of God were first expelled. It is nothing less than the healing of creation. It is apparent therefore that the church is to listen to two types of group story, its own and that of the community it serves. We need to listen to God so that he can show us what ails the church's story and causes it to stumble and miss its high calling to be salt and light within its community. To refer back to the language of 2 Chronicles 7, the people of God need to own their own group story and its faults and sins and bring them before God for forgiveness. The healing that God's people receive becomes the energy and vision it needs to be a resource for healing our community's group story. Not only will God forgive the sins and heal the consequences of the sins of the people of God, but he will move beyond us to heal our land, the community and the location we serve. William Storrar describes the church as being 'the acoustic community' for the needs of society at large.[11] The church is to be the people of God who listen to God for others. Having listened, then, and only then, are we empowered to speak and heal in the name of our Lord Jesus Christ. Jim Thwaites makes the connection between the church's recovery of a Hebrew world-view (in particular, with the focus on corporate story) and the church's calling to bless the fullness of creation, principally expressed in the healing of marriage, work and family stories.[12] What he is saying is that when the church recovers its spirit-filled group identity in Christ, it is better able to encourage wholeness of life in family and community group stories, to mention but two. This is similar to the point that Charles Elliott makes in his classic work on group memory and its function in bringing healing and redemption to society. He maintains that through its liturgies and life, the church is like an ark which carries the memories of Jesus which, when lived out and proclaimed by the church, serve as a form of counter-memory which delivers from the destructive effects of bad memories on individual and community alike.[13]

Conclusion

We have a model in Jesus of how to relate to our church's group story. It is intimately linked with our calling to mission within community. However, it is apparent that the church is itself damaged and in need of healing. Instead of sharing the story of Jesus in power, all too often the church carries in an uncritical and undiscerning manner the complaints and sins of its society. Consider how the Dutch Reformed Church in South Africa was too closely identified with the apartheid system of that country. A more complex example is the enmeshed relationships between the Roman Catholic, Church of Ireland and Presbyterian denominations in Northern Ireland. Each church group looks at the other through the filter of prejudiced history. Eoion De Bhaldraithe points out how the Catholic Emancipation Act of 1829 and the subsequent campaign for Irish Home Rule (which would give Catholics a voting majority in the North) seem to be one of the origins of Protestant fears for their future in that land – a fear which Catholics to some degree find hard to understand.[14] This is not the place to examine the complexities of Irish church history, but it serves to remind us that such incidents foster a partition of the mind within the church which sadly becomes a political reality that sometimes bends the church out of shape and out of all recognition as the body of Christ.

Consequently, we need to listen to God for the healing of the church, and in the next chapter we shall look at a particular service in the Old Testament which was designed purely to heal the place of ministry to be the place of ministry that God intended it to be. We know it as Yom Kippur, the Day of Atonement; so let us look at what I have called the Christian Day of Atonement.

10 THE CHRISTIAN DAY OF ATONEMENT

> Jesus gave up his life for her [the church] to make her holy and clean.
>
> (Ephesians 5.26 NLT)

In our study of how Jesus dialogued with seven churches in Asia we have noted how he presented each one with its corporate story, and in the case of five of those churches, how their unhealed story jeopardised their current and future effectiveness. If the story was not healed and changed, they were in danger of ceasing to be church, their candlestick of witness would be taken away. This theme of keeping the church's group story alive and holy is one of the recurring strands throughout the New Testament letters. In his first letter Peter links all the themes of building, group story and effective ministry into his picture of what constitutes being church. 'Come to Christ, who is the living cornerstone of God's temple . . . he is building you, as living stones, into his spiritual temple. What's more, you are God's holy priests, who offer the spiritual sacrifices that please him because of Jesus Christ' (1 Pet. 2:4–5 NLT). The emphasis is upon the spiritual vitality of being God's ministering agency in the community and not upon the formality of the type of building and the form of sacrifices used. This is not to undermine the importance of place and liturgy or style of ministry, but to underline that, for them to be effective, the community must be alive and energised by a living intimacy with the risen Jesus. However, both Peter and Paul are well aware that the church of Christ is not perfect and needs to keep on its toes if it does not want to be seduced by the spirit and values of a fallen world. Paul talks about the sad church which can go through all the motions of being the church but it is only an outward shell, a sham of the real thing, which has no real godliness nor power to save its society (2 Tim. 3: 1–5). Roger Mitchell describes this as a church which has lost its spiritual roots and is similar to a ship losing its compass-bearing: at best dangerous and at worst disastrous.[1] Consequently, threaded through scripture are continual encouragements for the church to be holy and united, to be loving and caring for each other and to keep the high standards set by Jesus Christ himself. In the light of the difficulties which would face the church in the future, Jesus emphasised the need to be forgivers. Matthew records in his Sermon on the Mount words of Jesus on the supreme importance of forgiveness and reconciliation before any other form of ministry at the altar (Matt. 5:23–4). It implies that if we do not attend to the breakdown in fellowship relationships within the body of Christ, no amount of gifts being placed on the altar will heal it, and it will serve as a festering wound in the life of the church's group story. It is interesting and disturbing to note that this message on the need to be forgivers comes in a section on the damaging effects of discord in the church and the resultant breakdown in church life. The supreme importance of forgiveness in the healing of the church's corporate life is made clear in the fact that Jesus selected it as one of the core teaching items in his upper room appearances to his disciples. 'Receive the Holy Spirit. If you forgive anyone's sins, they are forgiven. If you refuse to forgive them, they are unforgiven' (John 20:22–3 NLT). It is important to point out here that this is a reference to human activity and not divine. It does not mean that God does not forgive sins of the repentant, but it does imply that if we refuse to forgive another, then the effects of unforgiveness linger on in the life of the unforgiver and the group story to which they belong. Like any minister who wants to see his church grow, I also have experienced those occasions when we bring into the church life the ministry of the gifted. The blessings that accompany their ministry are showered on the church and many are helped and blessed. However, I have also to record that when the person with the gifted ministry departs, the group story of the church remains the same even though there are a number who have been helped. It is not until we own the unhealed group story of the church, no matter how few we may be, that the essential behaviour of the church is transformed for the better. This is because what has not yet been acknowledged and forgiven remains unhealed and its damaging consequences continue to shape the church story. As we have already mentioned in the previous chapter, some of these unforgiven stories have been around for a very long time.[2]

The Day of Atonement

In the Old Testament there is a healing service whose sole aim is to release the place of ministry to be the place of ministry God intended it to be. It is called Yom Kippur or the Day of Atonement. The original focus for such ministry was the portable tabernacle, but the rite was transferred to the later two temples and has been continued within synagogue life ever since. The Hebrew word *kippur* is one of the standard words for forgiveness in the Old Testament and basically means 'to cover, pacify or ransom'. William Gesenius said that it can also mean 'to be delivered from the effects of'. This comes from the fact that the word is also used for the 'wiping the face clean which has been blackened by displeasure'.[3] The New Testament word equivalent is *katallagē* which basically means 'reconciliation'. We can see therefore that intrinsic to atonement is a group experience of release and reconciliation. As part of their spiritual discipline, the people of God were instructed to hold an annual day of atonement for the healing and reconciling of community life and ministry. It will help us to understand its power if we now look at the reasons for the institution of this rite and therefore its prime purpose.

The historical reasons for instituting the Day of Atonement

'The Lord spoke to Moses after the death of the two sons of Aaron who died when they approached the Lord' (Lev. 16:1). The two sons in question were Nadab and Abihu who were consumed by the fire of God's punishment when they went into the tabernacle to make their own offerings to God (Lev. 10:1–5). Keil and Delitzsch suggest that their death was for wilfully drawing near to Yahweh and as such it served as a solemn warning to Aaron, the high priest, not to come into the holy place when it pleased him but only at the times which God specified and for the purposes which God laid down.[4] There is, however, some suggestion that their motivation was one of rivalry with that of Moses himself. In chapter 9 of Leviticus we read that Moses and Aaron, after spending time with God in the Tent of Meeting (tabernacle), came out and blessed the people, and the glory of the Lord appeared and fire came out from the presence of God and consumed their sacrifice (Lev. 9:23–4). It must have been an awesome moment of power and it is no wonder that they were impressed enough to want to repeat it through their own attempts. There are shades of similarity here with Simon who tried to buy the ability to give the Holy Spirit with the laying on of hands (Acts 8:14–24). It seems, therefore, that Nadab and Abihu had sought to bask in the same power and glory which accompanied the ministry of Moses and their father Aaron; their motivation was one of rivalry and possibly envy (cf. Num. 3: 1–4). They went through exactly the same motions of ministry as Moses and Aaron but their motivations were all wrong, their hearts were full of pride and they paid a high price for their disobedience. What is so devastating was that their ministry made ineffective that of their father, the high priest, and the effectiveness of the very building and all its ministries. In order to recover the ministry of the building and its leadership, it needed cleansing and atonement made for people and fabric alike.

Healing and atonement for ministers, building and the worshipping community

'Aaron is to offer the bull for his own sin offering to make atonement for himself and his household . . . and for the Most Holy Place and . . . for the Tent of Meeting and . . . for the altar' (Lev. 16:6, 16, 18). What follows is a detailed rite for the cleansing of the place of ministry and those who offer it. First there was to be atonement for the high priest and his own household (Lev. 16:6, 11) even though Aaron was not present and took no part in his sons' rebellious acts. Why is this so? Because Aaron belonged to the family and therefore the ministry team who perpetrated the defiling of the building. This is another example of corporate story needing to be identified, owned and offered for forgiveness and reconciliation. Therefore we read that Aaron offered the sin offering for himself and for his family group in recognition that it was his family which was at fault though he himself was personally innocent of their crime.

Next, atonement was to be made for the Most Holy Place which was not even used by Nadab and Abihu as this was the sole responsibility of the high priest (Lev.16:16). This was because the Most Holy Place, apart from being the most important ministry location in the building, is seen as a part of the whole building, and what is done in one section affects the whole. This is why there is reference to atonement being made for the whole of the Tent of

Meeting (Lev.16:16); it affirms for us the importance of place and how ministry, good or bad, offered in one part of the building affects the whole.

What follows next is atonement for the altar of sacrifice, which is a focus for the whole ministry of the building (Lev.16:18–20). It serves as a stark reminder that the places where we should meet with God and enjoy his healing care of our lives can be rendered redundant by bad ministry. However, they are not healed by pointing the finger at the various individuals who did not serve us well but by the congregation owning, through confession, not only their own sins but the sins of their group story. This is why the account in Leviticus now moves on to discuss making atonement for the corporate sins of the community of Israel. It is linked with the act of confessing the sins of the community by laying hands on the head of a live goat, known as the scapegoat (Azazel), which is then released to wander free in the desert (Lev.16:21–5). The community with its spiritual life and ministry now restored are freed to go on the journey of following after Yahweh into the land of promise. The connections with Christ our sin-bearer could not be more apparent. He is the Living One who represents the many through his act of sacrifice and confession upon the cross. As such, Jesus provides us with the potential to be forgiven personally and also to bring the wounded patterns of our various group stories to be healed also.

God also decreed that Yom Kippur was to be held annually, for the healing and renewal of the worshipping community, in order that their ministry might remain effective. Here was a healing service which delivered the people from the unforgiven effects of their sins and their ministry which may have accrued during the year. It is clear from this that the Day of Atonement was not only a response to a particular need to free people and ministry alike from the effects of Nadab and Abihu's actions, but also as a resource for continuous healing and forgiveness within the whole community on future occasions.

> It provided for the congregation of Israel the highest and most comprehensive expiation that was possible under the Old Testament . . . (and) formed a fitting close to the ordinances designed to place the Israelites in fellowship with their God and raise the promise of Jehovah, 'I will be your God', into a living truth.[5]

The Christian Day of Atonement

It seems that what we have here is an actual process by which forgiveness and release was brought to a whole community as well as to the place of ministry and worship in order to free it from the effects of anything spiritually unclean. The question is 'Can this procedure be applied to all other places of ministry or is it only applicable to the Tabernacle and Temple of the Old Testament community of Israel?' We have discussed this issue in more detail in Chapter 1, but suffice it to say here that as Christians, we are always looking at the principles embedded in the Old Testament and applying them through Jesus to our day and circumstances. This is why we look at the Servant Songs of Isaiah (Isa. 42:1–9; 49:1–6; 50:4–9; 52:13—53:12; 61:1–3); and although at the time they were written they were understood to refer either to a special prophet or even the renewed nation, for Christians they are supremely realised in Jesus.[6] I suggest that in the Day of Atonement we have a useful model service for healing the place of ministry to be the place of ministry. Consequently it is a powerful resource for the healing of wounded church stories. However, because of the once-and-for-all-sacrifice of Jesus on the cross for the sins of the whole world, for the sins of individual and group stories alike, it is to be carried out through the name and power of Jesus.

I was first led to hold one of these services when I was approached by the deacons of a Baptist church in the North West of England. They had a growing concern for their pastor and his family, who for some years by then had been continually dogged with ill health; there never seemed to be a time when someone in the family was not ill with something. This family had moved into the city some three years or so earlier and it was following this that the pattern of illnesses began to emerge. The pastor and his family had been prayed for, deliverance prayers had been offered as well as visits to the doctors to see if they were carrying viral illnesses. In all of these inquiries there had been no favourable result, and the illnesses continued. One of the leaders had pointed out to me that the church had a history of schisms, and as a result ministers who came tended not to stay very long. It was almost as if the ills of the church were being focused on the pastors and their families and I began to wonder if the real need was to heal the church's wounded story and remove the effects of it from the church and in particular from the minister's family. Since studying the prayers of Daniel, Ezra and Nehemiah, I suggested that we held a Christian Day of Atonement for the healing of the church's story where we would offer prayers of representational confession.

A day was arranged when the entire congregation was invited and informed of the purpose of the meeting which was to seek forgiveness and healing from anything, past or present, which was making the church sick. Those who did attend were invited not to be a spectator but to be prepared to confess their own sins either verbally or by writing them on pieces of paper. The papers would later be burnt but not read out. Next would be the owning of the church's story as their own and we were careful not to put the blame on various individuals from the past. Like those of Daniel, the prayers would be inclusive and take the form of 'Lord, forgive us for being a church where we have become divided and ill.' These prayers would be focused around the places of ministry within the building such as the pulpit, the communion table and the choir stalls. Appropriate space was given for the sharing of the peace or finding reconciliation between the people in the church itself. I am happy to report that apart from the usual round of coughs and colds, they were never again stricken with constant ill health within the family. The church was also enabled to pick up the experience of spiritual renewal and leave behind the frictions and animosities which had plagued its life. Since that first experience I have reflected more upon the ingredients of such a service and developed it into a liturgy for a Christian Day of Atonement which I suggest could become an annual event for the renewing of the church. As Christians, we have been called into a community committed to forgiveness within, and then from, the fellowship. 'By doing the will of God we shall belong to the covenant of forgiveness.'[7] Martin Luther said that forgiveness is that experience which allows the Holy Spirit to return to us and enliven us again.[8] The church must not allow itself to be like Samson, whose fellowship with God had long been broken but who nonetheless went out to battle thinking that everything was the same as before: 'But he did not know that the Lord had left him' (Judg. 16:20). He went through the familiar motions of confronting his enemies but there was no power there any more and he was badly mauled as a result. Consequently, we must keep our fellowship and church group story alive through the ministry of atonement and forgiveness. Therefore I would recommend that you give serious consideration to recovering the principles of Yom Kippur and holding a Christian Day of Atonement for the renewal and reconciling of your wounded church story. There is a full outline and liturgy for this service in the relevant chapter of the workbook which also has suggestions of how and when to hold it. I have taken part in a number of these services within the United Kingdom and the Republic of Ireland and have been greatly encouraged at the way in which churches have been renewed and better empowered to serve their community.

11 THE COMMUNITY GROUP STORY

Recovery of sight for the blind must never be separated from releasing the captives and enabling the broken victims of societal pathology to go free.

(Howard Clinebell[1])

As the soul is to the body, so are Christians to their city. (*Letter to Diognetus*)

From the very beginning of creation God has made us to live in community. We are made in the image and after the likeness of God who is after all a community of Father, Son and Holy Spirit. The Genesis stories describe how belonging in relationships is at the core of human experience. Adam is created in idyllic surroundings and enjoys fellowship with God but in a very essential way he is still alone and it is not good (Gen. 1:18). He is only fully humanised when he has companionship, although, as the accounts of the fall reveal, this is both risky as well as fulfilling. From Adam we trace the growth of community through the lives of the patriarchal family groups which lead to the formation of tribes and ultimately, the nation of Israel. As a way of understanding the story of nation and society at large, the scriptures focus on the city. There are at least 1,400 references to the city in the Bible and although most cities were not comparable with our modern metropolitan cities with their urban sprawl and decay, there were quite a few which were large by comparison. The archaeologist Sir Leonard Woolley reported that by 2000 BC the city of Ur, Abraham's homeland, numbered a quarter of a million people.[2] Ancient Nineveh was so large that it took three days to cross it on foot (Jonah 3:3). Babylon at the time of King Nebuchadnezzar had eleven miles of walls, and a water and irrigation system (perhaps even including flush toilets!) which was not equalled again until the end of the nineteenth century.[3] In New Testament times, Ephesus had street lighting along its famed Arcadius Street and Antioch had sixteen miles of colonnaded streets. Rome numbered more than a million people in Paul's day, and apparently the poor lived in forty-six thousand tenement houses many of which were eight to ten storeys high (pre-dating Chicago by two thousand years).[4] After Rome's demise it would take almost thirteen hundred years before another city, London of the 1820s, which would have a population so large.

The Bible and the city

Threaded throughout the scriptures is the ongoing importance of the community as the focus for God's ultimate purposes of redemption and healing of humanity. This can be traced by exploring the relative stories, spiritualities and final destinies of the two cities of Babylon and Jerusalem. Babylon is the model for the city which is dominated by the renegade powers of darkness. It is introduced in Genesis 11 as the community whose foundations are built upon rebellion and its final demise is revealed in Revelation 16—18. Babylon is painted as the city which is bureaucratic, self-serving and one with a dehumanising social system with economics geared to benefit its privileged minority and exploit its poor: its politics is one of oppression and its religion is bankrupt; cf. Isa. 14:5–11; Jer. 50:2–27; Dan. 3:1–7; Rev. 17:1–6, 18:2–19, 24.[5]

Jerusalem, on the other hand, is idealised as the city as it was meant to be, one belonging to God. Its social systems were to provide a living example of the shalom of the living God among them (Ps. 122:6–9; 147:2). It was to care for the poor and the stranger and exercise a fair and proper stewardship of its business practices (Isa. 26:1–6; 60:12; 65:17–25; Ezek. 48:35; Mic. 5:2; Zech. 2:4–5). The city was twice destroyed because its inhabitants had rejected the law of God for their community, but in the consummation of the ages it is to become the celebrated city in which the shining presence of God furnishes all its light and life, and it is the final home of the redeemed (Rev. 21 and 22) It is apparent, therefore, after this brief glimpse into city affairs, that the community group story is a significant and important issue in the purposes of God. Roger Greenway goes so far as to say that the prime mission of the church is to win the city for God. 'Failure in winning the cities means failure in winning the world. As cities go . . . so go the nations.'[6] The city has continued to fascinate Christian thinkers through the ages: in his treatise entitled *The City of God* Augustine envisioned a world won to God through the gradual growth of the church as the new city in which God's Spirit would rule supreme. This has influenced some to regard the church as the new Jerusalem as God abandons the city for the church as his new focus for the kingdom of God. Yet this would seem to run counter to Jesus' clear instructions for the church to be the salt and light of its community, its beating heart in fact (Matt. 5:13–16). 'The transformation that Jesus taught, and the Holy Spirit empowers, was not just for individuals and churches. It was nothing less than a radical change in society.'[7] In his book *The Challenge of the City*, Stuart Murray reflects this swing from extreme optimism and pessimism about the viability of the city. He mentions that in 1965 Harvey Cox published his book called *The Secular City* in which the author argues that the urbanisation of society and the secularism that accompanies it are to be seen as a fulfilment of the biblical message that we are all called to live in community. However, within five years of its publication, Jacques Ellul published his book *The Meaning of the City*, and concluded that the city was beyond redemption except by an act of God in establishing the new Jerusalem.[8] Murray implies the unsuitability of the city in God's economy by saying that although Jesus had a mission to cities, he did not settle in them.[9] He cites Jesus' words in Luke 4:42–3 where, in responding to the crowd's appeal to stay and teach them further, Jesus says that he has other towns to visit. This is more a reference to the determination of Jesus to visit the towns rather than a disinclination to avoid living in them. In order to have a more comprehensive understanding of community and city in the Bible we will explore this further under the following headings:

- the city as a corporate identity;
- the battle in the city;
- God's heart for the city;
- Jesus in the city.

The city as a corporate identity

'Every city is created with a life of its own, a corporate personality with a culture and a distinctive personality . . . In the fall, the city also symbolizes man's corporate rebellion against God; it becomes idolatrous and its idolatry leads to demonisation' (Tom Marshall[10]). Whereas Marshall's description of the city and its corporate identity seems to be over-focused on the demonic presence as representative of that group identity, he is nonetheless correct to point out that each city has its distinctive personality. Having grown up on Merseyside, I have had opportunity to compare the cities of Liverpool and Chester which are only fifteen miles apart, and yet they are so different. Liverpool is a city connected with slavery, shipping and a complex mixture of ethnic cultures. Chester, although once an ancient port, is a Roman walled town and is characterised by a largely white, middle-class society with little immigrant representation. Liverpool has experienced massive unemployment with the closure of its docks and many heavy industries whereas Chester seems largely to have escaped this sorrow. Consequently the Liverpool story is identified by a sense of depression and ethnic tension, and has recently recognised that one of the roots of this lies in its involvement in the infamous slave trade. In the year 2000 the city fathers hosted an apology to the black community in the city for its part in the affair. Chester, on the other hand, seems to exude an optimism for its present and future.

There are a number of ways in which the city as a corporate or group identity is represented in the scriptures. First is the familiar issue of *corporate punishment*. According to Deuteronomy, the entire town or city is implicated in the crimes of the few who may lead that city's inhabitants astray into idolatry. The penalty is that the whole community is to be put to the sword and the city itself to be burned to the ground (Deut. 13:12–18). It seems that in devoting the city and its inhabitants to God in this way, the rest of the community would be saved from its effects. In addition, the city was wholly accountable for its moral standards, the individual conduct of its citizens. This could mean that the loss of virginity of a single girl or the rebellious acts of a disobedient son could, under some circumstances, become a public issue and the individuals in question be brought before the elders of the city in order to keep the city's welfare intact (Deut. 22:15; 21:20–1). Perhaps this is nowhere more graphically expressed than in the story of Sodom and Gomorrah. Abraham pleads with God to spare the city if a number of righteous people can be found living in those cities (Gen. 18:16–33). The story of the righteous is resourceful enough to spare God's judgement on the story of the sinful city. However, the story is even more startling when we learn that the original Hebrew text of Genesis 18:22 does not say that Abraham waited before the Lord, but that God waited before Abraham as he struggled to ask for the cities to be spared. E. A. Speiser says that this is one of the very rare instances when the Masoretic text was interfered with by editors working in the post-exilic period.[11] It seems that the picture of God waiting (lingering, according to Gerhard von Rad[12]) upon man was too risky for their belief. Yet it is tremendously heartening to think of the Lord being so committed to the sparing of an entire community, that he lingers in the presence of humanity, daring us to hope and pray for more! The town of Sodom surfaces in Jesus' challenge to the communities where some of his greatest miracles were performed. Jesus, the urban evangeliser, is also the one who is the city's righteous remnant; he denounces Korazin, Bethsaida and Capernaum because they would not repent (Matt. 11:20–4). He addresses the entire city as if a single or collective personality, and calls it to account for its story of unrepentance in the face of the miracles he had performed among its people.

The second indication of cities having a group identity is that they *represent nations*. A typical example of this is how Judah and Jerusalem are used interchangeably in the prophecies of Zechariah who is addressing the whole theme of the renewed community of Israel and of how the nations will, despite their hostile intentions, become allies of the people of God (Zech. 12:1–10; 13:1, 12, 21). Another example is the city prophet Isaiah who, when prophesying against the nations, addresses their ruling cities:

- Babylon for the nation of Babylonia (Isa. 14 and 15);
- Ar, Kir and Dibon for the nation of Moab (Isa. 15: 1–4);
- Damascus for the nation of Assyria (Isa. 17);
- Jerusalem for the nation of Judah (Isa. 22).

Ezekiel, another urban prophet, retells the story of Jerusalem as if describing an individual, pointing out her beginnings in the land of Canaan (surely a reference to the beginnings of nationhood) and then, like a battered woman, she is washed and restored by the loving hands of God, only to rebel and worship idols (Ezek.16). This suggests to us another indication of corporate identity for cities and that is the *descriptions of the city as a female personality*. These descriptions seem almost exclusive to the prophet Ezekiel.

> Son of Man, will you judge her? Will you judge this city of bloodshed? Then confront her with all her detestable practices and say 'This is what the Sovereign Lord says: O city that brings on herself doom by shedding blood in her midst and defiles herself by making idols . . . therefore I will make you an object of scorn to the nations.' (Ezekiel 22:1–4)

Elsewhere he paints the picture of the two cities of Samaria and Jerusalem as two adulterous sisters who engaged in illicit relationships with Assyria and Chaldaea (Ezek. 23). In the final battle between God and the forces of darkness which inhabit society, one of the principle culprits for the fallen state of humanity is identified as the harlot city of Babylon. 'Fallen! Fallen is Babylon the Great! She has become the home for demons and a haunt for every evil spirit' (Rev. 18:2). The faithful people of God who still live within the city are told to come out of her so that they do not share in her judgement (Rev. 18:4). Most commentators see the reference to Babylon as a description of Rome and all that its empire stood for in its conquest of society and its lust for power and control. This is why it is described as the great city which rules over the kings of the earth (Rev. 17:18). Whatever the full identity of this corrupting city, it is presented in the form of the corporate personality of an adulterous woman sitting astride the Satanic systems of oppression and lawlessness.

We can conclude from this survey that the city or community is treated as a corporate story and will be blessed or judged according to its dominating spirituality or relationships. As Ray Bakke points out, if a city is anything, at least in an idealised form, it is an organic, dynamic series of relationships, interwoven in a common crucible.[13] The ideal guiding relationship for the city is the one with God which is why Jerusalem, in this context, is called the city of peace, the heavenly or holy city (cf. 2 Chron. 6:6; Isa. 65:18–19; Joel 3:17; Gal. 4:26; Phil. 3:20; Heb. 12:22; 13:14; Rev. 21:2). This is the goal which God initiated and is always working towards, that of community redeemed and renewed through its predominant relationship with God. This is of course the prime challenge to the church which is to represent and manifest God-centred community not for its own benefit, but for the healing of the city. 'The signposts and placards of the eternal city must be erected in our finite cities. God's judgement and promise must be testified to in the city' (Luther Copeland[14]).

According to the biblical accounts, each city has a separate and distinctive story – what Robert Linthicum describes as a 'spirit', an almost palpable essence different from every other city. It is a combination of that city's history, surroundings and systems, the people (key personalities) who have moved through it and shaped it to some degree and that city's accumulated story and consequences.[15] We can perhaps reflect on the essential spirit of our own city and try to identify it from its story and lived out consequences. We have already noted (p. 106) that one of the factors shaping the Liverpool story was the dumping there of the unwanted. And to quote Robert Linthicum again:

> No matter how matronly a face someone tries to paint on her, Chicago is never far from the honky-tonk, bootleg gin, gangsters and the smell of 'naughty' excitement. One cannot walk the streets of Rome without hearing the tramp of the ancient Legions and the whispered intrigue in emperors' courts and papal palaces. The spirit of Hong Kong is commerce, whether legal or illegal, whether under capitalism or communism. Scratch the skin of Mexico City and you find the grandeur and gore of its Aztec past. Rio means 'festival' and Moscow is firm, with unyielding walls regardless of perestroika; and London keeps a proper face and stiff upper lip in the midst of crumbled dreams and empires.[16]

In order to conduct its mission in and to the city effectively, the church needs to know and understand its community's group story. This will to some degree unmask the spiritual as well as social 'powers' which need to be confronted and where necessary, opposed and deposed. The importance of researching the history of community and what it may teach about the healing and regeneration of that community is now being taken seriously at a political and economic level. Dr Paul Syms has been appointed as Britain's first Visiting Professor of Land and Property at Sheffield Hallam University. In a project funded by the Rowntree Foundation, he is researching how new life can be breathed into contaminated land so it can be used for housing. 'The first thing is to look at historical research,' he says. 'You need to go out and walk on the site to look at the historical aspect . . . you might have to go back 200 years to the beginning of the Industrial Revolution.'[17] Syms is focusing primarily on digging out the pollutants within the soil in order to make the site environmentally safe. However, he sees the importance of knowing the story of a place and learning the lessons it gives about the necessary action which follows in order to restore the land.

The battle in the city

One of the fascinating features which the Bible gives to the city is the concept of the spirit or angel of the city. We are told that it was the angel of the Lord who presided over Jerusalem which was responsible for the dramatic defeat of the Assyrian armies which were gathered outside of its walls. During the night this angel destroyed 185,000 soldiers (2 Kings 19:35–6)! In the Book of Revelation there is the description of one of the seven angels of destruction giving a guided tour of the new Jerusalem and measuring its dimensions rather as in the book of Ezekiel (Rev. 21:9–21; Ezek. 40). In the Acts of the Apostles Luke records how the worship of Artemis was the core dynamic which shaped the city of Ephesus (Acts 19:23–40). The impact of Christianity was undermining the trade of silversmiths who made idols for worship and the whole prestige of the town was jeopardised and its economic growth in danger of collapsing. The anxiety was so strong that it led to rioting in the city. A similar connection between confronting the spirit of the city and threatening its commerce happened in Philippi when Paul cast out a spirit of divination from a fortune-teller (Acts 16:16–22). What started as a one-on-one confrontation soon escalated to include the business community, the magistrates and the mob. Walter Wink points out that in the Bible, the major cities also had their city deities. Rome had its *genius*, Athens its goddess Athena, Ammon its god Chemosh and Babylon its Marduk.[18] This needs to be contrasted with the fact that Israel does not have an angel or spirit watching over it but the Lord God himself dwells in the city (Ps. 48:3, 14).

Wink suggests that it is inevitable that every expression of corporate life will have its spirit, god or angel. This is because every group story will have its inner spirituality which is to some degree projected outwards in its focus on a representative deity. In other words, worship of the god(s) was the spiritual expression of what it meant to be that particular city, nation or tribe.[19] If this is so then we need to exercise discernment and caution in order to engage these angels or spirits in our desire to see God's kingdom planted in the city and upon the earth. We have already explored earlier in this book the fact that the principalities and powers are not always demonic, even when they are sinful. Wink suggests that part of the church's mission is to acknowledge the existence of these powers, love them as creations of God but unmask their idolatries and then stir them up to fulfil their heavenly vocation. Like the angels of the churches, the angels of communities need to repent and rediscover their true vocation which is that given to the community by God. However, for Wink, because the angel and the community are so closely bound up with each other as to be inseparable, the route to healing fallen angels is to enable the community to regain its calling and specific vocation in the scheme of things. He is remarkably similar in this to John Dawson who sees the work of the Spirit in calling nations and communities to own their redemptive gifts which they were given at the time of their original formation. I realise that there are dangers in oversimplifying the gifts of communities as they are multi-layered, but it occurs to me that Liverpool, as a port, had the gifting to be a welcomer of peoples and the distributor of goods to the needy. Instead it has abused its gifts through slavery and crowded its ethnic minorities into urban ghettos which have become a focus for drugs and prostitution, a further abuse of the poor and disadvantaged. As a consequence, the city has to some degree turned in on itself and become poor and needy, having one of the highest rates of unemployment during the twentieth century. In reconciling its divided communities both ethnic and religious it could reclaim its gifts to be a city of welcome and renewal for the poor and the broken. Here is a challenge to take to heart for the churches of that great city.

Understanding the nature of evil in the city requires some investigation into the primary systems that make the city function and then analysing them biblically. These systems are economic, social, political and religious, the last often giving the city its reason for existence. There is a need to explore the connections between the story of the city and how it has shaped its primary systems and subsequently affected the community. The sins and wounds of such stories take on a structural and corporate dimension which affects all the members of the community. This is in essence the goal of what George Otis Jr refers to as spiritual mapping or researching the corporate story of the city. An example of this research is to be found in the workbook and it contains some suggestions for following through with the information gathered from this exercise. Basically we need to take into account the nature of the city's group story and consequences and what this tells us about the powers with which we may be battling. The answers to these questions will help us decide on an appropriate course of action for mission and warfare in the city. It was George Otis Jr who first suggested a link between aspects of the city being impervious to the preaching of the Gospel and the presence of certain powers or angels who oppose the ministry of the church.[20] I have already suggested that the prime criterion is the group story with its repeating pattern; this can be just as much a block to the kingdom as the presence of fallen powers. I was once involved in a mission audit in preparation for a city-wide witness to the city of Warwick in Great Britain. The church leaders reported that there was a part of the city which traditionally the church had found very hard to work in. Through researching the story it was discovered that historically it was an area of poor housing once inhabited by the unwanted or extremely poor. Even though there was now new housing on the site, people living there still spoke about feeling unwanted and were therefore suspicious of the church. In order to confront this story and the powers that might wish it to stay that way, the church leaders held a service of the Christian Day of Atonement in which they apologised to each other for their divisions and to the people of that part of the city for the cycle of poor housing conditions. The mission then went ahead with encouraging results.[21] However, we do need to check out whether the wounded group story has given space and prominence to a spiritual power which fosters and increasingly distorts the repeating pattern.

As a final element in discussing the battle for the city we need to consider a strategy of prayer and listening which will help us understand the story we are dealing with and the powers which may possibly affect it. Stuart Murray gives a fascinating and expansive approach to praying for the city. His book, *The Challenge of the City*, has a series of chapters exploring the various relationships between the prophets and evangelists and the city. For example, 'Abraham and Prayer', 'Jeremiah and Presence', 'Jonah and Prophecy', 'Paul and Proclamation'.[22] In all of them he picks up on the need to know the story of the city and become a resource for its healing by intercession; to share what God thinks of the city aims at uncovering the systemic abuse beneath the surface of things. He underlines the need for the church to be emphatically present in the life of the city rather as the soul or spirit is present to the body. He rightly sounds a caution about the danger of so-called power ministries, which may be all too taken up with binding the powers of darkness but neglect to get their hands dirty and tackle the injustices of urban decay such as disease and disability, pollution, stress and poor medical help. The Prayer Track Movement which originated in the United States has produced a number of prayer strategies particularly associated with the works of George Otis Jr, Cindy Jacobs and Ed Silvoso. In his book *Informed Intercession* George Otis Jr lists five essential factors for the transformation of communities.[23] They are as follows:

- persevering leadership – he cites the example of Nehemiah who did not buckle under pressure (Neh. 6:1–6);
- fervent, united prayer – consider the fasting and prayers of the city of Nineveh as it repented of its evil ways (Jonah 3:5–10);
- social reconciliation – by this he means the healing of fellowship before mission (Matt. 5:23–4; 18:15–20);
- public power encounter – this refers to dramatic physical healings carried out in the public arena as in the case of Aeneas and Dorcas in the towns of Lydda and Sharon which were obviously impacted by the experience (Acts 9:32–8);
- research/spiritual mapping – getting the right information about the group story and its strengths and weaknesses as in the case of the mapping of the land prior to the settlement by the various tribes (Josh. 18:8–10).

Otis identified persevering leadership and fervent, united prayer as the two essential core factors in the transformation of any community and signals of the divine involvement without which there is no real change. I readily agree and would just point out that to bring renewal to the city-wide story it will take the whole church, and this in itself is a challenge to repent of our divisions which have been maintained through time and toil and have contributed to some degree to the wounding of our communities. 'United prayer is a declaration to the heavenlies that a community of believers is prepared for divine partnership.'[24]

The actual prayer process is described in the language of military strategy against an enemy dug in to the fabric of society. Otis suggests four phases of development, *spiritual beachheads* made when revived believers enter into united prayer; *spiritual breakthrough* characterised by rapid and substantial church growth; *spiritual transformation* where social and political life is transformed and *spiritual maintenance* which is consolidating the victories won through focusing on unity, prayer, humility and holiness. This is very similar to the work of Ed Silvoso in Argentina where cities like Cordoba experienced phenomenal growth in the churches and a parallel drop in crime and disease. Statistics like these have to be listened to and taken seriously.[25] Silvoso's strategy is modelled on the story of King Hezekiah who, when he came to the throne, set about restoring the spiritual life and cohesion of his city and nation (2 Chron. 29—32). The basic outline is one of establishing and securing a divine perimeter in the city and this is the restored community of faithful, praying believers. He parallels this with the cleansing and restoring of the temple in Jerusalem so that the liturgies of worship could once again be for the renewal of community. This has always been the case and is the usual pattern in all revivals: the transfiguration of the church results in the transformation of society! Next, this perimeter is expanded into the secular city and this is principally done by uniting the different churches so that they work together and are seen to do so, and by a confident sharing of the Gospel without compromise to the community. Wallace Brown, after years of experience of developing faith communities within decayed housing estates on the edges of Birmingham, is convinced that a lack of sin awareness is a major issue in the breakdown of society. 'Godliness leads to lawfulness' is a maxim he holds to.[26] The conclusion of Silvoso's recommended strategy is to infiltrate Satan's perimeter and destroy it, so founding God's perimeter in its place. Both Silvoso and Otis and others use the language of spiritual warfare as the prime issue in winning the city for God. They all appreciate the place of accurate research as a part of the preparation for this warfare, but they do not always give enough attention to the power of wounded group stories to repeat themselves, as is the nature of wounds until they are healed. There is a need to balance our understanding of the city in the purposes of God so that we do not just see them as the domain of demonic powers which make the city evil in itself. To do this we shall conclude this chapter by looking at God's heart for the city.

God's heart for the city

The city is important because in the scriptures it forms the central feature of a restored land and community in which God himself lives. Isaiah, the court and city prophet, shares his vision of Jerusalem as the strong city whose walls echo the saving presence of God and whose gates are never shut; but only the righteous may live there (Isa. 26:1–6; 60:11). In language prefiguring the book of Revelation, the prophecies of Isaiah look to a new heaven and earth, the central feature of which is the restored capital in which God delights. It is a favoured and protected community without disease and war (Isa. 65:17–25). Two other prophets, Ezekiel and Zechariah, both urban and in exile, envisage the return to their homeland which will be healed. The hallmark of this renewal is the recreation of the city which is without walls and whose gates are open to the scattered communities offering them shelter (Ezek. 48:35; Zech. 2:4–5). It is an idealised picture reflecting the longing of the exiles for home and prosperity, free from the harassment of their enemies.

The focus of the city continues into the New Testament where the consummation of the ages is not focused on the church but the city. It is the city where God lives and where all mourning and pain will be banished (Rev. 21:1–5: 22:1–6). However, the city is also described as a bride which is an image the Apostle Paul uses to describe the church's relationship with Christ (Eph. 5:22–30). This has led some to believe that the church will replace Jerusalem as the special city of God.[27] It is certainly true that the reward for faithfulness is to live in the city named 'The Lord is There!' (Rev. 3:12; cf. Ezek. 48:35). The city is indeed populated only by the righteous which seems to reflect the description of the church community being like living stones being built into a spiritual house (1 Pet. 2:5f). Yet the church is also described as a holy nation, which exceeds the boundaries of any city image. Perhaps it is enough to say that the church in God's purposes is to reflect the true community which is headed by the living Christ and which demonstrates to all communities the principles by which it ought to live and be governed. There are a number of conclusions we can make about God's relationship with the city and how this challenges us today.

God wants to live in the city

We must not think that God only wants to dwell in the idealised city of the last days – he longs to be in the city that is open to him. Of the 150 Psalms, 49 are city psalms describing how God dwells in the middle of the city and defends it (Ps. 42:1–2; 46:1–3; 48:1). Psalm 122 describes how God encourages the faithful to go about the walls of the city and proclaim the peace of Yahweh not only to the inhabitants but to the buildings also. It is the earliest form of prayer-walking the city!

God loves the city

A clear demonstration of the lavish love of God for the city is found in his relationship not only with Jerusalem but also with the pagan city of Nineveh. The city was loathed in Israel because it was the royal city of the Assyrian oppressors who had caused so much destruction in their land. The reason for the prophet Jonah's reluctance to go and challenge them to repent was based on this racial hatred. He wanted God to destroy them, not forgive them (Jonah 4:1–3). Yet God had compassion on the city because its leaders led them into repentance. Even though Jerusalem was twice destroyed for its corporate unfaithfulness, God promised to restore it so that he could once more enter into a loving relationship with it (Jer. 30:18–22; Amos 9:13–15; Mic. 3:12—4:5). As an act of love for the city we are encouraged to celebrate the good that is in it. 'Walk about Zion, go around her, count her towers, consider well her ramparts, view her citadels, that you may tell of them to the next generation' (Ps. 48:12–13). Linthicum says that this is a good way of reminding its occupants that it is intended to be the city of God.[28]

Celebration is so important in the process of healing because it helps us keep the balance between the extent of evil needing to be confronted and the good that remains that needs upbuilding. It is all too easy to demonise the city entirely and just see it as the stronghold of demonic forces, and to become preoccupied with evil rather than keep a true perspective on the presence of God which is still there to bless and heal. We must remember that the whole purpose of God in rescuing his people from the first slavery in Egypt was to bring them into the city where they could develop their group relationship with

God. The city was in fact the gift of God for developing community (Deut. 6:10–12; Ps. 107:4–9).

God resources and restores the city

Isaiah gives us the picture of Yahweh who is restless and will not be silent until he has made the city (Jerusalem) whole and freed from its decay and brokenness (Isa. 62:1–5). We too have this calling to love and pray for the city in which God has called us to live and not cease from our labours until we see the healing that God has for it. It is important to remember that the Holy Spirit at Pentecost comes to the city and that this is in response to the last commission of Jesus to be witnesses first in the city (Acts 1:8; 2:1). The earliest disciples were not instructed to abandon the city but to be its lighthouse in order to call it to its proper destiny which is to be the dwelling place of God and a resource for encouraging social and economic justice. This is reflected by the fact that Paul wrote his letters to the churches in an urban setting and they contained a strategy for living godly and caring lives in a fallen community. However, this theme is to be found throughout the scriptures. Consider how Jeremiah encourages the exiles in Babylon to pray for God's peace and blessing on their cities and villages (Jer. 29:1–9). There may have been an element of self-protection in this kind of praying, but it was also to demonstrate that God's blessings are for all and not just for the faithful. Alongside the need to break spiritual strongholds which affect the city group story, we must also include the ministry of celebration and blessing to resource the city for good and for God.

The following are a few examples of the prayers offered for the city's blessing:

- for security and well-being (Ps. 122:6–9; Jer. 33:10–11);
- for political order and justice (Ps. 72:1–4);
- for restoration of the home (Mic. 4:4);
- for prisoners of faith and conscience (Heb. 13:3);
- for the stranger and marginalised to find a place of belonging (Isa. 56:3–8);
- for calling the city to become whole and established in God's plan (Isa. 62:6–7);
- for the release of gospel proclamation and charisms of healing (Acts 4:27–30).

Jesus in the city

To complete our understanding of city group story and how to be a channel for its healing and renewal, we will look at how Jesus relates to Jerusalem. The bulk of Jesus' ministry was in the context of the city, but there are some examples of how he attends to the city group story itself. As we shall see, there are occasions when he addresses the city as a whole and other times when he uses people and places as a means of focusing upon the group story connected with the community.

Jesus, witness to community story

> 'O Jerusalem, Jerusalem, you who kill the prophets and stone those sent to you, how often I have longed to gather your children together . . . but you were not willing. Look, your house is left to you desolate. For I tell you, you will not see me again until you say, "Blessed is he who comes in the name of the Lord."' (Matthew 23:37–9)

Jesus takes up a prophetic prayer stance towards Jerusalem. Before addressing the city's corporate story he records some of the events of its history and says how God had sent them prophets, wise men and teachers, but all alike had been rejected and persecuted. Luke records Jesus' later and second visit to the city directly following his triumphal entry. As he approached Jerusalem, with the sound of the Pharisees' objections in his ears over how he was being welcomed by the crowd, he weeps for the city and looks into the future to a time when it would be ruined (Luke 19:41–4).

Jesus' prophetic prayer summarises the story of Jerusalem: he looks at the central feature which has characterised its group story and it is one of rejecting the word of the Lord. The amazing thing is that Jesus does not condemn the city but reveals the picture of God longing for a relationship with the entire community; he is like a mother hen wanting to gather chicks together in order to nurture and protect (Matt. 23:37–8). However, because the city has a repeating pattern of rejecting and persecuting the prophets, the result is that they are blinded from seeing the compassion of God and the community is in danger of reacting in its old and familiar and self-destructive ways.

The city's spiritual capacity has been shaped by its history and this needs to be challenged and changed. This is why Jesus hints at their need to know the blessings of God in the city streets and be shaken to undo the consequences of the sins of their shared history.

Many years ago when I was preaching in Belfast I was told that the area was 'gospel-hardened'. When I asked what this meant I was told that all too often the evangelism, largely carried out by the Protestant community, was aggressive and usually included unsavourary references to the Roman Catholic Church. In other words, the style of evangelism was rather like a military campaign which evoked in the minds of many the age-old battles between the English and the Celtic peoples of Ireland. The people in the street may well understand the message of the Gospel but they could not separate it from the scars of history.

Whatever we may think about the viability of healing and salvation on a group level, we must take seriously the model of Jesus challenging a city to repent. Consequently we must learn the story of our city or town and know its core features and how they have shaped the community subsequently. We need to take time and explore the shape of the structural sin and woundedness of our communities and give consideration to a cohesive policy of witness and engagement that involves all those churches which share the pastoral commitment with us. It may be helpful to go to the actual sites in the community where the word of God has been rejected and, on behalf of our city, confess this to God and ask for his forgiveness and a fresh release of gospel witness. Naturally we must back up such actions with appropriate initiatives of prayer and social action in the community.

Jesus, the listener to community story

> As he was leaving the temple, one of his disciples said to him, 'Look, Teacher! What massive stones! What magnificent buildings!'
>
> 'Do you see all these great buildings?' said Jesus. 'Not one stone will be left on another; every one will be thrown down.'
>
> (Mark 13:1–2)

I am fascinated by the fact that the disciples (Matthew's account mentions more than one disciple) and Jesus saw the same incredible temple building but gained a quite different insight as to how it reflected the story of the city. For the disciples the temple spelled magnificence and achievement; for Jesus, it was prophetic of the troubles about to engulf Jerusalem. Why is this so? I think the simple answer is that when Jesus looked at places he listened to what the place itself was saying and also to what God was saying to him through the story connected with the place.

The gospel records make constant reference to Jesus walking in, around and to Jerusalem and using these occasions to refer to events which would take place in the city. In a similar way we need to listen to what our cities tell us. Robert Linthicum offers some good suggestions about this kind of prayer-walking. He writes:

> In contemplative prayer listen to God and ask him to reveal to you seven sites in the city that are particularly precious to him. Take a full day off and visit these sites, on foot preferably. Slowly and reflectively observe them with all of your senses. When it is time, ask God why they are so precious to him or concern him particularly. Write down whatever thoughts and impressions come to heart and mind. Then, open your Bibles and read out loud passages of God's love for the city; a different one for each site. Now you will begin to see the city through the eyes of God.[29]

In listening to buildings and places within the city we may pick up much that will help direct what we pray for and where, in our desire to see Jesus more present and active in our communities. Are there places of poverty or power which make the inhabitants sceptical or too proud to see their need of Good News? As Stuart Murray points out, there may be cities which were bombed during the war and consequently have a legacy of fear or bitterness. In places with a history of unemployment there may be an overwhelming sense of powerlessness. Where occult practices are widespread, there may be an atmosphere of oppression. All these histories give us signals of root causes of the shape of spiritual battles, and we need to pay attention to them rather than carry out a Christian form of carpet-bombing with the Gospel which yields little good response.[30]

Jesus, celebrator of community story

> Jesus sat down opposite the place where the offerings were put and watched the crowd putting their money into the temple treasury. Many rich people threw in large amounts. But a poor widow came and put in two very small copper coins, worth only a fraction of a penny.
>
> Calling his disciples to him, Jesus said, 'I tell you the truth, this poor widow has put more into the treasury than all the others. They all gave out of their wealth; she out of her poverty, put in everything – all she had to live on. (Mark 12:41–4)

Here is the watcher Christ, finding faith in the city and celebrating it. The unnamed widow, full of faith and devotion, comes to the temple and gives away everything she has. It is a quiet and, up until now, an unsung song of deep devotion to God. Jesus, in the doomed city, stops and finds time to celebrate. There is a parallel in the actions of the aged prophetess Anna who was always watching for the redemption of the city, and when she saw the baby Jesus, she celebrated the moment because it spoke of God's presence in the city (Luke 2:38). It is a fact of life that what we do not celebrate, shrinks through lack of affirmation. It is true for us as individuals and we know the crushing power of not being recognised or appreciated or of being put down. Such wounds make us think twice before share our gifts with others again. The same is true for the city. It can become bound up and possessed by its own discouragements. Shallow as it may sound, it is a fact that because people in general looked down on Milwall, including its football team, supporters were known to sing at matches, 'Nobody likes us!' There is of course the biblical equivalent which says 'Can anything good come out of Nazareth?' (John 1:46). We too must learn the ministry of celebration and not forget to look for the good that still exists in the city, whether it be people or places. They all speak out the fact that God is still there, because every good and perfect gift comes from him. We must not allow God's presence to shrink because we do not know how to celebrate. Such celebration also prevents us from sliding into over-focusing on the demonic or evil in the city and becoming shaped by an overemphasis that is not all the truth of the city story.

Jesus, healer of wounded places

> 'Go,' Jesus told him, 'wash in the Pool of Siloam' (this word means Sent). So the man went and washed and came home seeing. (John 9:7)

Here the man born blind is sent to the local pool for his healing, where the washing with water is a sacramental agency for healing. John adds that the name of the place is 'Sent'. Rodney Whitacre says that this is a Messianic reference, as the words Siloam and Shiloh (or Shiloah) are similar and that the stream Shiloah flowed into the pool.[31] Shiloh is used as a reference to the coming ruler in the prophecy of Jacob to his sons (Gen. 49:10). Consequently, Whitacre links this up with references elsewhere in the Gospel of John which refer to Jesus as the sent one (8:16, 18, 29, 42; 10:36). This is undoubtedly part of the significance of choosing Siloam as the place for healing, but could the significance of the event be also connected with the place itself?

Siloam is only mentioned on two other occasions in the Bible, once in the book of Nehemiah (3:15), where the ruined city is being restored, and secondly in Luke's gospel (13:4) where the local disaster of the tower of Siloam falling down and killing eighteen men is referred to in the context of God's judgement upon community. The reference in Luke is one of a recent event the effects of which would still be felt by the local people. It is quite possible therefore that the blind man may have shown some reluctance to go and seek his healing in a wounded place. Yet I wonder which we remember Siloam more for today? The healing of a man born blind or the sudden and terrible death of eighteen men? I think it is obviously the former, which tells us that there were two healings that day, the individual blind man and the memory or story connected with the place and its consequent effects on those who lived there. How many wounded sites do we have in our community? It is astounding to think that Jesus models a way of praying for healing in sending the wounded people to wounded places. This would be rather like sending people to Dunblane to receive their healing. Who can forget that fateful day, Wednesday 13 March 1996, when Thomas Hamilton walked into the school and shot and killed sixteen children and their teacher and injured many more? That Scottish community was suddenly baptised into incredible pain and also tremendous love and support from around the world. John Drane, who lives in Dunblane, wrote a personal testimony of the powerful outpouring of spirituality he saw as a response to the insanity of the massacre. Dunblane cathedral was packed with over 6,000 people, all trying to get in at once to share in the vigil which took place. However, it was what he found outside on the pavement which affected him more profoundly.

> I made my way to the school gates which had become a centre for devotion, transformed by the floral and other offerings placed there by residents and strangers alike . . . The street was deserted except for a handful of police officers and a gang of youths aged about 17–20. As I watched, they took from their pockets sixteen night-lights – one for each dead child – and, kneeling on the damp pavement, arranged them in a circle, and then lit them – using glowing cigarettes to do so . . . One of them said, 'I suppose somebody should say something.' . . . One of them spotted me, and identified me as a minister, and called me over with the words, 'You'll know what to say.' So we stood, holding on to one another for a moment, and then I said a brief prayer. Then came a question first, 'What kind of world is this?' Another asked, 'Is there any hope?' Someone said, 'I wish I could trust in God.' 'I'll need to change,' said a fourth.
>
> As he did so he . . . glanced over his shoulder to the police who were on duty. He reached into his pocket and I could see he had a knife. He knelt again by the ring of candles and quietly said, 'I'll not be needing this now', as he tucked it away under some of the flowers. One of the others produced what looked like a piece of cycle chain, and did the same. We stood silently for a moment and then went our separate ways. Was God in Dunblane? Of course.[32]

It is significant that the story of the healing of the ten lepers happens in the border region between Samaria and Galilee: the place where there has been community breakdown and the hardening of hostilities between divided peoples (Luke 17:11). It is no small wonder that buried within the healing agenda was not just the need for physical restoration but the breakdown of relationships between communities. It is the irony of this account that the ten Jews and one Samaritan could associate with each other in their sickness but that, when all where healed, the Samaritan was returned to being not welcome among the Jews. He could not go to the temple and show himself to the priest to have his healing confirmed. Perhaps we need to be as daring as Jesus and prayerfully consider holding healing services either for people or for the place itself, where we offer the wounded history to God because it is our wounded history we are dealing with.

All this challenges us to think of ways to focus the healing presence and power of Jesus on parts of our community which have dark memories or which have been neglected. Jesus went about Jerusalem and the surrounding countryside, and while he did not avoid the issues of violence and sin nor romanticised the spiritual warfare that needs to be taken seriously, he nonetheless found places which could be challenged to change or transformed through healing power. He also found places and people to celebrate and in so doing deepened the awareness that God was still present in the city. May God give us vision to see the possibilities and potential for healing in our city.

12 THE TRIBAL OR NATION GROUP STORY

The border towns are black and white
and peaceful seeming to the sight,
although the stones below the mud
are stained dark and red with blood.

In border towns which violence built
there's commerce now of *Sais and Celt*,
false fair-day friends who sell and buy
in Amwythig, Henffordd, Caer.

You guilty cities, hear this song;
the stones recall the ancient wrong,
so let your prayers be lifted high,
Amwythig, Henffordd, Caer.

(Graham Davies, 1997)

Translated from the Welsh by the poet,
and used with permission.
(The three towns referred to in the poem are Shrewsbury,
Hereford and Chester.)

Graham Davies was taking a short weekend break with his wife when they visited Shrewsbury and he was reminded of A. E. Housman's poems entitled *The Shropshire Lad*. He decided to go and buy a copy in the town but first went to the castle from whose walls he would get a commanding view of the town and surrounding countryside.

> As I stood there looking north across the Shropshire countryside, I clearly heard the words 'The Guilty Cities' spoken to my mind. It was almost an audible voice, and was

certainly something totally unexpected and out of the ordinary. I knew immediately, because of my acquaintance with Welsh history, that the words referred to Shrewsbury, Hereford and Chester, and that the guilt referred to the fact that they were each established as strongholds of the Marcher Lords. Their task was to subdue Wales, and (these towns) had been bases for successive, and ultimately successful, aggressive military campaigns resulting in the Edwardian conquest of Wales.

That was all very well, but I could not see what I was supposed to do with this knowledge, so I simply went down and . . . bought a copy of Housman's *Collected Poems*. When I read the book that evening, I was astonished to come across the poem 'The Welsh Marches' which deals so powerfully with the very question of the guilt incurred during the subjugation of Wales . . . This was real guilt which needed to be expiated.

The Welsh Marches

. . .
The flag of morn in conqueror's state
Enters at the English gate:
The vanquished eve, as night prevails,
Bleeds upon the road to Wales . . .

The sound of fight is silent long
That began the ancient wrong;
Long the voice of tears is still
That wept of old the endless ill.

In my heart it has not died,
The war that sleeps on Severn side;
They cease not fighting, east and west,
On the marches of my breast.

Here the truceless armies yet
Trample, rolled in blood and sweat;
They kill and kill and never die;
And I think that each is I.

None will part us, none undo
The knot that makes one flesh of two,
Sick with hatred, sick with pain,
Strangling – When shall we be slain?

When shall I be dead and rid
Of the wrong my father did?
How long, how long, till spade and hearse
Put to sleep my mother's curse?
(A. E. Housman)

> I certainly feel that this question of the guilt resulting from border conflict is unfinished business. As devolution is now requiring the relationship between Wales and England to be redefined, perhaps now is the time for the question to be addressed and for reconciliation to be sought so we can move on from a position of forgiveness.[1]

Graham Davies is not alone when he believes that there are segments of history still waiting to be healed in order to improve relationships at a national level. We have already referred to Ireland, Rwanda, the United States, Canada and England, to name but a few, and new issues seem to emerge almost daily. In September 2000 a cross-party group of Members of the Scottish Parliament called for Parliament to 'regret' the infamous clearances and to 'extend its hand of welcome to the descendants of the cleared people who reside outwith our shores'.[2] Fergus Ewing, SNP member for Inverness, said that the genocide and ethnic cleansing that had taken place in America and Australia had been acknowledged long ago and that the time had now come for Scotland to follow what has become an internationally established activity. But regret was not enough, as they also recommended the setting up of a new Clearance Centre in the Highlands where descendants could come to search for information about their deported ancestors. The need to connect with our roots and their geographical location is an important issue for many.

However, it must be admitted that not all are convinced that corporate apology at a national level is either appropriate or helpful. One of the basic reasons for this is that history is never as simple as we paint it. It was illuminating for me to learn that Catholics fought on the side of William of Orange at the Boyne and Protestants for King James. The Irish famine or starvation was exacerbated by profiteering among the Irish business community. The Highland clearances were, according to John Farquar Munro, a Liberal MSP for Skye, aided and abetted by their own clergy telling their flocks that it was God's will for them to leave their homes for the benefit of the great white sheep.

Newsweek of 24 July 1995, in the context of VJ Day, doubted if there was any benefit in offering corporate forgiveness to whole nations, as there was no such thing as corporate guilt. The author maintained that nations should not be treated like people and that they were better off looking forward rather than backward. Paul Oestreicher describes this as being more like *corporate amnesia*.[3] He goes on to say:

> [This] well suits Japanese and – let's face it – Anglo-American, and most other national inclinations. But, illogically, it only works one way: forget our own crimes, but not those committed against us. Most Japanese will not forget Hiroshima. Many British, as our own official VJ Day events show, have no intention of forgetting Japanese cruelty . . . It should come as no surprise that many Germans deeply resent the call to repent (of their contribution to the holocaust) . . . they regret losing the war but not starting it.

Fred Halliday, in a lecture to the London School of Economics given in Belfast in 1997, doubts whether corporate identity plays a substantial role in the ongoing violence and intransigence between the Loyalist and Unionist groups in Northern Ireland. He sees it more as a result of a minority of committed political activists taking advantage of unsolved differences of history. 'It is the contemporary antagonism, not the artificiality of identity that counts. Both Catholic nationalism and Protestant unionism are ideologies, created in modern times, by writers and political leaders, to serve contemporary ends.'[4] I do not doubt that writers and leaders of more recent times have capitalised on the fears and hopes of the divided communities within Northern Ireland, but this is only possible because the people concerned do in fact have a strong perception, however partially informed, of their historical identity and tribal group membership. Such identity is important even though they are fed by the misperceptions of history. It does not help to minimise its importance – we must rather find ways to heal wounded history and its repeating cycles of pain and division. Even Halliday himself acknowledges this when in his introduction he says,

> A son of an Irish Catholic mother and an English Quaker father . . . I feel both personally and morally involved in the story of Ireland . . . My own parents crossed the divide in a mixed marriage. In keeping with the traditions of this island, no relative came to the wedding, and the witnesses were the gravediggers from the church.[5]

Perhaps what is important about tribe or nation is that it furnishes us with an identity which connects us to a history which we can more easily identify and examine and find a sense of belonging to, however peripheral. Yet, like all stories and memories, they can become simplified and we overlook the multi-layered nature of events. The story is summarised by its 'out-standing' events and these are repeated through symbols and ceremony; hence the importance of flags and police badges in Northern Ireland. Identity is important for our sense of well-being and belonging. In his book *The English,* Jeremy Paxman picks up the fact that for the English it has become increasingly hard to discern their identity. He attributes this to the end of the British Empire, the cracks opening up in the so-called United Kingdom through the process of devolution, the pressures for the English to plunge into Europe and the uncontrollability of international business.[6] Quoting a Conservative MP, who was comparing his nation with the French, he writes, 'Their problems are as great as ours. But they know who they are, even if they don't know where they're going. Not only do we not know where we're going. We don't even know who we are any longer.'[7] This thought is echoed by Peter Till when he writes about the paucity of cultural and symbolic representations of what it means to be English; even the language belongs to the international community.[8] 'April 23 is St George's Day. Not that you'd notice it. The Irish wear the Shamrock on St Patrick's Day; the Welsh the Leek on St David's Day; the Scots get piously drunk on Burns Night. But when have you seen the English sport the rose of England on the day of their patron saint?' However fanciful these thoughts may be they do at least underline the importance of identity as expressed at tribal and national level. They challenge us to ask the question, who or what are the nations?

Who or what are the nations?

The *New Collins Concise English Dictionary* defines 'nation' in two ways, as 'an aggregation of people or peoples of one or more cultures, races organized into a single state' and 'a community of persons not constituting a state but bound by common descent, language and history'. The *Concise Oxford English Dictionary* adds the ingredient of 'a territory bounded by defined limits'.[9] The biblical picture of nations ranges from the tribal confederacy of twelve tribes to the great city-states of Babylon and Damascus. Nationalism and nation as we know them today did not appear until the latter half of the nineteenth century. Coupled with this is the factor of mixed and plural ethnic descent which has become more common since the beginnings of the twentieth century. This can be confusing as well as challenging when we come to consider how to pray for the tribal group of which we are a part. John Loren Sandford suggests that in order to win the nations for Christ we must therefore crucify the nation that is with us. 'This means that from the moment of your new birth into Christ, you are engaged in a necessary and continual struggle to crucify all the "nationalities" that live within you, so that your walk with Christ might not be overcome.'[10] It is not clear if he is advocating a 'non-denominational' nation of believers, an homogeneous society of Christians with its own united brand of cultures and practices. Some do suggest that this is what the Apostle Paul was referring to when he wrote that there was no longer Jew or Greek, slave or free, male or female (Gal. 3:28). However, Paul was here addressing our oneness in Christ where our gender, culture and creed pale into insignificance in comparison. Sandford suggests this eradication of nationhood in order to be more sensitive to the differences within other cultures and to facilitate more effective evangelism. I do not think the solution to being sensitive is to disown our own roots – rather the contrary. It is often when we discover who we are that we can really begin to enter into relationship with others more authentically. If God challenges his believing people by saying 'If my people who are called by my name' (2 Chron. 7:14), then I always think we should say to ourselves, 'Who are my people which I carry in my heart and of whom I am a part?' It is only when we have owned our nation group story that we are in a position to be a healing resource to its wounded story.

The importance of nations in the Bible

This importance of nations in the purposes of God is underlined by the fact that they are mentioned over five hundred times in the scriptures. We have already noted that the final healing mentioned in the Bible is that of the nations, and it forms part of the climax of God's purposes in re-creating heaven and earth and godly community which resources the nations (Rev. 21—22). The judging of the nations forms the main feature of these references, which are couched in the form of eschatological prophecies and warnings. The nations will either be destroyed because of their hostility to the nation of Israel, or they will come to sit at the feet of Yahweh in the holy city of Zion (Isa. 4:5). Isaiah, perhaps, is the prophet of nationhood as he mentions the subject twenty times just in the last seven chapters as well as throughout all the prophecies written in his name. The nations are as a drop in the bucket compared to the powers of Yahweh to work his purposes out among them (Isa. 40:15). God will not rest until he establishes his justice among all the nations (Isa. 42:4) and brings them together to sit at his feet (Isa. 43:8–9; 60:3; 62:2). The servant song records the plan of salvation being revealed to the nations so that they might glimpse the pain and the power of Messiah's saving witness (Isa. 52:10–11).

Two themes emerge in the Old Testament regarding God's purposes for the nations: the covenant of blessing and the responsibilities for the nation of Israel as a resource for this blessing.

The covenant of blessing of the nations

From the beginning God intended that his blessings be distributed among all the nations. The very first promise that God made with Abraham was not only to constitute the nation of Israel as the focus of his plans but also to reach out to every people-group. 'I will make you into a great nation . . . and all the peoples on earth will be blessed through you' (Gen. 12:2–3). This encompassing of the nations is repeated and developed with each renewal of the covenant and Abraham and Sarah are described as the father and mother of many nations. The word used here is *goyim* which explicitly refers to the Gentile nations (Gen. 17:1–8, 16; 18:18; 22:18). At the heart of the constituting of the nation of Israel is the call to global stewardship.

Israel is to be the window through which God's relationship and blessing to nations are to be seen.

Israel and the nations

The range of responsibilities placed on Israel in order to be a blessing to all other people-groups are those of being *a model, a witness, a proclaimer* and *a prayer* for the healing of the nations.

A model of godly shared living

> 'Now, if you obey me fully and keep my covenant, then out of all the nations you will be my treasured possession. Although the whole earth is mine, you will be for me a kingdom of priests and a holy nation.' (Ezekiel 19:5–6; cf. Lev. 20:26; Deut. 10:15; 26:19; 1 Kings 8:53)

Israel is to demonstrate faithfulness in its relationship with God and this is balanced by its calling to priestly intercession for the care of all people-groups, which contributes to its own holiness and wholeness. It can be argued that this role of care of nations has not been rescinded and that, as Christians, we should pray for the revival of Israel's role as healer of nations. It is a sad travesty of their high calling that its political and spiritual focus has degenerated into self-preservation of its territories.

A witness to God's providence and care

> See, I have taught you decrees and laws . . . so that you may follow them in the land you are entering . . . Observe them carefully, for this will show your wisdom and understanding to the nations, who will hear about all these decrees.
> (Deuteronomy 4:5–6)

The book of Deuteronomy sets out the decrees of nationhood for the emerging nation of Israel, and they are not to treat this as an opportunity for boasting or exclusivism. These decrees are intended for the good of the nation but also as a witness to attract other nations to adopt a similar covenant commitment to God for their corporate lifestyle. This is often featured in prophetic form, such as when Isaiah describes the nations joining Israel on the mount of God in the last days (Isa. 2:2; cf. Jer. 3:17). It is also demonstrated in the ways in which the wise rule of Solomon attracted the leaders of other peoples to come to Israel to learn the patterns of living which would be good for their own peoples (1 Kings 4:29–34).

A proclaimer of God's word

> Give thanks to the Lord, call on his name, make known among the nations what he has done . . . Make known his glory among the nations. (1 Chronicles 16:8, 24; cf. Pss. 9:11; 18:49; 57:9)

David is celebrating the bringing of the Ark of the Covenant safely home to Jerusalem. It signalled the beginning of the newly united nation under his leadership and the favour of God upon the community, this latter issue being focused on the Ark residing in the city. It was before the Ark that sacrifices and prayers had been made for countless generations and as such it meant continuity of the nation with its roots in the Exodus from captivity. Consequently, the celebrations of nationhood were to include the proclamation to other peoples of the mighty deeds of God in the tribal community. The goal of such proclamation was not to heighten how special the nation considered themselves to be, but how wonderful God was in caring for his people. It is an appeal for the nations to discover this new relationship with God for themselves for that was always Yahweh's initial intention. Isaiah, in the servant song which more than any other points to the revelation of the sufferings and glory of Jesus as Messiah, refers to the kings of the nations being stunned as they too are caught up in God's plans to reveal to them the purpose of his suffering saviour (Isa. 52:15).

A prayer for the healing of the nations

> 'My house shall be called a house of prayer for the nations.'

At the heart of the daily sacrifices in the temple is to be the offering of prayers for the Gentile peoples as well as by the Gentile peoples. They are not to be excluded from the prayer life of Israel but welcomed, not in the form of a proselyte who converts to Judaism but as a representative of their own people with equal access to the holy presence of God. This is not to deny that the scriptures also speak of the judgement of the nations but this judgement is based on the nations' failure to live in response to God's call to be in relationship with him and also their hostility to Israel who models and demonstrates this relationship. The judgement on Israel also takes a similar form, their failure to fulfil their calling for themselves and for the nations' healing and restoration.

As we step into the New Testament we are confronted with disturbing revelations of the end times being characterised by nations rising up against nations (Matt. 24:7–8; Luke 21:10). The apostle Paul in his speech at Athens does point out that God set the various nations in their territorial location and wrote into their group story sufficient awareness for them to discover the purposes of God for their lives (Acts 17:26–8). This has been interpreted by John Dawson and others as a reference to the redemptive gifts that God has invested in every people-group: the precision and industry of the Germanic peoples, the colour and passion of the Latin peoples and the flamboyance and song and celebration among the nations of South America. The healing purposes of God are to call the nations to realise their gifts and offer them to the nations in the loving service of God. It is these gifts and the identity of such nations which will be celebrated around the throne in eternity (Rev. 7:9–12). There is no question that the destiny of nations is an important theme in the Bible and this is confirmed when we look at Jesus' mission to the nations.

Jesus and the nations

Jesus continually commits his disciples to keep as their vision the ultimate goal of bringing salvation to the nations. In the Great Commission of Matthew 28 he commands them to go into all the world and make disciples of the nations (Matt. 28:19). During his final discourse with them he repeats the exhortation and says that with the coming of the Holy Spirit to the church they must take this witness to the community of Jerusalem, but that they were also to move to the nations beyond (Acts 1:8). Further indications of his commitment to the nations are discovered in the parable of the sheep and the goats where the Gentiles as well as the Jews are liable to judgement or salvation (Matt. 25:31–46). However, this passage lends itself more to the idea of individuals from all nations being among the saved or the lost. Perhaps the passion of Jesus for the nations is seen most publicly in his confrontation with the money changers in the outer courts of the temple in Jerusalem. One observer, seeing Jesus overturn tables and whip people for putting profit before care of the nations, described it as a consuming zeal for the house of the Lord (John 2:17; cf. Ps. 69:9). The nations were being denied access to offer their worship to God also, and Jesus saw this as a travesty of God's intentions. Because this event is linked with the triumphant entry of Jesus into the city it has a strong messianic implication of fulfilment of prophecy for the nations. It is no wonder, therefore, that the New Testament paints a ministry for the church towards the nations as like that of Israel.

The church and the nations

Although I am not claiming that the church is the new Israel, a nation without walls or territorial boundaries, there are nonetheless parallels between the people called by God who constitute the nation of Israel and the people of many races called by God who constitute the church, the body of Christ. The church is called to *model* a community life which is likened to being a holy nation and a royal priesthood for all (1 Pet. 2:9). Once again, let me emphasise that this is not replacement therapy where the church is now treated by God as the real and true nation and Israel is reduced to supplying individual members, like any other nation, for the body of Christ. This is to run against the teaching of the Old and New Testaments which do speak of the renewal of Israel so that its calling to be a nation under God is renewed and realised (Zech. 14; Rom. 9—11) With the coming of the Holy Spirit to the church its first priority is to be a *witness* to the person and saving power of Jesus Christ (Acts 1:8). Sometimes this will be at great personal cost, as Jesus spoke of times when Christians will be dragged before governors and kings in order to bear testimony before them and the gentile nations (Matt. 10:18). The church is therefore called to go and be a *proclaimer* of the Good News of the love of God for all and to speak of the Lord's forgiveness for individuals and nations alike. We have already referred to this factor in Jesus' commissioning of his disciples. Finally, the church is encouraged to offer *prayers* for the leaders of nations, their kings and leading authorities (1 Tim. 2:2).

It is clear, therefore, that as Christians we have a responsibility to the nations and that, in some measure, our ability to reach beyond our own territory is reflected in the way in which we are able to own and work with our particular nation's story. It has been my joy and privilege to work in the Republic of Ireland for a number of years. On one occasion a group of us were having lunch in the Dail Eireann (Irish Parliament); among those present were a number of politicians who were very supportive of our work of listening, healing and reconciliation in that country. I was given several papers connected with the forthcoming business in the Parliament that day, and in particular oral questions for the Minister for the Environment and Local Government. My eye caught question number 28, which was being asked by John Perry. The opening sentence was 'To ask the Minister . . . the Government's position on the imminent threat of British multiple retail outlets to set up hypermarkets in Ireland'. When I raised this with my friendly politician, he replied by saying that any British enterprise in the Republic would be regarded as an intrusion, an invasion of privacy, reflecting that just underneath the surface of the nation there lay a deep wound that still needed to be healed. Such wounds are hooked into awareness by such events as these, and present us with an aspect of our national or tribal story which still shapes our opinions and perceptions of ourselves and others. Another such example is that mentioned by Naim Ateek, who is Canon of St George's Cathedral in Jerusalem and pastor of its Palestinian congregation. He is the author of *Justice and Only Justice*, a memoir and treatise on Palestinian liberation theology. Ateek comments on how the tribal memory of Israel focuses on only one of the two Exodus stories in the Bible and that this is fed by the memories of the Holocaust.

> The Old Testament has two Exodus stories. The first has an exclusive theology in which the native people are negated and exterminated. It has been used by some Jews and Zionist Christians to justify their conquest of Palestine and the expulsion of the Palestinians. Jeremiah and other prophets speak of another exodus after the exile. The returning exiles will live side by side with others. Ezekiel 47 speaks of sharing the land with the inhabitants who are already there.[11]

He goes on to speak of a modern-day generation of Israelis who did not experience the Holocaust *but who can still imagine it*. Instead of making the nation more compassionate, they act very brutally towards the Palestinians. Ateek thinks that by inflicting suffering upon others they imagine that they are preventing their own suffering as a nation. He makes the startling suggestion that in the mindset of the Israeli people, the Palestinian has become the new Nazi. He asks, 'Why would a soldier beat a Palestinian child? Does he see the Nazi in this child? Is this the way to express "never again"? Unless Israeli Jews begin to confront this part of their history and recognize that we are all the children of today . . . there will be no change.' Consequently, implicit in the healing of the nations is the taking of responsibility for our nation and tribal story. Each one of us is responsible for the sins of our own nation and we are not exempt, no matter how virtuous we think we are, from the judgement of our nation as we all share in the tribal group stories that have gone into the shaping of us. Walter Wink quotes, in support of this idea, the example of Martin Niemoller who spent eight years in a Nazi jail for his opposition to Hitler's policies. He was nonetheless the first to say about German atrocities during the Second World War, 'We are all guilty.'[12]

I believe that one of the challenges facing the church today is to locate and understand the story of its nation with its repeated patterns which are still waiting for the healing touch of Christ. This is a commitment not only to discover our people-group but also to develop a love for our tribe and nation. It is not an invitation to idolise our nation or fall into the trap of nationalism. I agree with Wink when he says that the only cure for the evil of nationalism, paradoxically, is genuine love for one's nation as a creature of God.[13] It is also a fact of life that we cannot enter into meaningful dialogue with other nations on the world's stage until we know who we are so that others can know this also. This is equally true at a tribal or local level. Bill Lowrey is a Christian minister who has been heavily involved as a facilitator in the healing and reconciliation process between the formerly warring tribes of Dinker and Nuer in the Southern Sudan where many thousands have been killed in the civil war. The long and painful journey to peace was dependent upon both tribes learning to listen to their own story as well as to that of their enemy. Once they had engaged with this stage of the process, representatives of the tribes came together to sign the Wunlit Dinka–Nuer Covenant. It was called a covenant because it signified that God was involved, without whom for the Dinka and Nuer no reconciliation was possible.

This covenant was made with God, self, each other and with the creation (land, water, grass and animals).[14] It necessitated the visiting of each other's holy places and as such was the beginning of re-establishing trading relations between the tribes, which allowed people to freely move through each other's territories.

The church of Christ has a mandate to be a resource and a channel for the healing of our nation's story and of the wounded relationships such stories have built up over generations with other nations. As John Loren Sandford has written,

> The healing of nations must first be a call to heal the history of those nations, much as inner healing restores the hearts of individuals. But the healing of nations must also include healing their lands, which includes healing the history of their lands, or troubles will most likely recur. We . . . must learn the fullness of our calling.[15]

Such group histories need to be owned in a confessional and celebratory way so that we do our best to keep a balanced response. This is the basic logic behind the many prayer and reconciliation events now being held all over the world, and more and more are including the political and business shapers of our societies. These events are invariably held on the site locations where the wounded stories were originally bedded into the soil and memory of the community. This brings back into focus the need to respect the land which God has made and bring confession and healing to the memories and the stories attached to places. As Christians we must use our God-given anointing to call our people to own our history and, through the power of confession and reconciliation, release our nations from the powers which perpetuate wounded stories, and create opportunities for our nation to be renewed in the service of Christ the healer.

EPILOGUE

This book has been written in conjunction with a workbook produced by myself and Michael Mitton. The workbook offers a number of practical ways in which to access the teachings I have given and apply them to your own particular circumstances. It is in the form of a small group course which can be taught at home or in the context of the local church or a group of churches. There are exercises based on the material of the book, and handouts so that everyone can follow the material for themselves. In particular there is a fully scripted liturgy for a Christian Day of Atonement which is crucial for this course and can be adapted to suit your own church situation and story. It is my hope that this textbook and workbook will prove to be a valuable asset in renewing your church and empowering it to be a healing resource to your community.

NOTES

Introduction

1. Larry Kent Graham, *Care of Persons, Care of Worlds* (Abingdon Press, 1992), p. 20.

Chapter 1: Healing the Land: An Overview

1. H. Wheeler Robinson, 'The Hebrew Conception of Corporate Personality' in *Corporate Personality in Ancient Israel* (Philadelphia: Fortress Press, rev. edn 1980), pp. 25–6.
2. E. A. Martens, *Plot and Purpose in the Old Testament* (IVP, 1981), p. 66.
3. Joel Kaminsky, *Corporate Responsibility in the Hebrew Bible* (Sheffield Academic Press, 1995), p. 12.
4. Ibid., p. 37.
5. J. D. Levenson, *Sinai and Zion, New Voices in Biblical Studies* (Minneapolis: Winston, 1985).
6. Kaminsky, *Corporate Responsibility*, p. 52.
7. Compare these four groups with the references to *territory/land, clan, nation* and *language* mentioned in Genesis 10:4, 20 and 31. These are all referring to the descendants of the three sons of Noah following the holocaust of the flood. The Genesis writer is setting out what is to become the context for God's dealing with the nations by favouring the family clans and descendants of Shem. It is surely no coincidence that the writer of the Revelation picks up these groups in his desire to paint the consummation of God's saving purposes. While these four groups are not identical, their similarities are striking:

   Genesis: territories (*erets*) – people in location
   clans (*mispahah*) – clan or family group
   nations (*goyim*) – nations other than Semitic
   language (*lashon*) – language or tongue

   Revelation: people (*laos*) – people assembled
   tribe (*phulē*) – tribe united by kingship
   nation (*ethnos*) – a people other than and distinct from Israel
   language (*glōssa*) – language or people group

Chapter 2: Land as Gift and Sacrament

1. Jeanie Wyle-Kellerman, 'Restoring the land', *The Witness* 78/4 (April 1995), 5.
2. The International Reconciliation Coalition, PO Box 3278, Ventura, California 93006, USA.
3. Wyle-Kellerman, 'Restoring the land', 5.
4. Walter Brueggemann, *The Land* (London: SPCK, 1978), p. 5.
5. Brueggemann, *The Land*, p. 52.
6. Cf. e.g. Judges 3:11, 30; 5:31; 8:28.
7. Cf. e.g. Jeremiah 12:4; 22:29–30; 34:1–3, 17–22.
8. W. D. Davies, *The Gospel and the Land* (Los Angeles: University of California Press, 1974), pp. 396–404.
9. Jürgen Moltmann, *God in Creation* (London: SCM Press, 1985), p. 68.
10. Peter Ackroyd, *Exile and Restoration*, Old Testament Library (Philadelphia: Westminster Press, 1968), pp. 89–90.
11. Jeffrey A. Fagar, *Land Tenure and the Biblical Jubilee* (Sheffield: JSOT Press, 1993), pp. 112ff.
12. John Howard Yoder, *Politics of Jesus* (Grand Rapids, MI: Eerdmans, 1972), pp. 64–78.
13. J. H. Wright, 'Jubilee' in *New Dictionary of Christian Ethics and Pastoral Theology* (Leicester: Inter-Varsity Press, 1996), pp. 512–13.
14. D. H. Field, 'Sabbath' in *New Dictionary of Christian Ethics and Pastoral Theology*, p. 754.
15. Michael Mayne, *This Sunrise of Wonder* (London: Fount, 1995).
16. Gerard Manley Hopkins, 'God's Grandeur' in *The Poems of Gerard Manley Hopkins* (OUP, 1952).
17. Michael Northcott, *The Environment and Christian Ethics* (CUP, 1996), p. 33.
18. Brian Swimme and Thomas Berry, *The Universe Story: A Celebration of the Unfolding Cosmos* (San Francisco: Harper, 1992), p. 237.
19. Lynn White Jr, 'The historical roots of our ecological crisis', *Science Magazine* 155/3767 (10 March 1967), 1204–7.
20. Matthew Fox, *Original Blessing* (Sante Fe, NM: Bear and Co., 1983), p. 11. Cf. also *The Coming of the Cosmic Christ* (San Francisco: Harper & Row, 1988), pp. 129–55.
21. John Calvin, quoted in David N. Livingstone, 'Is the church to blame', *Christianity Today* (4 April 1994), 26.
22. Ron Elsdon, *Green House Theology* (Crowborough: Monarch, 1992), p. 20.
23. Ian Bradley, *God is Green* (London: Darton, Longman & Todd, 1990), p. 42.
24. James Lovelock, The Age of Gaia: A Biography of our Living Earth (OUP, 1989), p. 212.
25. Gerhard von Rad, *Genesis: A Commentary* (London: SCM Press, 1961), p. 91.
26. Mary Grey, Editorial, *Ecotheology* 3 (July 1997), 5.
27. William Temple, *Readings in St John's Gospel* (London: Macmillan, 1939), p. 20f.

28. Northcott, *Environment and Christian Ethics*, p. 133.
29. 'The Deer Cry, The Hymn of St Patrick' in Kuno Meyer, *Selection from Ancient Irish Poetry* (Constable, 1928), quoted in David Adam, *The Cry of the Deer* (Triangle, 1991), pp. 3–4.
30. *The Apocalypse of Philip*, Irish tenth-century text, quoted in A. M. Allchin, *God's Presence Makes the World* (London: Darton, Longman & Todd, 1997), p. 12.
31. John Habgood, 'A Sacramental Approach to Environmental Issues' in Charles Birch (ed.), *Liberating Life: Contemporary Approaches to Ecological Theology* (Maryknoll, NY: Orbis, 1990), p. 51.
32. Winkey Pratney, *Healing the Land* (Chosen Books, 1993), pp. 24–6.
33. Chris Park, *Caring for Creation* (Marshall Pickering, 1992), pp. 146–8.
34. Peter Berg, quoted in Howard Clinebell, *Ecotherapy* (The Haworth Press, 1996), p. 56.

Chapter 3: The Importance and Power of Memories

1. Milan Kundera, *The Book of Laughter and Forgetting*, trans. M. Ileim (Harmondsworth: Penguin, 1983), p. 159.
2. David Woodhouse, 'Healing of memories', unpublished article (2000), p. 1.
3. Maurice Halbwachs, *The Collective Memory*, trans. F. J. Ditter (San Francisco: Harper & Row, 1980), quoted in Charles Elliott, *Memory and Salvation* (London: Darton, Longman & Todd, 1995), p. 9.
4. Dennis and Matthew Linn, *Healing Life's Hurts* (New York: Paulist Press, 1978), p. 7.
5. Gerhard Kittel and Gerhard Friedrich, *Theological Dictionary of the New Testament*, abridged in one volume by Geoffrey W. Bromiley (Grand Rapids, MI: Eerdmans, 1990), p. 56.
6. Elliott, *Memory and Salvation*, p. 29.
7. Anton Boisen, quoted in Gordon Lynch, 'Narrative ethics and pastoral practice', unpublished document (2000), p. 4.
8. For further exploration of this theme see K. Gergen and M. Gergen, 'Narrative and the Self as Relationship' in L. Berkowitz (ed.), *Advances in Experimental Social Psychology* (San Diego: Academic Press, 1988); Don Cupitt, *What is a Story?* (London: SCM Press, 1991); Gordon Lynch and D. Willows, *Telling Tales* (Oxford: Contact Monograph, 1998); Stanley Hauerwas and G. Jones, *Why Narrative? Readings in Narrative Theology* (Grand Rapids, MI: Eerdmans, 1989).
9. Elliott; *Memory and Salvation*, p. 11f.
10. Maya Angelou, 'On the Pulse of the Morning', poem for the Inauguration of the President of the United States © 1993 by Maya Angelou. Used by permission of Random House Inc.
11. Jürgen Moltmann, *The Trinity and the Kingdom of God* (London: SCM Press, 1980), p. 198.

12. Nicholas Frayling, *Pardon and Peace* (London: SPCK, 1996), p. 36.
13. Quoted in Frayling, *Pardon and Peace*, p. 25.
14. John Dawson, *Healing America's Wounds* (Regal Books, 1994), p. 20f.
15. Russ Parker, *The Wild Spirit* (London: Triangle, 1997), p. 104.

Chapter 4: The Powers that Shape Group Stories

1. Steve Turner, *Up to Date* (Hodder & Stoughton, 1994).
2. The Acorn Christian Foundation offers a number of taught causes in learning how to listen, and information may be obtained from Whitehill Chase, High Street, Bordon, Hants, GU33 7BW, or visit their website www.acornchristian.org.
3. Gerry Adams, *An Irish Voice: The Quest for Peace* (Roberts Rinehart Publishers, 1997), p. 79.
4. Oliver Holt, *The Times* (26 September 2000), p. 3.
5. Tom Hennessey and Robin Wilson, *With All Due Respect: Pluralism and Parity of Esteem, Democratic Dialogue*, Report No 7 (July 1997), p. 15.
6. Stephen Baker, 'Memory and the tradition of Northern Ireland', unpublished paper (1996).
7. Hennessey and Wilson, *With All Due Respect*, p. 85f.
8. Rudy and Marny Pohl, *A Matter of the Heart: Healing Canada's Wounds* (Belleville, Ontario: Essence Publishing, 1998), p. 20.
9. Albert Speer, quoted by Robert Elsberg, 'Truth makes demands on us,' *The Living Pulpit* 1/4 (1992).
10. Quoted in Nicholas Frayling, *Pardon and Peace* (London: SPCK, 1996), p. 110.
11. John Dawson, quoted in the International Reconciliation Coalition Brochure, Sunland, California (April 1996).
12. Rollo May, *The Art of Counselling* (Nashville, TN: Abingdon, 1967).
13. John Sandford, *Healing the Nations* (Crowborough: Monarch, 2000), p. 175.
14. Sandford, *Healing the Nations*, p. 182.
15. Walter Wink, *Naming the Powers* (Philadelphia: Fortress Press, 1994), p. 5.
16. Andii Bowsher, 'Time to wink at Wagner', 'Skepsis', *Anglicans for Renewal Magazine* (Summer 1995), 4.
17. Andii Bowsher, 'Time to wink at Wagner', 4.
18. Cindy Jacobs, 'Healing and Deliverance through Spiritual Warfare for the Nations', chapter in Sandford, *Healing the Nations* p. 206.
19. C. P. Wagner, *Breaking Strongholds in Your City* (Crowborough: Monarch, 1993), pp. 225–32.
20. Cindy Jacobs, *Dealing with Strongholds*, quoted in Wagner, *Breaking Strongholds in Your City*, p. 80.
21. Ed Silvoso, *That None Should Perish* (Regal Books, 1994), p. 103ff.
22. Silvoso, *That None Should Perish*, pp. 213–82.
23. George Otis Jr, 'An Overview of Spiritual Mapping' in Wagner, *Breaking Strongholds in Your City*, p. 35.

Chapter 5: The Role of Reconciliation

1. Hannah Arendt, *The Human Condition* (University of Chicago Press, 1958), p. 236f.
2. John Dawson, *What Christians Should Know about Reconciliation* (Sovereign World, 1998), p. 7.
3. Rhiannon Lloyd, 'Principles of Healing in Rwanda', Appendix 3 in *Discerning the Spirit in the Midst of Chaos* (Soma Publication, September 1999), p. 46.
4. Lloyd, 'Principles of Healing', p. 47.
5. W. E. Vine, *Expository Dictionary of New Testament Words* (Zondervan, 1982), pp. 261–2.
6. I am grateful to Jose Comblin who suggested these three levels in his paper 'O Tema de reconliacao e a teologia na America Latina', *Revista Eclesiastica Brasileira* 46/182 (1986), 272–314. This was brought to my attention through reading Robert J. Schreiter's book *Reconciliation* (Orbis Books, 1992).
7. It is a sad fact that perhaps the first wound in the church of Christ has been the separating of Jewish and Gentile believer. Quite early on in the life of the church certain resolutions were passed which discriminated against Jewish culture and practices. For example, towards the end of the second century Pope Victor, in intense written debate with Polycrates, forbade the use of Jewish lunar calendars for the dating of Christian holy days. For a detailed examination of this growing trend within the church and its long-term effects within the church today see, *Toward Jerusalem Council II: A Vision for Reconciliation*, published by the International Reconciliation Coalition, PO Box 3278, Ventura, California 93006, USA.
8. Schreiter, *Reconciliation*, p. 57.
9. Schreiter, *Reconciliation*, p. 58.
10. Schreiter, *Reconciliation*, p. 59.
11. *The Times* (17 January 2000), p. 10.
12. *The Times* (4 February 2000), p. 16.
13. Schreiter, *Reconciliation*, p. 19.
14. John Hughes, *Seminars on Reconciliation at New Wine Conference, August 1999*, p. 2.
15. Stanley Hauerwas, *A Time to Heal*, ECONI (Evangelical Contribution on Northern Ireland), p. 9.
16. Claus Westermann, *Praise and Lament in the Psalms* (Edinburgh: T. & T. Clark, 1981).
17. Walter Wink, *When the Powers Fall* (Philadelphia: Fortress Press, 1998), p. 28.
18. Wink, *When the Powers Fall*, p. 52.
19. Dawson, *What Christians Should Know*, p. 19.
20. Ibid.
21. For a fuller treatment of this subject see my book *Forgiveness is Healing* (London: Darton, Longman & Todd, 1996).

22. Schreiter, *Reconciliation*, pp. 34ff.
23. Hughes, *Seminars*, Talk 3, p. 6.
24. Ibid.

Chapter 6: Representational Confession: The Right to Reconcile

1. Kenneth Milne, 'A Church of Ireland response', *Doctrine and Life* 44 (December 1994), 582–3.
2. This has been produced in the document called *Toward Jerusalem Council II: A Vision for Reconciliation*. A copy can be obtained from the office of International Reconciliation Coalition, PO Box 3278, Ventura, California 93006, USA.
3. See Chris Seaton, *Identificational Repentance*, a Peaceworks Document (Summer 2000), pp. 24ff, for a fair and interesting treatment of what he calls 'bizarre behaviour and bad history'. A copy can be obtained from Peaceworks, PO Box 392, Southsea, PO5 2UD.
4. Jim W. Goll, *Father Forgive Us* (Destiny Image, 1999), p. 42.
5. Goll, *Father Forgive Us*, p. 45.
6. John Dawson, *Healing America's Wounds* (Regal Books, 1994), p. 30.
7. For a study of the advocates of Identificational Repentance consult such works as Brian Mills and Roger Mitchell, *Sins of the Fathers* (Sovereign World, 1999), Chs 2 and 15; Goll, *Father Forgive Us*, Chs 2 and 3; C. Peter Wagner, *Warfare Prayer* (Monarch, 1992), 'Remitting the Sins of Nations'; Seaton, *Identificational Repentance*.
8. Gary S. Greig, 'Healing the land: what does the Bible say about identificational repentance?', *Ministries Today Magazine* (1996), 10.
9. Mills and Mitchell, *Sins of the Fathers*, p. 29.
10. Ray Mayhew, 'Vicarious repentance in the theology of J. McLeod Campbell', unpublished paper (2000).
11. Goll, *Father Forgive Us*, p. 36.
12. Goll, *Father Forgive Us*, p. 55.
13. Cindy Jacobs, *Possessing the Gates of the Enemy* (Marshall Pickering, 1991), p. 134f.
14. Seaton, *Identificational Repentance*, p. 22.
15. Mills and Mitchell, *Sins of the Fathers*, p. 28.
16. Karl Jaspers, *The Question of German Guilt* (1948) quoted in Walter Wink, *When the Powers Fall* (Philadelphia: Fortress Press, 1998), p. 20.
17. Mills and Mitchell, *Sins of the Fathers*, p. 27f.
18. Jaspers, *The Question of German Guilt*, p. 20.
19. Quoted in John Hughes, 'Reconciliation seminar No. 4' (August 1999), p. 3 (unpublished paper).
20. Christopher Irvine (ed.), *The Pilgrim Manual* (Wildgoose Press, 1997), pp. 53–8.
21. A very helpful study of this subject is provided by the course *Ears to Hear*, which can be obtained from the Acorn Christian Foundation.

22. C. F. Keil and F. Delitzsch, *Commentary on the Old Testament* (Hendrickson Publishers, 1989), Vol. 9, p. 320.

Chapter 7: Jesus, the True Representational Confessor

1. Jim W. Goll, *Father Forgive Us* (Destiny Image, 1999), p. 12.
2. Jeff Day, *Forgive: Release and Be Free*! (Sovereign World, 1997), p. 15.
3. A. M. Hunter, *The Work and Words of Jesus* (SCM Press, 1958), p. 94.
4. Hunter, *Work and Words of Jesus*, p. 96.
5. For an interesting study in how the blood of Jesus becomes the vehicle for our salvation and healing and prayers of intercession, read pp. 224–33 of Goll, *Father Forgive Us*.
6. Donald Coggan, *The Servant-Son* (London: Triangle, 1995), p. 44.
7. P. T. Forsyth, quoted in F. W. Dillistone, *Jesus Christ and His Cross* (Lutterworth Press, 1953), pp. 75–6.

Chapter 8: The Family Group Story

1. Dave Carder, 'Passing the Torch: The Multigenerational Transmission Process' in Dave Carder, Earl Henslin, John Townsend, Henry Cloud and Alice Brawand (eds), *Secrets of Your Family Tree* (Chicago: Moody Press, 1991), p. 68.
2. Robert Bly, *Iron John* (Addison-Wesley, 1990). See also Michael Gurian, *The Prince and the King* (Jeremey P. Tarcher/Perigee, 1993), who focuses specifically on healing the father–son wound.
3. *Family Policies Study Centre Survey of Lone Parents* (1995).
4. Dennis Wrigley, *What on Earth Are We Doing to Our Children?* (Maranatha Community, 1995), p. 3.
5. Carder, 'Passing the Torch', p. 15.
6. Carder, 'Passing the Torch', p. 58.
7. Earl Henslin, 'Jesus Models Healthy Relationships' in Carder et al., *Secrets of Your Family Tree*, pp. 227–42.
8. For a fuller treatment of this subject you may like to read Russ Parker and Michael Mitton, *Requiem Healing* (Eagle Publications, 2001) or Kenneth McAll, *Healing the Family Tree* (London: Sheldon, 1989).

Chapter 9: The Church Group Story

1. Walter Wink, *Unmasking the Powers* (Philadelphia: Fortress Press, 1986), p. 77.
2. Bruce Reed, *The Dynamics of Religion* (London: Darton, Longman & Todd, 1978), pp. 41–3.
3. Charles Elliott, *Memory and Salvation* (London: Darton, Longman & Todd, 1995), pp. 221–44.
4. Elliott, *Memory and Salvation*, p. 224.
5. Wink, *Unmasking the Powers*, p. 70.
6. Ibid.
7. Wink, *Unmasking the Powers*, p. 73.

8. Dave Carder, 'Blest Be the Tie that Binds: Local Church "Family" Patterns' in Dave Carder et al. (eds), *Secrets of Your Family Tree* (Chicago: Moody Press, 1991), p. 131.
9. A study by Speed Leas of the Alban Institute, quoted in *Christian Century* 97 (December 1980), 1215.
10. Compare how this theme is followed through in the lives of the other churches. For the church in Pergamum, Jesus introduces himself as the one who has the double-edged sword and the exhortation is to encourage the church to confront pagan and heretical practices and to make sure that they do not infiltrate the church. Failure to do this results in Jesus himself judging the apostates with the double-edged sword of his word (Rev. 2: 12–17). To the church in Thyatira Jesus is the Son of God whose eyes blaze like fire and whose feet are burnished bronze. It is a picture of divine holiness and rule and the whole theme of the church's story is its failure to combat immorality of life among its members and community (Rev. 2: 18–29). To the angel of the church in Sardis Jesus reveals himself as the holder of the seven spirits and the seven stars which represent the very heart and life of the churches. The challenge is to a church which is on the point of dying out if it does not wake up and be transformed by the renewing power of the Holy Spirit (Rev. 3: 1–6). To the church in Philadelphia, Jesus is the one who holds the key of life and can open or shut whatever he chooses. To this persevering church he gives the promise of eternal security in the new Jerusalem (Rev. 3: 7–13). Finally, to the church in Laodicea, Jesus reveals himself as the faithful and true ruler of God's creation. This church, grown cool on its earthly riches, he challenges to change; and if they do so they will sit on the ruler's throne and oversee creation itself (Rev. 3: 14–22).
11. William Storrar, *Scottish Identity* (Handsel Press, 1990), p. 118.
12. Jim Thwaites, *The Church beyond the Congregation* (Paternoster Press, 1999), pp. 143, 179–83.
13. Elliott, *Memory and Salvation*, pp. 201–5.
14. Eoin de Bhaldraithe, 'A Roman Catholic response in corporate repentance and hope for peace', *Doctrine and Life* 44 (December 1994), 581.

Chapter 10: The Christian Day of Atonement

1. Roger Mitchell in Brian Mills and Roger Mitchell, *Sins of the Fathers* (Sovereign World, 1999), p. 168.
2. For a fuller examination of the subject of forgiveness and its links with all the dimensions of healing you might like to read my book *Forgiveness Is Healing* (London: DLT, 1997).
3. Francis Brown, S. R. Driver and Charles A. Briggs (eds), *Hebrew and English Lexicon of the Old Testament* (Clarendon Press, 1977), p. 497.
4. C. F. Keil and F. Delitzsch, *Commentary on the Old Testament*, Vol. 1 (Hendrickson Publishers, 1989), p. 395.
5. Ibid.

6. For a fuller development of this theme of the Servant Songs and their fulfilment in Jesus see Donald Coggan, *The Servant-Son* (London: Triangle, 1995).
7. *Second Letter of Clement* in *The Apostolic Fathers*, translated by F. Glimm, J. Marique and G. Walsh, The Fathers of the Church, Vol. 1 (Cima Publishing Company Inc., 1947), p. 74.
8. Martin Luther, quoted in William Telfer, *The Forgiveness of Sins* (London: SCM Press, 1959), p. 109.

Chapter 11: The Community Group Story

1. Howard Clinebell, 'Towards envisioning the future of pastoral counselling and AAPC', *Journal of Pastoral Care* 37/3 (1983), 189f.
2. Leonard Woolley, *Excavations in Ur* (New York: Barnes & Noble, 1955).
3. Lewis Mumford, *The City in History* (New York: Harcourt Brace, 1961), p. 62.
4. Robert Linthicum, *City of God: City of Satan* (Zondervan, 1991), p. 21.
5. Linthicum, *City of God: City of Satan*, p. 24.
6. Roger Greenway, *Apostles to the City* (Presbyterian Reformed Publishing Company, 1973), pp. 26–7.
7. Don Brewin, *The Healing of Community Memories* (SOMA Publication, August 2000), p. 4.
8. Stuart Murray, *The Challenge of the City: A Biblical View* (Sovereign World, 1993), pp 14–15.
9. Murray, *Challenge of the City*, p. 46.
10. Tom Marshall, from the Foreword to Murray, *Challenge of the City*, p. 7.
11. E. A. Speiser, *Commentary on Genesis*, Anchor Bible Series (Garden City, New York: Doubleday, 1964), p. 134.
12. Gerhard von Rad, *Genesis: A Commentary* (London: SCM Press, 1961), p. 206.
13. Ray Bakke, *A Theology as Big as the City* (Monarch, 1997), p. 63.
14. Luther Copeland in Roger Greenway (ed.), *Discipling the City* (Grand Rapids, MI: Baker Books, 1979), p. 70.
15. Linthicum, *City of God: City of Satan*, p. 66.
16. Linthicum, *City of God: City of Satan*, p. 64–5.
17. Paul Syms in Eve-Ann Prentice, 'Doctor who heals the poisoned planet', *The Times* (Wednesday 26 March 1997).
18. Walter Wink, *Unmasking the Powers* (Philadelphia: Fortress Press, 1986), p. 88.
19. Ibid.
20. George Otis Jr, *The Last of the Giants* (Chosen Books, 1991), p. 85.
21. For further examples of working in city areas which seemingly resist the Gospel more than other sections you might like to read C. Peter Wagner (ed.), *Breaking Strongholds in Your City* (Monarch, 1993).
22. Murray, *Challenge of the City*, pp. 74–141.
23. George Otis Jr, *Informed Intercession*, Ch. 2, quoted in Brewin (ed.), *Healing of Community Memories*, pp. 9–10.
24. Brewin, *Healing of Community Memories*, p. 9.
25. Ed Silvoso, *That None Should Perish* (Regal Books, 1994), pp. 205–81.

26. Wallace and Mary Brown, *Angels on the Walls* (Kingsway, 2000), pp. 248–52.
27. Murray, *Challenge of the City*, pp. 51–4.
28. Linthicum, *City of God: City of Satan*, p. 33.
29. Linthicum, *City of God: City of Satan*, pp. 37–9. You might like also to consult the Acorn Training Course entitled 'Ears to Hear' which is full of suggestions and ideas for listening in the city.
30. Murray, *Challenge of the City*, p. 76.
31. Rodney A. Whitacre, *Commentary on the Gospel of John* (Leicester: Inter-Varsity Press, 1999), p. 240.
32. John Drane, 'Dunblane: a personal testimony', unpublished.

Chapter 12: The Tribal or Nation Group Story

1. Quoted from private correspondence with permission. The extract from A. E. Housman, 'The Welsh Marches', from *A Shropshire Lad* is used by permission of The Society of Authors as the Literary Representative of the Estate of A. E. Housman.
2. *The Times*, 28 September 2000.
3. Paul Oestreicher, *Church Times* (4 August 1995), p. 7.
4. Fred Halliday, 'Irish nationalisms in perspective', *Democratic Dialogue* (May 1998), 18.
5. Halliday, 'Irish nationalisms', 5.
6. Jeremy Paxman, *The English* (Penguin Books, 1999), p. viii.
7. Paxman, *The English*, p. 16.
8. Peter Till, 'The death of England', *Times Magazine* (20 April 1996), p. 17.
9. *The Concise Oxford Dictionary* (Clarendon Press, 1970), p. 802.
10. John Loren Sandford, *Healing the Nations* (Monarch, 2000), p. 57.
11. Naim Ateek, 'Whose promised land?', *The Witness* 78/4 (April 1995), pp. 20–1.
12. Walter Wink, *Unmasking the Powers* (Philadelphia: Fortress Press, 1986), p. 97.
13. Wink, *Unmasking the Powers*, p. 105.
14. Bill Lowrey, content of e-mail to prayer supporters, 28 May 1999.
15. Sandford, *Healing the Nations*, p. 28.

BIBLIOGRAPHY

Abrams, Jeremiah (ed.), *Reclaiming the Inner Child*, Los Angeles, Jeremy P. Tarcher Inc., 1990.

Ackroyd, Peter, *Exile and Restoration*, OTL, Philadelphia, Westminster Press, 1968.

Adams, Gerry, *An Irish Voice: The Quest for Peace*, Roberts Rinehart, 1997.

Allchin, A. M., *God's Presence Makes the World*, London, DLT, 1997.

Bakke, Ray, *A Theology as Big as the City*, Monarch, 1997.

Bradley, Ian, *God is Green*, London, DLT, 1990.

Bradley, Ian, *Columba, Pilgrim and Penitent*, Wild Goose Publications, 1996.

Brown, Wallace and Mary, *Angels on the Walls*, Kingsway Publications, 2000.

Brueggemann, Walter, *The Land*, London, SPCK, 1978.

Carder, Dave, *Secrets of Your Family Tree*, Chicago, Moody Press, 1991.

Clinebell, Howard, *Ecotherapy*, The Haworth Press, 1996.

Coggan, Donald, The Servant-Son, London, Triangle, 1995.

Davies, W. D., *The Gospel and Land*, Los Angeles, University of California Press, 1974.

Dawson, John, *Healing America's Wounds*, Regal Books, 1994.

Dawson, John, *What Christians Should Know about Reconciliation*, Sovereign World, 1998.

Dillistone, F. W., *Jesus Christ and His Cross*, Lutterworth Press, 1953.

Elliott, Charles, *Memory and Salvation*, London, DLT, 1995.

Elsdon, Ron, *Green House Theology*, Monarch, 1992.

Facius, Johannes, *The Powerhouse of God*, Sovereign World, 1995.

Fager, Jeffrey A., *Land Tenure and the Biblical Jubilee*, JSOT Press, Sheffield, 1993.

Fox, Matthew, *Original Blessing*, Santa Fe, New Mexico, Bear & Co., 1983.

Frangipane, Francis, *The House of the Lord*, Word Publishing, 1992.

Frayling, Nicholas, *Pardon and Peace*, London, SPCK, 1996.

Gannon, Thomas M. and Traub, George W., *The Desert and the City*, Chicago, Loyola University Press. 1969.

Goll, Jim W., *Father Forgive Us*, Destiny Image Publications, 1999.

Graham, Larry Kent, *Care of Persons, Care of Worlds*, Abingdon Press, 1992.

Gurian, Michael, *The Prince and the King*, Jeremy P. Tarcher/Perigee, 1992.

Halpern, Baruch and Hobson, Deborah W. (eds), *Law, Politics and Society in the Ancient Mediterranean World*, Sheffield Acadamic Press, 1993.

Hauerwas, Stanley, *A Time to Heal*, ECONI, 1999.
Hicks, F. C. N., *The Fullness of Sacrifice*, London, SPCK, 1946.
Hopkins, Gerard Manley, 'God's Grandeur' in *The Poems of Gerard Manley Hopkins*, OUP, 1952.
Hunter, A. M., *The Work and Words of Jesus*, London, SCM Press, 1958.
Irvine, Christopher, *The Pilgrim Manual*, Wild Goose Publications, 1997.
Jacobs, Cindy, *Possessing the Gates of the Enemy*, Marshall Pickering, 1991.
Kaminsky, Joel, *Corporate Responsibility in the Hebrew Bible*, Sheffield Academic Press, 1995.
Keil, C. F., and Delitzsch, F., *Commentary on the Old Testament*, Vol. 9, Hendrickson Publishers, 1989.
Kraft, Charles H., *Defeating Dark Angels*, Servant Publications, 1992.
Kundera, Milan, *The Book of Laughter and Forgetting*, Harmondsworth, Penguin, 1983.
Lea, Larry, *The Weapons of Your Warfare*, Word Publishing, 1989.
Levenson, J. D., *Sinai and Zion, New Voices in Biblical Studies*, Minneapolis, Winston, 1985.
Linn, Dennis and Matthew, *Healing Life's Hurts*, Paulist Press, 1978.
Linthicum, Robert C., *City of God: City of Satan*, Zondervan, 1991.
Lovelock, James, *The Age of Gaia: A Biography of our Living Earth*, OUP, 1989.
McCoughey, Terence P., *Memory and Redemption*, Gill and Macmillan, 1993.
Marshall, Tom, *Explaining Principalities and Powers*, Sovereign World, 1992.
Martens, E. A., *Plot and Purpose in the Old Testament*, IVP, 1981.
Mayne, Michael, *This Sunrise of Wonder*, Fount, 1995.
Mills, Brian and Mitchell, Roger, *Sins of the Fathers*, Sovereign World, 1999.
Moltmann, Jürgen, *God in Creation*, London, SCM Press, 1985.
Molyneux, Brian Leigh, *The Sacred Earth*, Macmillan, 1995.
Muller, Wayne, *Sabbath Rest*, Lion, 1999.
Muller-Fahrenholz, Geiko, *The Art of Forgiveness: Theological Reflections on Healing and Reconciliation*, WCC Publications, 1997.
Murray, Stuart, *The Challenge of the City*, Sovereign World, 1993.
Northcott, Michael, *The Environment and Christian Ethics*, CUP, 1996.
Park, Chris, *Caring for Creation*, Marshall Pickering, 1992.
Parker, Russ, *Forgiveness Is Healing*, London, DLT, 1993.
Parker, Russ, *The Wild Spirit*, London, Triangle, 1997.
Paxman, Jeremy, *The English*, Penguin Books, 1999.
Pohl, Rudy and Marny, *A Matter of the Heart: Healing Canada's Wounds*, Belleville, Ontario: Essence Publishing, 1998.
Pratney, Winkey, *Healing the Land*, Chosen Books, 1993.
Von Rad, Gerhard, *Genesis: A Commentary*, London, SCM Press, 1961.
Ruether, Rosemary Radford, *Gaia and God*, HarperSanFrancisco, 1994.
Reinhold, Margaret, How to Survive in Spite of your Parents, London, Heinemann, 1991.
Sandford, John Loren, *Healing the Nations*, Monarch, 2000.

Sanford, Agnes, *Creation Waits*, Plainfield, NJ, Logos International, 1978.
Schama, Simon, *Landscape and Memory*, HarperCollins, 1995.
Schreiter, Robert J., *Reconciliation; Mission and Ministry in a Changing Social Order*, Orbis Books, 1992.
Silvoso, Ed, *That None Should Perish*, Regal Books, 1994.
Sjoberg, Kjell, *Winning the Prayer War*, New Wine Press, 1991.
Sjoberg, Kjell, *The Prophetic Church*, New Wine Press, 1992.
Storrar, William, *Scottish Identity*, Handsel Press, 1990.
Swimme, Brian and Berry, Thomas, *The Universe Story*, San Francisco, Harper, 1992.
Temple, William, *Readings in St John's Gospel*, London, Macmillan, 1939.
Thwaites, James, *The Church Beyond the Congregation*, Paternoster Press, 1999.
Wagner, C. Peter, (ed.), *Wrestling with Dark Angels*, Monarch, 1990.
Wagner, C. Peter, *Territorial Spirits*, Sovereign World, 1991.
Wagner, C. Peter, *Warfare Prayer*, Monarch, 1992.
Wagner, C. Peter, *Prayer Shield*, Monarch, 1992.
Wagner, C. Peter, *Breaking Strongholds in Your City*, Monarch, 1993.
Wallis, Jim, *The Soul of Politics*, Fount, 1994.
White, Tom, *The Believer's Guide to Spiritual Warfare*, Kingsway Publications, 1991.
White, Tom, *Breaking Strongholds*, Servant Publications, 1993.
Wilson, Rod, *Counseling and Community*, Word, 1995.
Wink, Walter, *When the Powers Fall*, Philadelphia, Fortress Press, 1998.
Wollaston, Isabel, *War Against Memory: The Future of Holocaust Remembrance*, London, SPCK, 1996.
Wrigley, Dennis, *What on Earth Are We Doing to Our Children*? Maranatha Community, 1995.
Yoder, John Howard, *Politics of Jesus*, Grand Rapids, MI, Eerdmans, 1972.

Periodicals and Reports

Agreement Reached in the Multiparty Negotiations, Joint Statement of Accord Issued by the British and Irish Governments (1997).
Arrowhead: The Bulletin of Prayer Expeditions (1996). (John Presdee, Reconciliation Walk, PO Box 61, Harpenden, Herts AL5 4BB).
Catching the Dream: New Start for the Millennium, Action of Churches Together in Scotland (1999).
Christians Aware (Easter 2000).
Dail Eireann, *Questions for Oral Answer* (Thursday 11 June 1998).
Democratic Dialogue: Two-Tiered Policing, A Middle Way for Northern Ireland? (March 1998); *Politics: The Next Generation, Report 6* (1997); *With all Due Respect: Pluralism and Parity of Esteem, Report 7* (1997); *New Order? International Models of Peace and Reconciliation, Report 9* (1998); *Irish Nationalisms in Perspective* (May 1998); *Scottish Parliament: Lessons for Northern Ireland* (September 1998); *Making Consent Mutual* (October 1997).

Discerning the Spirit in the Midst of Chaos, SOMA Leader's Manual (September 1999), ed. Don Brewin. Obtainable from Anglican Renewal Ministries, 4 Bramble Street, Derby DE1 1HV.

Doctrine and Life (December 1994), Dominican Publications, Dublin.

ECONI, *Lion and Lamb* 5 (October 1995).

Ecotheology 5 and 6 (Sheffield Academic Press, 1998).

Father Heart for Ireland, ed. Malcolm P. Chisholm (February 1998). (Community of the King, 'Crinan', 13 Dundela Gardens, Belfast BT4 3DH.)

Green Christians, Journal of Christian Ecology Link (August–October 1995).

Healing of Community Memories, Diocese of Maridi, Sudan, SOMA (September 2000).

Intercessor (August 1997), Journal of the Brisbane House of Prayer for all Nations.

Maranatha Paper: *The Healing of Creation* (1994). (Maranatha Community, 102 Frean Road, Flixton, Manchester M41 6JT.)

The Common Good and the Catholic Church's Social Teaching, Catholic Bishops' Conference of England and Wales (1998).

Peaceworks Reports: Chris Seaton, *Whitby Reconciliation* (April 1999); *Celtic Mission* (August 1999); *Identificational Repentance* (Summer 2000). (Peaceworks, PO Box 392, Southsea PO5 2UD.)

Reconciliation Walk: A Project to Promote Better Understanding between Christians, Muslims and Jews, by John and Yvonne Presdee (1995). (See above, under *Arrowhead*.)

Statement on war responsibility of Nippon Sei Ko Kai, Minutes of 49th regular General Synod, (23 May 1996).

Tithe An Oireachtais: *The Irish Parliament, Democracy at Work* (1996).

'Wunlit Dinka–Nuer Covenant' (Bill Lowrey), report on the reconciliation of tribal conflict in the Southern Sudan (28 May 1999).

Articles

Baker, Stephen, 'Memory and the tradition of Northern Ireland' (1996), unpublished.

Blair, The Right Honourable Tony, MP, the Prime Minister, speech to the Oireachtas, Dublin (Thursday 26 November 1998).

Bowsher, Andii, 'Time to wink at Wagner', 'Skepsis', *Anglicans for Renewal Magazine* (Summer 1995).

Brady, Archbishop Sean, the Corrymeela Sermon, Corrymeela Sunday Ecumenical Service, the Cathedral Church of St Thomas of Canterbury (Anglican), Portsmouth.

de Bhaldraithe, E., Milne, K. and McCaughey, T. P., 'Corporate repentance and hope for peace', *Doctrine and Life* 44 (December 1994).

Dow, Graham, 'Healing in society: a theological overview' (1998), unpublished.

Dunlop, John, 'Prophetic ministry: questioning the ideologies', *Doctrine and Life* 43 (November 1993).

Gilmore, Inigo, 'Archbishop refuses to let bygones be bygones', *The Times* (8 February 1996).
Greig, Gary S., 'Healing the land: what does the Bible say about identificational repentance, prayer, and advancing God's kingdom?' Regent University (29 October 1996), unpublished.
Jebb, Stanley, 'The heresy of surrogate repentance', *Evangelicals Now* (1994).
Juster, Dan, Hocken, Peter and Dillon, John, 'Toward Jerusalem Council II: a vision of reconciliation', International Reconciliation Coalition, PO Box 3278, Ventura, CA 93006, USA, unpublished.
Kilcourse, George, 'Thomas Merton and racism: Letters to a White Liberal reconsidered'.
Lynch, Gordon, 'Narrative ethics and pastoral care' (1999), unpublished.
Maxwell, Joe, 'Racial healing in the land of lynching', *Christianity Today* (10 January 1994).
Selman, Michael, 'The Christian, power and powers', 'Skepsis', *Anglicans for Renewal Magazine* (Autumn 1996).
Sladden, David (InterPrayer), 'Identificational repentance' (25 January 2000), unpublished.
Smyth, Geraldine Marie, 'Church denominations and precious diversities', *Doctrine and Life* 47 (October 1997), 450–60.
Starkey, David, 'The death of England', *The Times Magazine* (20 April 1996).
Waldman, Martin J., 'Reconciliation: a Jewish–Gentile issue facing the church today' (1997), unpublished.
Wilkins, Richard, 'Thinking of England', *Third Way* (February 1998).
Wilson, Joan, 'Lessons from Enniskillen', *UKFocus* (April 1997).
Woodhouse, David, 'Healing of memories' (June 2000), unpublished paper.

Angel of the church p138-39
inner spirituality of the church

Other Books from The Pilgrim Press:

GODZONE

A Guide to the Travels of the Soul

Mike Riddell

This is a guide to Godzone—the space inhabited by God. It is a book for travelers, those who have never quite settled in the world, who follow an inner urge, a voice that calls from the depths, and a desire to explore the territory. Join Mike Riddell on a journey not unlike that in *Zen and the Art of Motor-cycle Maintenance*—a journey that is humorous, captivating, and above all, inspiring.

ISBN 0-8298-1516-3 / Paper, 112 pages / $11.00

HENRI'S MANTLE

100 Meditations on Nouwen's Legacy

Chris Glaser

In biblical terms, *mantle* is the equivalent of legacy. Henri Nouwen's mantle consists of more than 40 books on how to cultivate a spiritual life. Glaser, a student and friend of Nouwen for over 25 years, presents 100 meditations on Nouwen's words, in the hope that his ministry will continue to thrive.

ISBN 0-8298-1497-3 / Paper, 224 pages / $18.00

THE LABYRINTH AND THE ENNEAGRAM

Circling into Prayer

Jill Kimberly Hartwell Geoffrion and Elizabeth Catherine Nagel

The labyrinth has become one of the most recognized symbols of contemporary spirituality. The enneagram is a psychological model of how individuals understand and organize their perceptions about experience. This book brings the two together so that readers may enjoy the transformation that arises from new learning and insights.

ISBN 0-8298-1450-7 / Paper, 128 pages / $15.00

LIVING THE LABYRINTH

101 Paths to a Deeper Connection with the Sacred

Jill Kimberly Hartwell Geoffrion

Living the Labyrinth offers beginners and seasoned labyrinth users a multitude of new ways to approach this sacred tool. The short, devotional-like chapters may be used however the reader chooses because—as author Geoffrion tells us—any way we live the labyrinth is the "right" way.

ISBN 0-8298-1372-1 / Paper, 88 pages / $16.95

LIVING WITH CANCER

Meditations on Patience and Love

Melody Kee Smith and Richard A. Smith

This book will uplift people living with cancer and their families and friends. The authors, the late Melody Kee Smith (who died of cancer shortly before this book was published) and her husband Richard A. Smith have compiled a collection of meditations that include short prayers and the invitation to write or think through issues, such as being frustrated with health care, building support systems, and building a sense of the sacred in one's life.

ISBN 0-8298-1436-1 / Paper, 128 pages / $8.00

OUTSIDE THE LINES

Meditations on an Expansive God

Andrea LaSonde Anastos

19 meditations to encourage those looking for a more meaningful relationship with God to discover that "The Holy One who creates and cherishes a universe filled with anteaters and supernovas, with sea anemones and solar systems, will speak to every human being in a unique voice....Trust that God loves and needs your uniqueness, and then seek the unique imprint of God within you."

ISBN 0-8298-1471-X / Paper, 144 pages / $13.00

PRAYING THE LABYRINTH

A Journal for Spiritual Exploration

Jill Kimberly Hartwell Geoffrion

The first book in its series, *Praying the Labyrinth* is a simple, meaningful approach to preparing for, taking, and meditating on labyrinth walks. This is a journal that will lead the uninitiated seeker into a unique spiritual exercise of self-discovery through Scripture selections, journaling questions, poetry, and space for personal reflection.

ISBN 0-8298-1434-8 / Paper, 112 pages / $15.00

SACRED JOURNEY

Spiritual Wisdom for Times of Transition

Mike Riddell

This inspiring and challenging book is for anyone who has ever asked "What now?" or "What will be left of my life when I'm gone?" Storyteller and writer Mike Riddell brilliantly identifies the malaise that is particularly common in midlife and shows us how to make it a time for refocusing on what really matters.

ISBN 0-8298-1456-6 / Paper, 224 pages / $16.00

TRANSFORMING THE ORDINARY

Caroline A. Westerhoff

An extraordinary book of essays conducive to comtemplative thought and prayer. *Transforming the Ordinary* encourages readers to look at the world in original and enlightening ways. A selection from the Book of Psalms is used at the beginning and end of each essay. The book also contains study questions and will be especially useful during Advent and Lent.

ISBN 0-8298-1476-0 / Paper, 96 pages / $10.00

To order these or any other books from The Pilgrim Press, call or write to:

The Pilgrim Press
700 Prospect Avenue East
Cleveland, OH 44115-1100

Phone orders: 800.537.3394 (M-F, 8:30am-4:30pm ET)
Fax orders: 216.736.2206

Please include shipping charges of $4.00 for the first book and 75¢ for each additional book.

Or order from our web site at *www.pilgrimpress.com*.

Prices subject to change without notice.